DATE DUE

A HISTORY OF THE
FIRST BULGARIAN EMPIRE

A HISTORY
OF THE FIRST
BULGARIAN EMPIRE

BY

STEVEN RUNCIMAN

FELLOW OF TRINITY COLLEGE
CAMBRIDGE

LONDON
G. BELL & SONS LTD
1930

DEDICATED BY GRACIOUS PERMISSION
TO BORIS III, TSAR OF THE BULGARIANS

Printed in Great Britain by the Camelot Press Limited
London and Southampton

PREFACE

IN the Balkan Peninsula memories linger long. The centuries of Turkish rule have passed like a single night, and the previous ages have kept all the living passions of a yesterday. In a land where races have perpetually overlapped and where frontiers have been seldom natural and never permanently just, a spirit of rivalry and bitterness has inevitably permeated international politics and their records far back into the past. Inevitably, Balkan historians have succumbed to this spirit. All too sensible of the support that a kindly history can bring to their countries, they cannot restrain themselves from ensuring the kindliness, from painting history in a light that is favourable to them. It is natural enough, but a mistaken policy. Not only does it often inherently defeat its ends—as when the Slav writers in unison pour contempt on the East Roman Empire, because it was chiefly Greek, quite forgetting that to belittle your enemies is the least effective way of magnifying yourself—but also it has long since ceased to achieve its object abroad. In Western Europe, where national rivalries are less unendingly acute, and so learning has freed itself from patriotism, the words of Balkan historians no longer carry conviction.

It is a pity; for there are many passages in Balkan history interesting and important enough to deserve recording. But few have been recorded satisfactorily. In Eastern Europe there has been too much passion; while Western Europe has adopted the attitude that nothing of consequence happened in Eastern Europe till the growth of the so-called Eastern Question in the course of the eighteenth century. Thus the First Bulgarian Empire has remained a vague and ill-known period, whose very name falls as a surprise on most Western ears. But its story deserves attention, both for its significance in the history of Europe, and also for its own qualities and the study of the great men that were its rulers. It is in the hope of winning for it some of this attention that I have written this book. Following the rule that it is not for the historian to meddle in modern politics, I have restricted myself here to the history of the First Bulgarian Empire and no more. But, if its history can arouse any interest in and sympathy with the country that is its modern heir, I shall be well pleased; for that result is, I think, within the legitimate aspirations of the historian.

The First Bulgarian Empire presents one great initial difficulty for historians. We know its history almost exclusively from external sources. Except for a valuable but meagre dated list of the early monarchs, a few hagiographical writings, and a few inscriptions, mostly of recent discovery, we only possess the evidence provided for us by chroniclers of the East Roman Empire, with occasional sidelights from Western Europe. I deal more fully with the original sources elsewhere; but, all the while, it is necessary to remember that there are inevitable gaps in our information, particularly with regard to the internal history and the history of the frontiers on the side away from the civilized world. Such lacunæ are excellent playgrounds for the Chauvinists, where their imaginations can play the most riotous games; but for the serious historian they are highly discouraging, forcing him to advance with a timorousness or a confession of ignorance that is most distasteful to his pride. It is possible that more evidence may arise—that more inscriptions may be found to throw light in many places; but that only deters the historian the more; he can never hope to say the last word on early Bulgarian history.

Consequently, few historians have attempted to deal

with the First Empire as a whole. In Western Europe it has only been treated in one or two chapters in histories that deal with the whole history of the Balkans or Bulgaria; and the most important of these, Jireček's *Geschichte der Bulgaren*, excellent in its day, is now out of date. The others are of little value. In England, however, there is also a chapter, readable but necessarily superficial, in the *Cambridge Mediaeval History*, vol. iv. It is only in books dealing with various periods of the history of Constantinople that early Bulgaria has received concentrated attention from Western writers, and then only in patches. But some of these works are of great importance, as, for example, Bury's *History of the Eastern Roman Empire, 802–67* (his *Later Roman Empire, 395–800*, was written too long ago to be of much use to-day), Rambaud's *Empire Grec au Xme Siècle*, and Schlumberger's great monographs on the Emperors of the later Macedonian period. The careers of Cyril and Methodius have given rise to a large crop of literature, dealing largely with Bulgaria, and remarkable chiefly for its various religious prejudices. The most temperate of these books is Dvornik's admirable *Les Slaves, Byzance et Rome*. In addition, writers such as Bury, Jireček, Marquart, and others have written articles and monographs on various questions affecting Bulgarian history; I cite them in my bibliography, and, where they are relevant, in my footnotes. I myself, in my *Emperor Romanus Lecapenus*, have given a detailed account of Symeon's later wars.

But it is only when we come to Slavonic writers that we find a fitting interest taken in early Bulgarian history. For some time now Russian historians—such as Palauzov, Drinov, Golubinski, Uspenski, and Vasilievski—have written on various aspects and periods of early Bulgarian history and have undertaken excavations and unearthed inscriptions of very great value. Of recent years the

Bulgarians themselves have turned to its study. Particularly I must cite Ivanov, to whose book on Bogomil literature I am deeply indebted, and, most important of all the historians of early Bulgaria, Professor Zlatarski. Zlatarski, besides having written many very useful short articles and monographs, is the only historian to have attempted a full-length history of the period; his great history of his own country has been brought so far, in two thick volumes, down to the close of the First Empire. It is a work packed with learning and ingenuity, and is absolutely essential for any student of early Bulgarian history.[1] I have ventured to disagree with Professor Zlatarski on various points of judgement and interpretation; but his writings, together with the personal help that he has given me, put me under an obligation to him that it is difficult adequately to acknowledge.

An explanation is needed for the method of transliterating that I employ. With Greek names I have adopted the traditional Latin transliteration; with Cyrillic the problem is more difficult. I have not attempted to alter forms that are time-honoured and well-known—I write Sofia rather than Sofiya; as for the rest, I follow, with one or two modifications, the rules approved by the British Academy,[2] rather than the forms employed by the European Slavists, whose ornamental additions to ordinary letters look unfamiliar to English eyes and some of whose usages, such as 'c' for 'ts,' definitely invite error among the unwary. Proper names provide a further difficulty. With

---

[1] Its only great defect is an absence of any maps.

[2] *Proceedings of the British Academy*, vol. viii. (1917–18), p. 529. I transliterate the Russian 'e' after a softened consonant as 'ie' rather than ''e,' and I render the letter 'yat' as 'ie,' rather than 'ê.' Apostrophes and accents, though necessary for minute phonetic accuracy, serve only to make restless the average eye. I transliterate the nasal 'a' which Bulgarian has inherited from old Slavonic as 'â.' I also divide the strings of consonants which Bulgarian joins together with only a hard sign with a 'u,' as in the name Bulgaria itself. The hard sign in Bulgarian has more of the quality of a vowel than in Russian.

regard to the persons whose Christian names have English equivalents, I have used these equivalents. It would be pedantic to write of Tsar Petr or the Empress Aecaterine, or even Pope Johannes. But many of the Bulgarian proper names are only known to us through alien, principally Greek, versions. Where guidance has been given as to the names of the early Khans in the Old Bulgar List, I have followed such guidance, save only that I have preserved the Greek form Asperuch rather than Isperikh. [1] When the List ends, difficulties arise. Occasional inscriptions help; but my rule, on the whole, has been to use the original Bulgar or Slavonic name where it is obvious, but in doubtful cases to transliterate the Greek. [2] I adopt the same rule with regard to Slavonic place-names. With Imperial place-names I have, except for obvious exceptions such as Adrianople, transliterated the Greek form then current. In one case I have been deliberately inconsistent; in the earlier parts of the history I call the city now known as Sofia by its Imperial name, Sardica; but after the ninth century I call it Sofia. Actually in the tenth and eleventh centuries it was known in Greek as Triaditza, or in Slavonic as Sredetsa ; but as the name did not survive I considered it merely confusing to employ it.

I have drawn a distinction between the words Bulgar and Bulgarian. The former I use to mean the race of Hunnish invaders that formed the nucleus of Bulgaria, the latter the nation composed by the amalgamation of the Bulgars and the Slavs. The terms the Empire, the Emperor, and Imperial all refer to the East Roman Empire,

---

[1] I have acted illogically with the name Kubrat—in Greek, Crubatus or Crobatus; in Bulgar, Kurt. The form Kubrat has no better justification save that it is now generally employed. I use Asperuch's Greek form because he is best known from the story of the Greek chroniclers.

[2] In the discovery of the Slav original forms I have relied very largely on Professor Zlatarski's judgement. In most cases it is easy; 'Ιβάτζης clearly was Ivatsa to his people.

x   PREFACE

misleadingly known as Byzantine.[1] To the contemporary
world this Empire was simply the Empire, and the Emperor was the Basileus that reigned at Constantinople; and
to the East, at any rate, the situation was not altered by
the appearance of rival Emperors in Germany.

I give a brief discussion of the original sources in Appendix I; and I have appended at the close of the volume a full
bibliography. The page-references in the footnotes of the
text refer to the editions that I have cited there.

In conclusion I wish to thank very warmly my Bulgarian friends who have been of great assistance to me, not
only on my visits to Bulgaria, but also in supplying me
with maps. My one regret is that I have been unable to
visit in person the splendid examples of old Bulgarian
architecture at Prespa and Ochrida, now under Jugo-
slavian dominion. I wish also to thank Miss R. F. Forbes
for her help over the proofs.

---

[1] The term Byzantium is, I think, legitimate for describing the civilization of the Empire, but the Empire itself was consciously the heir of the
universal Roman Empire, and in no way local.

CONTENTS

xi

Book I

THE CHILDREN OF THE HUNS

Chapter I

THE FIVE SONS OF KING KUBRAT

ONCE upon a time, when Constans was Emperor in Byzantium, there lived a king called Kubrat on the shores of the Sea of Azov. In due course he died, leaving five sons behind him, whom he bade live in concord together. But the brothers in a short time quarrelled, as princes often do, and, dividing the inheritance between them, departed each his own way, bearing his portion of the people with him. The eldest brother alone, Baian, remained where he was born; the second brother, Cotrag, crossed the Don, to the northward, and lived on the farther bank; the fourth brother moved far to the westward, and, crossing the Danube, came to Pannonia, where he fell under the domination of the Avars; the youngest wandered even farther, and ended his days in the Pentapolis of Ravenna. But the third brother, whose name was Asperuch, crossed the Dnieper and the Dniester and settled on the banks of the Lower Danube.

There he dwelt with his people, until the Emperor Constantine, displeased at the presence of these barbarians on the very borders of the Empire, determined to stamp them out. The Imperial armies marched to the Danube and invaded the wild country; where Asperuch's hordes in terror hid for four days in their fastnesses. But the Emperor's feet were tender and sore; he decided to retire and rest them in his city of Mesembria. The barbarian spies were alert; on his departure the barbarians came out from their strongholds and attacked. The Imperial troops found themselves leaderless; their Emperor had fled, they thought, so they too would flee. Close on their

3

heels came the barbarians, across the Danube, into the province of Moesia. The land pleased Asperuch and his people; they were victorious, and the Emperor could not withstand them. So there they remained, and there their descendants remain, even to this day.

For all its air of a fairy-tale, this story, told by the Greek chroniclers,[1] is in the main a true description of the entry of the Bulgars into Bulgaria. This was not, however, the first time that the Empire had come into contact with Bulgarian tribes. The kingdom of Kubrat, 'of old called Great Bulgaria' (though actually its greatness was very newly established), had a past known in part to the historians of Constantinople. We can go back, and, noticing their former raids into civilization, peer into the mists that hang over the Steppes, to see if we can discover who were these Bulgars whose final incoming, in the seventh century, disturbed so lastingly the untranquil Balkans.

The Huns and their tempestuous onrush over Europe made a story that has often been told. But whence they came and whither they went are lost in mystery. Some say they were the Hiung-Nu, the race that was the terror of China; but the Goths, who knew them best, thought otherwise. They told of the wicked sorceresses that King Filimer the Goth banished from his Scythian kingdom, who mingled on their wanderings with the evil spirits of the desert; and from that wild union were born the Huns.[2] Their going is as shrouded as their coming. Not long ago a wave of militarism swept over Europe, and an awful ancestry became the boast of every bellicose nation; Attila was proudly called cousin, if not grandfather, by them all. Of all these claims, it seems that the Bulgars' is the best justified; the blood of the Scourge of God flows now in

[1] Theophanes, pp. 546–9: Nicephorus, pp. 33–5.
[2] Jordanes, *Getica*, p. 89.

the valleys of the Balkans, diluted by time and the pastoral Slavs.

At the time of the Huns' passing, the Empire was still the only civilized State in Europe; and so it is to the Imperial writers that we must go for information. They cannot tell us much; the Steppes were turbulent and very mysterious, and they could not get things clear. They made their attempts at ethnological elucidation, but often it was easier to give them up and seek instead a literary flavour, calling every oncoming tribe the Scythians or Cimmerians. Nevertheless, certain facts emerge. On Attila's death, his empire crumbled. His people, who had probably been only a conglomeration of kindred tribes that he had welded together, divided again into these tribes; and each went its own way. One of these tribes was soon to be known as the Bulgars.

It was in 482, some thirty years after Attila's death, that the Bulgars first appear by name. The Emperor Zeno, fighting against the two Theoderics and their Goths, found it necessary to call in to help him the Bulgars, a tribe living apparently to the north-east of the Danube.[1] The incident taught the Bulgars that the Empire could be put to some use; during the next few years they made several successful raids on the Balkans, in 493, 499, and 502.[2] They also entered again into the career of the great Theoderic. In 504 they were allied with the Gepids against him.[3] In 505, when a brigand chief called Mundo (a relative of Attila, but by some said to be Getic and by others Gepid) was attacked at Margum (the junction of the Morava and the Danube) by the 'Greeks' (the Imperial

---

[1] John of Antioch, *Fragmenta*, p. 619.

[2] Marcellinus Comes, *Chronica Minora*, pp. 94, 95, 96. Marcellinus calls them Scythians in 493, but Bulgars in 499, and, in 502, Consueta gens Bulgarorum. Theophanes (p. 222), writing several centuries later, mentions only the 502 raid, calling it the first entry of the Bulgars into history.

[3] Cassiodorus Senator, p. 160.

troops), Theoderic's general, Pitzia, went to his aid; the
Greeks called in Bulgars to fight for them, and the Bulgars
there suffered their first defeat.[1]

In 514 the rebel Vitalian employed Bulgars to help him
in his attempt against the Emperor Anastasius.[2] In 535
they invaded Mysia; in 538 large numbers of Bulgars, led
by two kings, invaded the Balkans and succeeded in defeating and capturing various Imperial generals, including
a baptized Hun called Acum.[3] Next year Mundo re-
appeared into prominence; he was now ruling in Sirmium,
and, his old patron Theoderic being dead, he turned for
patronage to the Emperor Justinian. He proved a useful
vassal, defeating Bulgar raiders so efficiently that no other
Hun dared cross the Danube.[4] And so for a while we
hear no more of the Bulgars.

Indeed, the Bulgars of whom we have so far heard were
a race of no great importance, a wandering, predatory
off-shoot of greater nations that lay behind to the east.
To these nations the historians of the days of Justinian,
when the world was for a while more orderly, direct our
notice.

According to Procopius, there once lived a nation of
Huns or Cimmerians in the districts to the east of the Sea
of Azov and north of the Caucasus. The king of these
Huns had two sons, Cuturgur and Uturgur. On his death
they divided the people, and Cuturgur went off to conquer
new territory. He succeeded at the expense of the
Tetraxite Goths of the Taman peninsula, the Crimean

---

[1] Marcellinus Comes, p. 96: Jordanes, *Romana*, p. 46, *Getica*, p. 125:
Ennodius, pp. 210, 211.

[2] Malalas, p. 402, calling Vitalian's allies πλῆθος Οὔννων καὶ Βουλγάρων:
Theophanes, p. 247, using same words: Georgius Hamartolus, ii., p. 619,
adds Γότθων.

[3] Malalas, p. 437, calling them Huns: Theophanes, p. 338, calling them
Bulgars, adding the words καὶ δρούγγου, which have never been satisfactorily explained: Anastasius (ii., p. 141) in his paraphrase of Theophanes
takes 'Droggo' to be the name of a Bulgar king, a partner of Vulger.

[4] Theophanes, pp. 339–40.

Goths, and other tribes that lived along the northern shore of the Black Sea; and his people made the country their base, from which they raided farther afield. Uturgur, however, stayed in his old home.[1] The eponymous princes probably were born in the simplifying mind of Procopius; but certainly in the sixth century there were two close kindred Hunnish tribes, of the Bulgar branch of the Huns,[2] situated on either side of the Sea of Azov, the Cotrigurs to the west and the Utigurs to the east; and the diplomats at Constantinople found themselves forced to pay them attention.

There were several Hunnish tribes with which the Empire had dealings then existing on the Steppes; there were the Sabirs, whose ruler, a tempestuous widow called Boa, sought the alliance of the Emperor,[3] there were the Ultizurs and the Burugundi, near relatives of the Cotrigurs and Utigurs, whom Agathias mentions merely to tell of their destruction[4]; there were the Saraguri, the Urogi, and the Onoguri, victims of the growth of Sabir power.[5] But, with the possible exception of the Sabirs, the Cotrigurs and the Utigurs alone seem to have enjoyed a formidable power and an efficient organization.

In 528 there was a king of the Crimean Huns called Grod—Theophanes euphonized his name into Gordas, and John of Antioch even more mellifluously into Gordian —who came to Constantinople to be admitted into the Christian Church. His Crimean Huns were probably

[1] Procopius, *De Bello Gothico*, iv., 5, pp. 475 ff. He calls them Cuturguri and Uturguri or Utiguri: Menander and Agathias call them Cotriguri and Utiguri: Theophanes only mentions the Cotragi.

[2] None of the sixth-century writers actually call the Cotrigurs or Utigurs Bulgars, but the identification is made certain by later writers. See below, pp. 11, 15.

[3] John Malalas, pp. 430–1. Theophanes, p. 269, who calls her Boarex. Sabir alliance was considered useful against the Persians.

[4] Agathias, p. 365, talking of Cotrigurs, Utigurs, Ultizurs, and Burugundi, says, ' οὗτοι δὲ ἅπαντες κοινῇ μὲν Σκύθαι καὶ Οὖννοι ἐπωνομάζοντο.'

[5] Priscus, *Fragmenta*, p. 341.

Procopius's Cimmerian Huns—that is to say the Cotrigurs, who had settled in the Crimean lands of the Goths, themselves a Christian race. Grod was certainly a personage of some power; his help had already been sought by the Emperor for the Iberians against the Persians. However, the Imperial diplomats overreached themselves; this early evangelization was a failure. When Grod returned home, determined to destroy his people's idols of silver and electrum, his people objected, and slew him, setting up his brother Mugel in his place. Mugel preferred to remain a heathen.[1]

Meanwhile the Cotrigur power grew. The Tetraxite Goths, crushed by the Cotrigurs, lingered on under Utigur patronage. They were orthodox Christians, and in 548 they sent to Constantinople nominally to ask for a new bishop, but actually to give alarming reports of affairs on the Steppes.[2] Their warnings were justified; in 551 twelve thousand Cotrigurs, under their leader Chinialus, incited by the Gepids, invaded and ravaged the Balkans. The Emperor Justinian, remembering the information of the Tetraxites, hastily sent an embassy and gifts to Sandilch, Khan of the Utigurs, to urge him to attack the Cotrigurs in the rear. Sandilch was delighted to comply with this request, and did his work only too thoroughly. So Justinian, with all the subtlety of Byzantine diplomacy, told the Cotrigurs of the attack on their homes, and gave them money to retire, and even offered to find them homes within his dominions, should they find themselves dispossessed on their return. The Cotrigurs anxiously retreated; and soon afterwards two thousand of them, under a chief called Sinnion, who had once served under Belisarius, came back to the Empire and were settled in

[1] John Malalas, pp. 431–2: Theophanes, ad ann. 6020, pp. 269–70: John of Ephesus, *Historia Ecclesiae*, p. 475: Procopius, *De Bello Persico*.

[2] Procopius, *De Bello Gothico*, iv., 4, p. 475.

Thrace. Sandilch was annoyed at this volatile policy of the Emperor, and sent a long remonstrance—verbatim through ambassadors, as the Huns could not write. But Justinian ignored the complaints, and merely continued to send the Utigurs a yearly income.[1]

There was a short respite; but the Cotrigurs were incorrigible. In 558, under their king, Zabergan, they came again, in even greater force. Their armies divided into three; one invaded peninsular Greece, one attacked the Thracian Chersonese, and one, the greatest, led by Zabergan himself, forced its way through the Long Walls to the very suburbs of Constantinople. The Emperor was terrified; and the aged Belisarius was summoned to save the Empire. His strategy was successful, and the Cotrigurs were outwitted and routed: while their first army was held up by the defences of Thermopylae, and their second was defeated by the Emperor's nephew, Germanus, at the entrance to the Chersonese. In the meantime the Emperor sent again to the Utigurs. Fearing lest they should be shy after their first experience of the Imperial alliance, he told them that the Cotrigurs had carried off the money destined that year for them; he could have recovered it himself, but he preferred to test their friendship by leaving it for them to do so. Sandilch was impressed by the argument and wanted the money; and so the Cotrigurs and the Utigurs started gaily on an internecine struggle that kept them fully occupied until a new factor appeared on the scene and brusquely silenced them both.[2]

In the early years of the sixth century a race, known among the powers of the far East as the Zhen-Zhen or the Zhuan-Zhuan, dominated over the inhabitants of Turkestan. As time went on, the Turks tired of this oppression;

[1] Procopius, op. cit. iv., 18–19, pp. 550 ff.: Menander Protector, p. 3: Procopius calls the Utigur king, Sandil, Menander and Agathias (see next note), Sandilch. The Tetraxite Goths sent 2,000 men to help the Utigurs.

[2] Agathias, p. 367: Theophanes, pp. 360–1.

and in the ensuing convulsions the Zhen-Zhen moved off to seek new worlds to conquer in the West. There they received a new name, and as the Avars they played their terrible part in history.[1] The Huns of the Steppes lay right across their path. But nothing could withstand the Avars and Candich, their Khagan. The Utigurs were beaten, the Sabirs utterly destroyed; the Cotrigurs were subjugated, and the Avars passed on, to cause panic-stricken turmoil among the Slavs that were quietly filling the Balkans, and to crush the Antae, the bravest of them all. And so they entered deep into Europe, and spent their days now raiding Germany, now attacking the walls of Constantinople. In 562, Candich was succeeded by Baian, who seems to have organized and ordered the vast Avar Empire, stretching from the Don to the middle Danube. Among their sternly repressed subject-races were the Cotrigurs.[2] Meanwhile the Turks, seeking to emulate their erstwhile masters, also moved westward to conquer. The weary Utigurs were no match for them; in 568 they fell under Turkish dominion—the first time that the Bulgars experienced a taste of their future destiny.[3] Thus, with the Cotrigurs enslaved by the Avars and the Utigurs enslaved by the Turks, the curtain goes down on the first act of Bulgarian history.

When next the curtain rises, the scene is utterly changed. The stage is held by Kubrat, King of Old Great Bulgaria.

Hitherto we have only known the Bulgars as they emerged into the view of Imperial history. It is an inevitable limitation; for the Empire alone was civilized

---

[1] I assume the identification of the Zhuan-Zhuan of the Chinese with the Avars to be generally now accepted. See Marquart, *Streifzüge*, p. 43.

[2] Menander Protector, p. 5.

[3] Ibid, pp. 55, 87. Menander's Uguri and Uiguri must be careless spelling for Utiguri; though, on the other hand, the Hunnish tribes all enjoyed remarkably similar names.

enough to produce witnesses capable of writing history, or even of writing at all. But there is one other important testimony, which it is now time to consider; the Bulgars that settled in the present-day Bulgaria produced, in the eighth century, a List of their previous rulers, with dates attached—a work unaffected by any of the historians of the Empire. Unfortunately they gave their dates in their old dead language, so as to provide posterity with an innumerable series of puzzles, philological and mathematical; it is only very recently that new evidence has allowed historians to arrive at any satisfactory conclusions.[1]

Fourth on this List we meet the Khan Kurt, who reigned from 584 to 642. Name and date alike identify him as Kubrat or Crobatus, King of Old Great Bulgaria, King of the Bulgars and their kindred the Cotragi. Of Kubrat's ancestry the Imperial historians say nothing; but the List tells us that he was of the family of Dulo. Two of his predecessors had belonged to this family, though the third, whom he immediately succeeded, was of the house of Ermi.

The first monarch mentioned was Avitokhol, of the house of Dulo, who reigned for the portentous period of three centuries, from A.D. 146 to 437. His successor, Irnik, did not compete with such tenacity of life; a mere century and a half was all that he could manage (437–582). Next came Gostun, of the Ermi family, with a meagre reign of seventeen months (582–4). And so we come to Kurt, who inherited sufficient longevity from his Dulo ancestors to reign close on sixty years (584–642).

The name Avitokhol seems meaningless: unless we remember that, by the seventh century, Christian, Jewish, and even Moslem missionaries were spreading Old

[1] I accept Zlatarski's dating. See Appendix II.

12 THE FIRST BULGARIAN EMPIRE

Testament stories all over the Steppes. The Turks improved on the Scriptures, and told of the later history of Japheth, whose eldest son and heir was called Turk, and surnamed Yafeth-Oghlâni (son of Japheth). Yafeth might easily modify itself into Avit, itself a word meaning 'ancestor.' Thus, perhaps, Avitokhol, ancestor of the first royal house of Bulgaria, was none other than a grandson of Noah himself. Certainly no member of the Patriarch's august family would have thought anything of a reign of a mere three hundred years.[1]

Irnik's parentage was definitely less holy. On the contrary, his father was the Scourge of God. Attila, King of the Huns, left a son whose name was Ernach or Hernak (the Greeks by now dropped their h's). The Bulgars, we know, were Huns; and Attila died in 453, when, according to the List, Irnik was on the Bulgar throne. That Irnik and Ernach were the same person there can hardly be a doubt.[2] But Ernach lived in Little Scythia—in Bessarabia—and Old Great Bulgaria lay on the shores of the Sea of Azov, stretching to the River Kuphis (Kuban). Ernach's descendants must, therefore, have some time moved to the east; possibly one of them early assumed control over the Cotrigurs when that tribe migrated westward; but more probably during the dark days of Avar rule it was a prince of the house of Attila— whose family had some time acquired the surname of Dulo and had no doubt kept the headship of one of the many Hunno-Bulgar tribes of the Steppes—that was able to supply the unifying force which rallied all the Huns and

[1] Mikkola, *Die Chronologie der Türkischen Donaubulgaren*, p. 23. He there quotes a Turkish inscription found by Desmaisons at Abulghasi which told of the history of Japheth. Marquart, *Die Chronologie der Alttürkischen Inschriften*, pp. 75–6, identifies Avitokhol simply with Attila. This is possible, but I think the biblical origin is more convincing; see Appendix III.

[2] Zlatarski, *Istoriya*, i., 1, pp. 40–2, denies the identity of Irnik and Ernach. I give my reasons for disagreeing with him in Appendix III.

Bulgars and so built the kingdom of Old Great Bulgaria. This unifier was, I believe, King Kubrat.[1]

The List, then, permits the following deductions. First, from Avitokhol's three centuries, we may assume that the Bulgar nation had consciously existed for some time past, perhaps even from 146—time enough for it to have acquired a Patriarchal origin: secondly, from Irnik's century and a half, that the Bulgars of the List belonged to the branch of Attila's family founded by his son Ernach, and that roughly from 453 till 582 his descendants, known as the house of Dulo (why, we cannot tell), were nonentities overshadowed by the memory of their ancestor: finally, from 582 to 584, the Dulo were replaced by a new but short-lived dynasty, the Ermi and their head, Gostun, till in 584 the Dulo returned in the person of Kubrat or Kurt, the Liberator, who reigned for fifty-eight years.

It was in the days of the Emperor Heraclius that Kubrat's name was first heard at Constantinople. John, Bishop of Nikiou, writing from the depths of Egypt, told a story of the rumoured alliance between Heraclius's widow, the Empress Martina, and Kubrat, King of the Huns; and he explained it by mentioning that Heraclius had befriended the Hun at Constantinople in his youth. Kubrat had become a Christian, and then had returned to rule triumphantly in his own country; and he always henceforward regarded the family of Heraclius with grateful affection. Hence it was that when Martina and the Patriarch Pyrrhus plotted to depose her stepson, the Emperor Constantine III, people suspected Kubrat of being an accomplice.[2]

The Ethiopian Bishop was romancing when he pictured

[1] John of Nikiou (see below) says that Kubrat made himself supreme over other tribes. Old Great Bulgaria was clearly a composite kingdom of all the Hunno-Bulgars of the Steppes.

[2] *Chronique de Jean de Nikiou*, p. 580.

Kubrat being brought up at Constantinople. Heraclius, his kind Emperor, began to reign in 610, when Kubrat had been a king already for twenty-six years. Nevertheless, it seems certain that Kubrat visited Constantinople a little later. In 619, according to the Patriarch Nicephorus, the ruler of the Huns came there with his suite seeking to be baptized. The baptism took place, and the Hunnish monarch returned, having been made a patrician. A few pages later, after speaking of the Avars, Nicephorus tells of Kubrat, ruler of the Unogunduri, who revolted from the Avar Khagan and sent to Heraclius to make an alliance: which was kept throughout his lifetime. Kubrat was also made a patrician.[1] Both Nicephorus and John of Nikiou when they mention Kubrat call him nephew of Organâ.

Clearly Nicephorus's two accounts refer to the same visit. The second indeed is dated in the margin 635, but from its context it certainly may be a digression into the past. And John of Nikiou's story of Kubrat's youth at Constantinople is clearly an embroidered improvement on the same visit. Kubrat's life-history thus fragmentarily emerges.

Kubrat reigned fifty-eight years; he must, therefore, have been a child when his reign began, and as a child he would need a regent. The regent was no doubt his uncle Organâ, probably a maternal uncle; otherwise, as an adult member of the house of Dulo, he would certainly have preceded his child nephew on the barbarous throne.[2] Gostun was either a usurper or possibly an Avar-appointed governor, and it was Organâ who restored the power of the Dulo. In 619, Kubrat, having taken the government into his own hands, visited Constantinople to secure help

---

[1] Nicephorus, pp. 12 and 24.

[2] It seems to me to be quite unnecessary to identify Organâ with Gostun. It is unconvincing and nothing is gained by it.

against the Avars, against whom he had recently revolted. At this time he was probably just a Hunnish chieftain; his great kingdom was not yet founded. He secured Imperial help—the Emperor was only too grateful for allies against the Avars—at the price of baptism; and on his return he established, not only his independence, but also a supremacy over the neighbouring tribes. When he died, he was ruler of a land lying round the lower Don and south to the Caucasus, the kingdom called Old Great Bulgaria. And he left the five sons of the fairy-story.

It is a little difficult to identify the tribes that made up this kingdom. In his early life, Kubrat is called lord of the Huns or (once by Nicephorus) of the Unogunduri. Theophanes, telling of his sons, calls him lord of Bulgaria and the kindred race the Cotragi (the Cotrigurs), and talks of the Onogunduri, the Bulgars, and the Cotragi as forming his subjects. But the situation of this Bulgaria, from the Don to the Caucasus, is the same as that occupied by the Utigur kingdom. We have heard no more of the Utigurs since their conquest by the Turks. The Turkish tide had ebbed by now, but it must have been strong enough at its fullness utterly to swamp the Utigur power; for it is strange that, while the Cotrigur name survived, the Utigur name vanished. However, considering the geography, it is impossible not to see in the Bulgars of Theophanes the bulk of the old Utigur people, stripped no doubt of its old ruling class, whereas the Cotrigur aristocracy continued an unbroken career. The Onogunduri or Unogunduri present a new difficulty. Before Kubrat's time we never hear of them, but during the next few years the Imperial writers use their name, the Huns', and the Bulgars' indiscriminately to describe the same race. It is possible that the word is a composite affair, a blend of the Huns and the Bulgars, invented by the source from whom Theophanes and Nicephorus both drew, in vague confusion with memories of such early Bulgar tribes as the Onoguri and Burugundi. But all the Hunnish tribes had names of a most unenterprising inter-resemblance, and so it is dangerous to see in any of them an artificial composition. More probably the Onogunduri were the tribe over which the descendants of Ernach ruled. Kubrat in his youth was only lord of the Onogunduri, as Nicephorus says; but he led the revolt against the Avars, and, extending his power eastward over the Cotrigurs and the leaderless Utigurs, founded the new kingdom. The Cotrigurs were probably never completely absorbed. They remained in their old home across the Don, and in the next generation separated again. The second of the five sons in the fairy-story was called Cotragus, and he crossed the Don. Clearly, he owed his name to the nation over which he ruled.[1]

In 642, soon after his rumoured intrigue with the Empress Martina, Kubrat died, at a ripe age and, we may hope, in the odour of sanctity—but we hear no more of his Christianity after his visit to Constantinople; indeed, for two more centuries the Bulgars remained unmistakably heathen. According to the List, his successor was Bezmer, who reigned three years, but after a few months, in February 643, we hear of the accession of Isperikh—we have come here to Asperuch—who reigned fifty-eight years. But, according to the Greek story, the five sons of Kubrat, after living in peace together for a little, presumably under the headship of the eldest, Baian, separated and each went his own way.

---

[1] These problems are fully discussed in Zlatarski (*Istoriya*, i., 1, pp. 84–96). Briefly summarized, his conclusions are (i.) that the house of Dulo has nothing to do with Attila, (ii.) that the Utigurs are the basis of Old Great Bulgaria, and (iii.) that Onogunduri is a composite word—Οὔννοι καὶ Βούλγαροι—and does not describe a separate tribe. For (i.) see my Appendix III. For (ii.) I think his geographical arguments unanswerable, and I am in agreement with the result, with the legitimate modifications suggested above. (iii.) I think unconvincing.

It is possible that Baian (or Batbaian, as Theophanes calls him) and Bezmer were the same person.[1] On the other hand, it is rash to identify names merely because it is convenient to do so and they both have the same initial letter; besides, it would really be more convenient to interpose a generation between Kubrat and his sons. Asperuch, the List tells us, reigned fifty-eight years. The similarity of his reign to Kubrat's is suspicious, though Asperuch's was a few months longer; but that is not sufficient reason for rejecting it. Certainly both Kubrat and Asperuch enjoyed long reigns. But it seems unlikely that a son should only die one hunded and nineteen years after his father's accession. Moreover, Asperuch appears to have had younger brothers. Even allowing for the lengthy lives that their excellent sour milk is said to grant the Bulgarians, the matter remains unconvincing. Kubrat's sons were more probably—some, if not all of them—his grandsons.[2] Their father was Bezmer; but, sandwiched as his paltry reign was between the great Kubrat's and the great Asperuch's, his fame never reached Constantinople.

Soon after Bezmer's accession, the kingdom broke up and the tribes were divided up between various princes of the house of Dulo. The reason was the pressure from a new conquering Turkish race, the Khazars, whose later conversion to Judaism was to be a strange phenomenon in the Christian-Moslem world. At present the Khazars were ruthless militant savages; and Old Great Bulgaria lay in their path. The eldest of the Bulgarian brothers, Baian, stayed at his post; his kingdom, depleted by terrified emigration, fell an easy prey to the Khazars, and he became their tributary. Gradually, it seems, his

---

[1] Zlatarski identifies them, which simplifies his history; but he does not face the difficulty of Kubrat's and Asperuch's age.

[2] I shall continue to call them, for convenience, the sons of Kubrat.

Cᴇ

people were mostly absorbed by the conquerors, without much difficulty, for Huns and Turks came both from the common Turanian stock; and the remainder lasted only to be wiped out by the Maygars. Thus Old Great Bulgaria quietly vanished.[1]

The second brother was known to the Greeks as Cotragus, clearly because he ruled the Cotrigurs. Probably he was a viceroy who declared his independence at the collapse of the central power. According to the fairy-story, he crossed the Don and lived on the far side, the northern bank. This crossing would be merely his inevitable journey when he went to govern the Cotrigurs. Later, however, when the Khazar dominion increased, the Cotrigurs moved farther to the north, recrossing the Don during its upper eastward course, and settling by the middle Volga and the Kama. There their descendants remained for many generations to come, known to the world as the Black or White ('White' is synonymous with 'Great'), or even the Silver (an improvement on 'White'), or merely the Kama Bulgarians. In time they acquired a certain civilization, probably through the Khazars; their capital city, Bulgar, by the junction of the Volga and the Kama, became an important emporium, the centre of the trade of the Volga plain. Early in the tenth century they became converts to Islam, and even imported a Moslem missionary whose gifts included castle-building—indeed he fortified, not only their souls, but their capital—the writer Ibn-Foszlan. Their empire endured till the twelfth century, when they fell before the withering might of the Mongols.

---

[1] Zlatarski, *Istoriya*, p. 114, says that Batbaian founded the Black Bulgaria (on the River Kuban) of Constantine Porphyrogennetus's day. But not only Constantine, but also the tenth-century Arab geographers clearly knew only of one Bulgaria on the Steppes, the Kama-Volga Bulgaria, called also, it is true, by such contradictory names as Black and White Bulgaria. See Constantine Porphyrogennetus, *De Administrando Imperio*, pp. 81, 180: also Maçoudi, *Les Prairies d'Or*, p. 16; Ibn-Foszlan, *De Bulgaris, passim*. It seems, however, that till its extinction Old Great Bulgaria was also called White Bulgaria.

To the last they remained notorious and efficient raiders.[1]

The third brother was Asperuch, whose fortune, following the pattern of the Greek story-tellers, we shall trace later. The fourth brother crossed the Carpathians and the Danube and came to Pannonia, where the Avar Empire had its main seat. There he became a vassal of the Avars. Probably this migration was due to a desire to combine with the Bulgars that had come with the Avars into the central Danubian plain. That there were Bulgars there is incontestable. Indeed, the Bulgars that accompanied the Avars to the great siege of Constantinople in 626 were almost certainly of this branch; for Kubrat's Bulgars were at that time intriguing with the Emperor against the Avars. Moreover, in 630 the German historians tell of a strange, tragic episode. In that year, they say, there was war in Pannonia between the Avars and the Bulgars. The latter were beaten, and nine thousand of them, men, women, and children, migrated to Germany and asked King Dagobert to assign them quarters. He bade them go to Bavaria, but told the Bavarians to kill them all. This was almost completely done; only the leader, Alciocus, and seven hundred of them survived, and fled for refuge to the Wendic Mark.[2] Probably this war was a revolt of the Western Bulgars in connection with Kubrat's successful revolts farther to the east. But, despite Alciocus's emigration, there were probably many Bulgars remaining in Pannonia; and it was in reinforcement of these that the fourth son of Kubrat came. The Pannonian Bulgars remained under Avar suzerainty till the opening of the ninth century, when we shall hear of them again.[3]

[1] See references given in preceding note.

[2] Fredegarius Scholasticus, p. 187: *Gesta Dagoberti*, p. 411, ad ann. 630, gives the same story, leaving out the name Alciocus and allowing no survivors from the Bavarian massacre. Zlatarski (*Istoriya*, pp. 119–20) says that the name Alciocus was an invention, made in confusion with Alzeco; see p. 21.

[3] See p. 50.

From the years 675 to 677 the great city of Thessalonica was besieged by a horde of Bulgar tribes, allied with insurgent Slavs of the neighbourhood. Various Bulgar tribes are mentioned by names that occur there and nowhere else; but their leader was a certain Kuber who had recently revolted against his Avar overlords, and crossed the Danube to settle in the Cormesian plain, near the city. As in the previous great sieges by the Slavs, it needed the personal intervention of their patron saint, Demetrius, to save the Thessalonians.[1] The appearance of Kuber and his Bulgars, who had already crossed the Danube by 675, raises certain problems. To solve them, Kuber has been identified as the fourth son of King Kubrat. He went first to Pannonia and there fell under Avar domination; but, disliking it, he revolted and moved south across the Danube and up the Morava, and so to the confines of Thessalonica.[2] It is possible, but it seems improbable, that Kubrat's fourth son should have been so energetic. On the other hand, the obvious similarity between the names Kubrat and Kuber must not tempt us into a fast identification. But the similarity may not be entirely pointless. Kubrat was still the only great Bulgarian of whom men had hitherto heard. The Thessalonians may well, therefore, have given his name in a debased form to their local Bulgarian; or the martyrologist may simply have made a general muddle of names. But it seems best to attempt no embroidery on the known facts, and to leave Kuber unconnected by relationship or name to King Kubrat. Kuber was merely a stray Bulgarian chieftain, who may have been in the vanguard of Asperuch's invaders, but more probably, considering the geography of the Balkans, came from Pannonia. He may have been a

[1] *Sancti Demetrii Martyris Acta*, pp. 1364 ff. The date of the siege is approximate; we know it began between the years 670 and 675.

[2] Zlatarski, *Istoriya*, pp. 121–2, 148–51.

well-travelled son of Kubrat, or he may have revolted
against the Avars with Alciocus, or independently at a
later date. Anyhow, after the long, divinely frustrated
siege, we hear no more of Kuber. His tribes mingled and
were absorbed with their allies, the Slavs, and thus laid
the first foundation of the Bulgar claims to Macedonia.

The youngest son went to Ravenna. Here the Greek
chroniclers made a small, pardonable mistake. Ravenna,
they knew, was a great Italian city, and round it in these
troublous times of depopulation many barbarians had
settled, Bulgars amongst them[1]; so they used Ravenna for
Italy. In truth, the youngest son went farther. In the
days of the Lombard King Grimoald (662–671), the
Bulgar 'duke' Alzeco peaceably invaded Italy and
offered himself and his army to be the King's vassals.
Grimoald sent them to Benevento, to his son Romoald,
who assigned them three villages near his capital—Sepi-
num, Bovianum, and Isernia. They settled there, and
'to this day'—a century later—still partially spoke their
old language.[2] There is no reason to doubt that herein we
see the fate of the fifth division of Kubrat's Bulgars—a
weak, straggling division by the end of its long journey.
The name Alzeco is suspiciously like Alciocus; but that
proves nothing. The two chieftains were clearly not the
same.

Thus the Bulgar family split up, and spread over
Europe, from the Volga to the shadow of Vesuvius. It
remains now only to consider the strongest branch of all,
the only branch to survive the tempests of the centuries.
Asperuch, less restless than his younger brothers, but more
enterprising than his elders, moved along the Black Sea
coast, across the great rivers of the Steppes, to the land of
lagoons and marshes where the Danube joins the sea.

[1] Paulus Diaconus, *Historia Langobardorum*, lib. ii., p. 87.
[2] Ibid., op. cit., p. 154.

Chapter II

BARBARIANS IN THE BALKANS

FOR centuries past, the Balkan peninsula had been the playground of barbarians, a land that the fierce tribes pillaged and destroyed and left deserted. But till the sixth century none of them made of it a lasting home. The Goths and Gepids, the Sarmatians and the Huns, had all passed through, trailing blood and fire, and moved on to seek richer countries. It was left for a gentler race, the Slavs, to inherit the Balkans.

Gentle is here a comparative term; but the Slav penetration was covert, an almost unnoticed work achieved under the shadow of more terrible and spectacular movements. In the fourth century the Slavs were still, it seems, hidden in their home, the forests of Western Russia; by the beginning of the sixth century, the world, having hitherto ignored them, was astonished to find that all over Central Europe, from the Elbe and the Alps to the Russian rivers, from the Baltic to the Save and the Danube, Slavs were thick upon the ground. The statesmen of the Empire, anxiously watching the Danube frontier, grew alarmed. The Slavs might be less savage than the Huns, but they were very numerous, and one of their tribes, the Antae, now by the mouth of the Danube, was renowned for its warlike qualities.

In the reign of the Emperor Justinian the storm broke—softly at first, in isolated raids. In 534 the Slavs made their first excursion across the river. In 545 and 549 they penetrated to Thrace, in 547 to Dyrrhachium; in 550 they threatened Adrianople and the great city for which they

had struggled so long, and still in vain, Thessalonica.¹ In
558 they followed in the train of the Cotrigurs, to the walls
of Constantinople.²

As the century passed on, the Avars loomed larger in
the background; and the Slavs decided to seek safer homes
across the Danube. In 581, for the first time, they
entered the Balkans and remained.³ In the following
years their settlements feverishly increased; between 584
and 589 there were no less than ten invasions of the Greek
peninsula.⁴ The Avars followed the Slav refugees, and
the two would even combine against the Empire. In 597
Thessalonica suffered at their hands the first of its great
sieges, when Saint Demetrius had to come to the rescue
of his city.⁵ In 601 the Emperor Maurice, victorious
against the Avars, made a treaty in which the Imperial
frontier was still placed at the Danube.⁶ But it was an
idle boast. During the next years the troubles of Phocas's
usurpation and the Persian war denuded the Balkans of
Imperial troops; and the Slavs could do as they pleased.
They overran Dalmatia, destroying Salona, the old
metropolis, and spread eastward over the peninsula: till,
by the fourth decade of the century, only the great maritime cities and the Albanian mountains were untainted;
even the Peloponnese had its Slavic settlements.⁷

At the same time the Avars were growing in strength,
even in the Balkans, to reach their high tide at the great
siege of Constantinople in 626: in which the Slavs joined,

¹ Procopius, *Bello Gothico*, pp. 329, 331, 441, 444, 592.
² Agathias, p. 367: Theophanes, p. 360.
³ John of Ephesus (trans. Schönfelder), p. 8: Michel le Syrien, p. 347.
⁴ Michel le Syrien, p. 361: Evagrius, p. 228.
⁵ *Sancti Demetrii Martyris Acta*, pp. 1284 ff.
⁶ Theophylact Simocatta, pp. 250–60: Theophanes, p. 432 (he calls the
Avars Bulgars, mixing them with their vassals).
⁷ *Sancti Demetrii Martyris Acta*, p. 1361: Niederle, *Slovanské Starožitnosti*,
ii., p. 224. Thessalonica had twice again been nearly besieged (*S. D. M.
Acta*, pp. 1336, 1341 ff.).

as their vassals.[1]   After the failure of the siege the Avar power ebbed.   In the distant north of their empire, King Samo freed the Czechs and the Moravians; farther to the south, the Balkan Slavs were strengthened by new invaders of their kindred, the Croats and the Serbs.   As the Avar dominion receded, the Imperial dominion grew; and the Emperor Heraclius, victorious at last from the Persian and Avar wars, induced the Balkan Slavs to recognize his suzerainty.   He even attempted to strengthen his hold by Christian missions; but, except along the Dalmatian coast, where local missionaries from the holy Latin cities aided the work, the evangelization had little result.[2]

From the Avar decline till Asperuch's advance from the Danube delta, the peninsula enjoyed a few decades' comparative quiet.   The Empire had recovered a certain control.   The coast cities had never passed into Slav hands—though Thessalonica's escape had more than once been thought literally miraculous—and now with the peace were able to spread their commercial, and therefore political, influence over their neighbours.   In the centre of the peninsula, Upper Macedonia, and the Morava plain, and in the Greek watershed, the Slavs were to all intents independent; but farther east, along the ranges of Haemus and Rhodope, the Empire kept a few inland garrison cities, to guard the roads to Constantinople— cities such as Adrianople, Philippopolis, and, far into the heart of the barbarians, Sardica (Sofia).[3]   The Slavs by themselves did not constitute a great menace.   They were brigands and pirates, but never systematic conquerors.

---

[1] Theophanes, p. 485.   [2] See Appendix IV.

[3] The extent of the destruction of the old city life can to some degree be gauged by the various lists of bishops and signatures to the Councils. These have been admirably analysed in Dvornik, *Les Slaves, Byzance et Rome*, p. 74 ff.   I am inclined to think that the organized establishment of garrisons in the inland cities probably only dates from Constantine V's campaigns; but presumably some defence was always maintained in towns like Adrianople or Sardica.

Of old, the Antae alone had achieved any sort of political organization; and though soon the Croats, and a little later the Serbs, were to feel their way out of chaos, as yet the Balkan Slavs were disunited and disorganized. They all spoke much the same language, and probably indulged in the same heathen religions. But there their unity ended. In other respects they were divided up into small tribes, each with its petty chieftain,[1] and inclined to be jealous of its neighbours: some of the tribes were purely predatory, but more, it seems, were peacefully inclined and pastoral. They were too prolific not to be restless; but once they had overrun the whole country there was no reason why they should not have settled down and, from their disorganized weakness, fallen gradually under the recovering power of the Emperors from Constantinople. In the past the Slavs had only been an aggressive menace when they had attacked in the train of the Cotrigurs or the Avars. If now no fresh invaders were allowed to enter in, the Slavs as a political force might fail, and the Balkans be saved to Byzantium.

But Asperuch the Bulgar came to the Danube, and crossed.

This first resting-place of Asperuch, after he left his home, has always been a puzzle. He crossed the Dnieper and the Dniester, and came at last to a place called Onglos or Oglos; but neither of our informants, Nicephorus and Theophanes, seems sure on which side of the Danube to situate it. Subsequent generations have remained in equal doubt, arguing each side in turn. The answer probably is both sides, but more particularly the middle of the river. Oglos was one of the islands of the Danube delta, probably

---

[1] Called in the *Sancti Demetrii Martyris Acta*, ῥήγες. The accounts of the sieges of Thessalonica provide a good picture of the Slavs at that time. See references above.

Peuce.[1] The muddle is certainly helped by the fact that neither Theophanes nor Nicephorus, each deriving his matter from the same lost source, understood the situation, which was probably incompletely described in the source; and so each improved on it in his own way. Anyhow, it is useless to attempt great accuracy. Asperuch's Bulgars were a numerous race. Oglos, or Peuce, was their temporary centre, but there was probably a vanguard in the Dobrudja and a rearguard in Bessarabia. All that we know is that it was a country difficult of access and full of natural fortresses, marshy and rocky—though the rocks may only be one of Nicephorus's improvements. Such a description might well be applied to the Danube delta and the country surrounding it.[2]

Wherever it was, it was inconveniently close to the lands of the Empire, those difficult Balkan provinces where the Slavs were being gradually tamed. We cannot accurately tell the date of Asperuch's move to Oglos. It must have been a gradual affair, taking place between the years 650 and 670.[3] During these years the Empire was occupied in a sanguinary war with the Arabs in Asia, and in Europe in the religious and diplomatic intricacies of the Monothelite controversy; and in 668 the murder of the West-loving Emperor Constans by a chamberlain with a soap-bowl was followed by a short rebellion. But by the year 679 the throne was secure and the Arab war was ending. The Emperor Constantine IV, Pogonatus, the Bearded, was alive to the danger of allowing new invaders into

---

[1] Identified by Zlatarski (*Istoriya*, i., pp. 123 ff., 387 ff.), who discusses the question convincingly. Additional difficulties have been created by a persistent attempt of historians from Theophanes onward to derive Ὄγλος from the Slavonic âgul, 'a corner' (cf. the Greek ὄγλος, 'an angle or corner'). Really it can be equally well derived from agul, 'an enclosure.'

[2] See Zlatarski, loc. cit.: Theophanes, pp. 546–9: Nicephorus, pp. 33–5. Bury (*Eastern Roman Empire*, p. 338) thinks that the earthworks of Preslav-on-the-Danube date from this occupation. He is probably right.

[3] The outside dates are 643 and 679.

the Balkans, to disquieten or, worse, to organize the Slavs. Asperuch's Bulgar hordes must be driven back or crushed.

And so the Imperial armies marched to the Danube; and there followed that campaign that was ruined by the Emperor's sore feet—a euphemism, probably, for gout. The result was very different from the Emperor's hopes. The Bulgars, victoriously driving back the Imperial invaders, themselves invaded the Empire. Their hordes overran the country as far south as Varna, pillaging and making innumerable captives. And where they came they settled. They conquered the Slavs that inhabited the countryside, and threatened the Imperial cities. The Balkan world had been taken by surprise; it could effect no resistance. Thus, rapidly and unexpectedly, early in the year 680, Asperuch founded modern Bulgaria, Bulgaria south of the Danube.

The Emperor bowed to fate. Shocked at the numbers of captives from his people, he hastened to make peace. All the land beyond the northern slopes of Haemus as far as the Danube and the Avar frontier (an unknown distance) was ceded to the Bulgar monarch; and he was further promised a yearly tribute if he abstained from raiding the Empire—a humiliating concession, but one according to the canons of Byzantine economy, which found tributes less expensive, on the whole, than wars.[1]

The exact extent of Asperuch's new kingdom is impossible to discover. South of the Danube its eastern boundary was the Black Sea, its southern the Haemus (Balkan) range, and its western probably the River Isker; but there was also considerable territory on the northern bank, including Bessarabia as far as the River Dniester, and probably the bulk of the Wallachian plain. Along

[1] Theophanes and Nicephorus, loc. cit.

this vague northern line it abutted on to the Avar empire.[1] But it was to the south of the Danube that Asperuch now transferred the seat of his government. Asperuch was not only a conqueror, but also a statesman. From the first he saw that the success of his kingdom depended on the Slav population. The Slavs of the north-east Balkans, haunted by the memory of the Avars and a fear of the Imperial restoration, had submitted to Asperuch with a good grace, almost welcoming him as a leader against the dangers. Asperuch made use of their compliance to organize them, placing them in tribes along his various frontiers and controlling them from the centre, where he built his palace of Pliska and held his Court.

Pliska was no more than a fortified camp, a collection of tents or rude habitations surrounded with great earthworks. It was situated on the low, rolling hills that lie inland from Varna and join the Dobrudja plain with the heights of Haemus. This district was the nucleus of the new kingdom. It was probably cleared of the Slavs; their business was to provide padding along the frontier. The relations between the Bulgars and their subject Slavs are difficult to decipher clearly. It is highly unlikely that they blended all at once, as some Slavophil Bulgar historians have maintained. It is also unlikely that the Bulgar invaders were the mere handful that they are usually depicted to be. The tribe that settled at Oglos and so easily defeated a large, well-trained Imperial army must have been, to judge from the Imperial historians' accounts, a tribe of considerable dimensions. It is impossible to lay down a dogma on the subject; but it seems that round the edge of the Bulgar kingdom there were these Slav tribes, which kept their old chieftains—we soon find a Slav aristocratic element at the Bulgar Court—but

---

[1] See Zlatarski, *Istoriya* i., 1, pp. 151 ff. I do not think that Asperuch extended his power as far west as the Isker till after the 689 war.

were controlled by Bulgar commissioners: while in the centre was the Bulgar king, the Sublime Khan, and his Bulgar officials and Bulgar armies. During the next century the Imperial historians, when talking of the Bulgar wars, usually call the enemy the 'Bulgars and Slavs,' implying an alliance, but not a fusion; and at the end of the century we find Slavs fleeing to the Empire for refuge against the Bulgars[1]—a movement that suggests that the Bulgars were not yet a predominantly Slav nation.

Of the organization of the Bulgars themselves we are better informed. Like all the Finno-Turkish tribes they had a clan system; and the Sublime Khan was actually only the most exalted of the Khans, the chiefs of the clans. At present the house of Dulo, with its high Hunnish past, was firmly established in the supremacy; but later, when the dynasty faded out, the dangers of the clan system made themselves apparent. The two chief Ministers were called the *kanarti* (possibly the same as the *kavkan*) and the *tarkan*; the latter, it seems, was in charge of the provincial administration. The nobles were divided into two classes: the superior consisted of the *boliars* or *boyars*—in the tenth century there were six *boyars*, but before Boris's day they were probably more numerous; the lower of the *bagaïns*. There were also other titles, such as the *bagatur* or the *koulourat*; but their functions are unknown. During the ninth century the title of Khan was changed to that of Knyaz, the Slavonic 'prince'; but the other old Bulgar titles lasted till the fall of the Bulgar Empire, and one even longer—the title *boyar* appears throughout the Slavonic world.[2]

Asperuch lived on for more than twenty years after the invasion, organizing his realm. He was not left entirely in peace. In 685 there succeeded to the Imperial throne a

[1] During Constantine V's Bulgar wars (see below).
[2] I discuss the Bulgar titles in Appendix V.

fierce, restless youth, Justinian II. Annoyed at paying a
tribute to the barbarians, he soon broke the peace of 680,
and in 689 invaded Bulgar territory—a land now called
by the Imperial chronicler 'Sclavinia and Bulgaria,' the
Bulgar kingdom and its Slav fringe. The Bulgars fled
before Justinian, and he turned and came down the
centre of the peninsula to Thessalonica, bringing great
numbers of Slavs in his train, some of them captives,
others gladly escaping from Bulgar domination. All these
he sent across to Asia to settle in the Opsician theme. A
few years later thirty thousand of them went out under his
banners to fight the Saracens. Satisfied with his good
work, Justinian marched back through enemy country;
but on the way the Bulgars ambushed him. His army
was routed, and he himself barely escaped alive back
to Constantinople. And so the Bulgars were left in
peace.[1]

In 701, Asperuch died, fifty-eight years since his separa-
tion from his brothers. His successor was Tervel, of the
house of Dulo, his son, or perhaps his grandson. Tervel
continued in Asperuch's path, quietly consolidating his
kingdom: till once again, in 705, the sinister figure of
the Emperor Justinian II, an outlaw now, with his nose
and his tongue slit, entered into Bulgar history. The ex-
Emperor, since his deposition in 695, had been living in
exile at Cherson, and latterly at the Court of the Khan of
the Khazars, whose daughter he had married. But the
Khan turned against him and he had to flee for his life.
Angrier and more determined than ever, he came to
Tervel and asked for help. Tervel was delighted; the
troubled waters were admirable for an ambitious angler.
He placed his army of Bulgars and Slav vassals at Jus-
tinian's disposal, and the two monarchs marched on
Constantinople. The walls of the city baffled them, and

[1] Theophanes, p. 557: Nicephorus, p. 36.

the citizens within mocked at the ex-Emperor. But, after three days, Justinian crept in along an aqueduct. His sudden appearance suggested treachery, or magic, or the undermining of the walls. The city was seized with panic. The Emperor Tiberius fled; and Justinian was quickly established in the palace and on the throne. He remembered his Bulgar benefactor; Tervel was invited into the city, and, seated at the Emperor's side, was given the title of Caesar.

The title is significant; but it is probable that the Emperor and the Khan interpreted it differently. Caesar was the second rank in the Imperial hierarchy; but it was *in* the Imperial hierarchy, under the Emperor. Tervel, in accepting the title, might seem to be acknowledging himself as being under the suzerainty of the Emperor, almost the Imperial viceroy in Bulgaria. But certainly Tervel intended no such thing. He was not versed in Byzantine history and etiquette. He merely saw that the Emperor was willing—was almost obliged—to give him a high-sounding title and a seat at his side; and he accepted it as a tribute to his power, that would raise his prestige in his own country and over the whole world. His view of the transaction was strengthened by the fact that Justinian gave him an immense amount of presents and ceded to his realm the small but valuable district known in Slavonic as Zagoria, 'Beyond the Mountains,' the district that slopes from the eastern end of the Haemus range down to the Gulf of Burgas. The towns on the Gulf, however— Mesembria, Anchialus, and Develtus—remained in Imperial hands. Tervel had also been promised the hand of the Emperor's daughter; but she was still a little child, and the marriage never took place. Bulgaria had to wait two more centuries for its first foreign queen.[1]

[1] Theophanes, p. 572–3: Nicephorus, p. 41–2: Georgius Hamartolus, ii., p. 622. See also Zlatarski, *Istoriya*, i., pp. 163 ff.

Meanwhile the Byzantine enjoyed the interesting spec-
tacle of the Bulgar Khan distributing largesse to his
soldiers, and measuring the gifts of the Emperor with his
barbaric whip.[1]

The peace was of short duration. Justinian, who never
forgot his injuries, soon forgot his benefits. In 708, no
doubt because Tervel demanded more presents or tribute,
Justinian prepared to invade Bulgaria. His army encamped by Anchialus, where his fleet rode in the harbour.
The troops felt secure, and their discipline was slack: so
that a surprise attack from the Bulgars utterly routed
them. Justinian himself took refuge in the citadel; after
three days' siege he escaped to his ships and returned in
disgrace to Constantinople. But Tervel seems to have
won no material benefit by his victory. Moreover, he
showed a strangely forgiving nature; he sent three
thousand of his Bulgars to accompany Justinian in his
flight to Bithynia in 711. They stayed with him till his
cause was desperate, and left him then to his death.[2]

Imperial troubles during the next few years gave Tervel
fresh opportunities for interference. In 712, as though to
avenge his friend Justinian, he invaded Thrace, ravaging
as far as the Golden Gate of Constantinople itself, and
retiring laden with booty and unhurt.[3] In 716, when an
Arab invasion was imminent, the ephemeral Emperor
Theodosius III sought to consolidate his position by
making a treaty with Tervel, the first Bulgarian treaty the
terms of which we know. These terms first fixed the
frontier: which was to pass by Meleona—an unknown
place that must be some peak on the great Monastery
range, such as the heights of Bakadzhik. Probably the
frontier now followed the line later fortified by the Bulgars

---

[1] Suidas, *Lexicon*, p. 761.
[2] Theophanes, pp. 575–6: Nicephorus, pp. 43–4, 47.
[3] Theophanes, pp. 586–7: Nicephorus, pp. 48–9.

and known as the Great Fence of Thrace—a line running roughly for some miles from the northern shore of the Gulf of Burgas in a west-south-west direction, through Bakadzhik to the Maritsa. Farther west the country was too unsettled for a definite frontier to be drawn. The second article of the treaty provided for a yearly payment by the Imperial Court to the Khan of robes and skins to the value of 30 lb. of gold (about £1,350). The third provided for an exchange of prisoners and the return of refugees, even refugees who were hostile to the present Governments—the Imperial civil wars must have obliged many intriguers from the Empire to take refuge in Bulgaria. The fourth article stipulated the free intercourse of merchants and merchandise between the two countries, provided that the merchants had passports and seals; those without passports were to have their goods confiscated.[1]

Theodosius barely outlasted the treaty; but his successor, Leo the Isaurian, apparently confirmed it, through his ambassador, Sisinnius Rendacius. In 717, when the Arabs made their second great siege of Constantinople, Tervel helped the Imperial defenders by making a raid, considerably to his profit, on the Arab encampment.[2] But next year, after the Arabs had fled in rout, Tervel grew less well-disposed towards the Emperor Leo, and even involved himself in an intrigue in favour of the ex-Emperor, that emanated from Thessalonica and was supported by Sisinnius. However, the affair amounted to nothing, and shortly afterwards Tervel died, in May 718.[3]

[1] Theophanes, p. 775. He only refers to it retrospectively, when dealing with Krum's wars, a century later. He says it was made between Theodosius and the Patriarch Germanus, and Cormesius (Kormisosh) of Bulgaria. Clearly Tervel is meant. With regard to the Great Fence, which some historians think dates from this time, see Appendix VI.

[2] Theophanes, p. 611: Cedrenus, p. 790: Zonaras, p. 726.

[3] Theophanes, p. 615: Nicephorus, p. 55. The date of Tervel's death is given in the List.

DE

Tervel's reign had been restless, and his policy variable and perverse. He was justified by his achievements. His readiness to interfere helpfully in the internal troubles of the Empire, in spite of the Emperors' breaches of the peace, made him too valuable a figure in Imperial politics. In those difficult years no Emperor could afford to embark on the natural course of stamping out the aggressive barbarians. Justinian II, who alone made one short and disastrous attempt to do so, did not dare to repeat the experiment, lest it might be successful and he lose his best support. Meanwhile the indispensable Tervel improved his own position. His frontier was pushed farther south over the Haemus to embrace Zagoria and to stretch even to the mountains of Rhodope. How far west it ran we do not know; Sardica and Philippopolis were both Imperial fortresses, but Bulgar influence was spreading; it was alarming that Thessalonican intriguers should be in close touch with the Khan. But more alarming was the firmness with which the Bulgars were now established in their home. The newly come nomads of thirty years before now ruled a kingdom from beyond the Danube into Thrace, and ruled it in sufficient tranquillity to enjoy the blessings of commerce. They were still distinct from the Slavs; and, except round their centre—which, it seems, was more purely Bulgar—they were only the landowning, organizing aristocracy, similar no doubt to the Normans that three centuries later were to order the backward Anglo-Saxons. But a certain blending between the races was inevitable; though there yet remained many Slavs to resent the Bulgar intrusion.

Of the details of this consolidation we are necessarily ignorant, but that it certainly existed was proved by the story of the next half-century. For thirty-seven years after Tervel's last intrigue the Imperial chroniclers have nothing to tell of the Bulgars. Even the Bulgar List cannot give us the name of his successor, who reigned for six years, till 724. There then followed the Khan Sevar, till 739; but of him we know nothing, save that, like his predecessors, he was of the family of Dulo. In him this great house, the House of Attila, died out.[1]

The end of the old reverend dynasty meant an era of civil wars. The Bulgar lords and *boyars* were too jealous of each other to submit long to the rule of any one of their number. Moreover, they were splitting into two factions. The one, misunderstanding Tervel's policy, were all for concord with the Empire and eyed longingly the comforts of Byzantine civilization. The other hated the seductive luxuries and Imperial conceptions of Byzantium, and were determined on war. The successor of the last Dulo was a *boyar* named Kormisosh, of the family of Vokil or Ukil. Kormisosh belonged, it seems, to the Byzantine faction; for sixteen years, by maintaining peace, he maintained himself on the throne, till, in 755, circumstances forced him into war.

Under the great Isaurians, Leo III and Constantine V, the Empire had been undergoing religious schism but political re-organization, and the latter Emperor was now in a position from which he could strike at his neighbours. The common people of Byzantium might mourn for their lost images and surname their persecutor Copronymus, the Dung-named, but the army was devoted to him; and he had made the army supreme in the State. In the year 755, Constantine had transported large numbers of Armenians from Theodosiopolis and Syrians from Melitene to the Thracian frontier, where he constructed fortresses for them, to be their homes and their defence. The Bulgars demanded tribute and an indemnity on account of these new fortresses; their construction was probably a breach

[1] The dates and dynasties are to be found in the List (see Appendix II.).

of the Theodosian peace.[1]   But Constantine dismissed the
Bulgar ambassadors with contumely, and so Kormisosh
had to yield to the pressure of his war party, and invaded
the Empire.

The Bulgars raided triumphantly as far as the Long
Walls; but suddenly Constantine fell on them and routed
them utterly.   Even during their headlong flight the
Emperor inflicted heavy losses on them.[2]   The story of
the ensuing campaign is a little hard to decipher; our
two informants, Theophanes and Nicephorus, disagree,
the former's account merely mentioning a terrible victory
of the Bulgars at Veregava in 759, the latter's, the more
detailed but less dated, telling of a considerable campaign
that followed on the 755 raid but was over by 762, cul-
minating in an Imperial victory at Marcellae.   Neither
chronicler appears to have heard of the other's battle.
Nicephorus is the more convincing; it is necessary to follow
his accounts interspersing dates and a disaster at Veregava
as best we may.   It seems, then, that Constantine determined to follow up his victory.   Soon afterwards he took
an army by sea to the mouth of the Danube, and, landing
there, marched down victoriously through Bulgaria, pillaging and making captives as he came, and finally routed
the Bulgar army near a fort called Marcellae, close to the
Imperial frontier.[3]   This must have occurred during the
years 756 or 757.   In 758, as we know from Theophanes,

[1] Both Nicephorus, p. 66, and Theophanes, p. 662, say that the Bulgars
claimed tribute at the sight of the new fortresses, Theophanes adding, 'according to the πάκτα.'   I do not think it is necessary to give as complicated an explanation as Lombard (*Constantin V, Empereur des Romains*,
p. 43) gives.   It simply was a breach of the treaty, entitling the other party
to compensation.   I believe that neither side was to fortify the frontier;
and that is why the Fence was not built by the Bulgars as yet.

[2] Theophanes, p. 662, says that the Bulgar raid was successful, using
almost the identical words which he used to tell of the successful Bulgar
raid of 712.   Here he must be wrong; Nicephorus is too positive.

[3] Identified by Bury (*Eastern Roman Empire*, p. 339) as Karnobad. Zlatarski places it at Bakadzhik (pp. 204–5).

Constantine was busy subduing the Slavs of the Thracian and Macedonian frontiers—they had no doubt taken advantage of the war between their two overlords to aim at independence. Constantine firmly reduced them to obedience. In 759 it is quite possible that Theophanes's battle of Veregava took place. Probably Constantine himself was not present, and that is why Nicephorus ignores it. Nicephorus implies that Constantine had conquered a large number of the tribes in Bulgaria; but by the end of the campaign it is clear that he did not still hold them. It is, therefore, likely that he left behind an army of occupation, which, however, was heavily defeated by the Bulgars as it passed through the defiles of Veregava, on the Diampolis–Pliska road, and forced to evacuate the country. Among the dead were the strategus of the Thracesian regiment, and many other distinguished soldiers. But, in spite of this reverse, whose importance Theophanes probably exaggerated, the campaign had been highly favourable to the Emperor, and the Bulgars were anxious to sue for peace, possibly forfeiting their tribute, and certainly providing hostages.[1]

During these troubles, Kormisosh had died, in September 756, soon after the first defeat. It was his successor, Vinekh (of the same family, probably his son) who had to bear the brunt of the war. Its disasters were his undoing. His subjects supported him through it all, but the humiliating peace exasperated them. At the close of 761 they rose up against him, and massacred him and all the representatives of the house of Ukil; and in their place the throne was given to a sinister *boyar* of the house of Ugain, called Telets, the leader of the war party.[2]

[1] Theophanes, pp. 662–5: Nicephorus, pp. 66–7: see Lombard, op. cit., pp. 43 ff.

[2] Dates given in the List: Theophanes, p. 667: Nicephorus, p. 69, also his *Antirrhetici*, p. 508.

Telets (whose age, we are told, was thirty) at once embarked on a vigorous policy, and forcibly levied troops
from among his subjects.   This was not altogether agreeable to the Slavs, and in consequence a horde of some
208,000 of them left Bulgaria to seek an asylum in the
Empire.   The Emperors had always been glad to mix up
populations so as to break down nationalism; and Constantine received them gladly, allotting them a home in
Bithynia, by the River Artanas.

The Khan began the war with an invasion of Thrace,
during which he even captured some of the frontier fortresses.   Then, knowing that he would have to face re-
prisals, he took the precaution, rare among the barbarians,
of fortifying his frontier, and waited behind in a strong
position with a great army, to which he had added no
less than 20,000 auxiliaries, chiefly Slav.   But Constantine
was equally impressed by the seriousness of the war, and
the Empire could command better organized resources.
First he dispatched an expedition by sea to the mouth of
the Danube (as he had done on his first campaign)—
mainly a cavalry force, each boat carrying twelve horses.
Then, as his horsemen rode down through the Dobrudja,
he marched up through Thrace, and in June 763[1] the
armies met and encamped by Anchialus, the great Imperial city at the head of the Gulf of Burgas.   Telets attacked them there, on June 30, and a terrible battle
raged from daybreak to nightfall.   The carnage was immense, but in the end the Bulgars were routed.   The

[1] I agree with Zlatarski (*Istoriya*, i., 1, p. 213) in dating the battle of
Anchialus 763 rather than 762, which Theophanes gives and which Lombard (op. cit., pp. 47–8) accepts. Theophanes dates Telets's revolution and
the battle before the great winter of 762–3; Nicephorus dates them both
after; the natural deduction seems to me to be that the revolution, Telets's
first expedition (which Theophanes does not mention), and the Slav
emigration occurred in 762, but Constantine had to wait till after the winter
(which was severe enough to freeze the shores of the Black Sea) to start his
punitive campaign.   Telets, as we know from the List, did not fall till the
close of 764.

Imperial army was too heavily reduced to follow up the
victory; so Constantine returned to his capital, to hold
triumphal games in the Circus and to slaughter ceremoniously his thousands of captives. [1]

The disaster had crippled the Bulgars, but it did not
break their spirit. Telets's government lingered on for
a year discredited. It failed to repair the position, so
eventually Telets was murdered with the nobles of his
party by his angry subjects. The throne was now given
back as nearly as possible to the annihilated dynasty of Ukil;
Sabin, a son-in-law of Kormisosh, became Khan. Sabin at
once tried to negotiate with Constantine; but a peace was
not at all to the temper of the Bulgars. Accused of handing
over the country to the Empire, he found it a necessary
precaution to flee to the Imperial city of Mesembria, where
he threw himself on the protection of the Emperor. In
his place the Bulgars appointed a Khan called Pagan. [2]

Constantine received Sabin gladly, and even sent for
his wives and relations from Bulgaria, thus collecting the
whole Bulgar Royal family at Constantinople. Meanwhile Pagan realized that further war was impossible,
and sent an embassy to the Imperial court. It was not
received. Instead, Constantine prepared a new expedition. Pagan was desperate; with his *boyars* he came in
person to Constantine to beg for clemency. Constantine
received them with the ex-Khan Sabin seated by his side,
and harangued them sternly as rebels against their legitimate sovereign; but making it quite clear that he considered their sovereign as his vassal. Peace was made,
but, it seems, at the price of Pagan's deposition. We do
not know if Sabin returned to Bulgaria, or if he appointed

[1] Theophanes, pp. 667–9: Nicephorus, pp. 69–70.
[2] For the chronology of this period and for the sequence of the Bulgar
Khans see Appendix II. I believe that both Theophanes and Nicephorus
(who disagree between themselves) are wrong, and that Theophanes's
Paganus and Nicephorus's Campaganus (Khan Pagan) are one person,
and Nicephorus's Baianus quite separate.

a viceroy. According to the List, he died in 766, and was
succeeded by his relation, Umar. Meanwhile the Emperor
was able to reduce the Slav brigands that had taken advantage of the wars to frequent the Thracian frontier.[1]

Again the peace was of short duration. Umar's reign
only lasted a few months; before the end of 766 he was
deposed by a certain Tokt, who, we are told, was the
brother of Baian and a Bulgarian. The latter epithet
seems superfluous; probably it means that Tokt belonged
to the nationalist war party, as opposed to the pro-Greek
house of Ukil. Constantine answered the revolution with
a fresh expedition, which found the frontier fortresses deserted, and over-ran the whole country. The Bulgars that
could escape fled to the forests of the Danube. Tokt and
his brother Baian were captured and put to death; the
ex-Khan Pagan was killed by his slaves as he attempted
to escape to Varna.

For the next few years there was anarchy in Bulgaria;
but the Bulgars nevertheless still resisted the Emperor.
His next campaign was apparently fruitless; he advanced,
ravaging, only as far as the River Tundzha, very close to
the frontier, and then was obliged to retire, probably
owing to trouble at home. But he persevered, determined
to administer the *coup de grâce*. Accordingly (probably
in 767) he set out again with vast preparations, and penetrated as far as the Pass of Veregava. But the expedition
was not as final as he had hoped; 2,600 transports that
set out along the Black Sea to bring additional troops to
Mesembria were driven by the north wind on to the coast
of the Gulf of Burgas, and totally destroyed. Still, the
Bulgars were glad to sue for peace, and hostilities ceased
for some five years.[2]

[1] Theophanes, pp. 660, 673–4: Nicephorus, p. 70.

[2] Nicephorus, pp. 70–3: Theophanes (p. 674), following his habit of
recording for preference Constantine's unsuccessful actions, only tells of
the Tundzha campaign. But there is no need, therefore, to assume with

During these years—we do not know exactly when, for the List stops with Umar—a new, abler Khan mounted the Bulgar throne, a certain Telerig, of unknown birth. By May 773 Telerig was well enough established to alarm the Emperor. Constantine adopted his usual tactics. A fleet of 2,000 ships was sent to the Danube, where the Emperor disembarked, while the generals of the themes invaded Bulgaria by land. When the Emperor in his southward march reached Varna, the Bulgars in terror asked for peace. Constantine agreed, and returned to Constantinople, where the *boyar* Tsigat came to discuss terms. But in October, while the negotiations were still going on, Constantine was informed by his spies that Telerig was preparing an expedition of 12,000 soldiers under a *boyar* against the Berzetian Slavs, who lived in Thessaly, intending to deport them into Bulgaria—probably the Bulgars were anxious to increase their population, depleted by the war, and the Berzetians, kindred to their own Slav subjects, seemed the most amenable tribe. But Constantine was too quick for them. Deceiving the Bulgar ambassador by pretending that he was arming against the Arabs, he invaded Bulgaria with forced marches and, with an army 80,000 strong, fell on the Bulgars at Lithosoria,[1] and put them to flight without the loss of a single man. His return to Constantinople was celebrated in a triumph, and the campaign was surnamed the Noble War.[2]

The Noble War no doubt accelerated the peace. We

Lombard (op. cit., p. 51) that he is lying; the second campaign mentioned by Nicephorus (p. 71) was apparently abortive, and clearly Theophanes alludes to it, not the previous campaign.

[1] Probably the Blue Rock in the Balkan Mountains by the River Sliven (Zlatarski, *Istoriya*, i., 1, p. 232).

[2] Theophanes, pp. 691–2. His chronology is obscure. The May campaign is given as being in Ind. XII, and the Noble War which follows it in the text in October, Ind. XI. It does not seem necessary to transpose the campaigns as Lombard does (op. cit., pp. 53 ff.); we know that peace negotiations were proceeding at the time of the Noble War. It is simplest to assume

do not know its terms save that Khan and Emperor undertook never to invade the other's country. It was soon broken. Early in the next year (774) Constantine planned another combined land and sea campaign, this time accompanying the land forces. The expedition was apparently resultless; again the weather intervened and wrecked some of his ships: though Theophanes's story of an almost universal disaster is too like the previous story of the Anchialus wrecks to be convincing. Theophanes was always impatiently eager to exaggerate the disasters of the heretic Emperor.[1]

Later in the year Telerig outwitted the Emperor. Theophanes says that the Khan sent to Constantine to tell him that he was likely to have to flee to Constantinople and to ask him who were his trustworthy friends in Bulgaria. Constantine was simple enough to send Telerig in reply a list of all his spies and agents in the country; and so Telerig was easily able to arrest and execute them all, and utterly upset the Imperial intelligence department. It is a little unlikely that an Emperor as invariably astute as Constantine Copronymus should play so naïve a rôle; but certainly somehow Telerig managed to acquire the list of Imperial agents, and acted on it, to his great advantage.[2]

The Emperor was furious, and once more roused himself to action. But, as he started out with his ninth expedition, a terrible fever took hold of him, and he died

---

that the Ind. XI is a mistake for Ind. XII. The whole chronology is complicated by the fact that Ind. XII was spread over two years, Sept. 772 to Sept. 774, so as to bring the Indictions into line with the A.M., a divergence having crept in in 726, probably because the Emperor Leo III wished to extort two years' taxes during one year—see Bury, Appendix 10 to Gibbon's *Decline and Fall*, vol. v. pp. 524–5, and Hubert, *La Chronologie de Théophane*, B.Z., vol. vi., pp. 504 ff.—or because for this period Theophanes was simply muddled between his two distinct schemes of chronology. (Brooks, *The Chronology of Theophanes*, vol. viii., pp. 82 ff.) We no longer now have Nicephorus to provide confirmatory evidence.

[1] Theophanes, pp. 692–3.   [2] Ibid., p. 693.

in agony at the fort of Strongylus, on September 14, 775.[1]

Bulgaria had been saved again. Constantine's campaigns had been a glorious chapter in the history of Byzantine arms, and they had reduced Bulgaria very low. Her army had again and again been routed, her population depleted; her Khans sat precariously on their throne. It surely seemed as though another Constantine, or even another campaign, would be the end of her. And yet the *coup de grâce* had so often been administered, and still the Bulgars lived on. Asperuch and Tervel had rooted them too firmly for them now to be dislodged. And the disasters had probably the result of binding them closer to the Slavs. We have seen how they forcibly sought to encourage Slav immigration; and there was gradually rising a Slav aristocracy, that first became evident early in the next century, and that must occasionally have intermarried with the Bulgars. Misfortunes have a unifying effect.

But, though the Bulgars could not be dislodged, they had certainly been subdued; it might be possible to absorb them in the Empire, as so many other tribes had been absorbed. Even after Constantine's death their troubles did not cease. In 777 Telerig himself was forced to fly from his country. He came to the court of the Emperor Leo IV, and there accepted baptism and was accorded the honour of a Greek bride, a cousin of the Empress. Had the Empire been inclined to intervene, then again Bulgaria might have been utterly reduced; but the Empire was weary and still torn between iconoclast and iconodule. Bulgaria was so obscure a state now—even Telerig's successor is unknown—it would be safe to let her linger weakly till another opportunity arose. The barbarians might remain in the Balkans; they were negligible.

[1] Theophanes, loc. cit.

Book II

THE GREAT POWERS OF EUROPE

Chapter I

AN EMPEROR'S SKULL

THE Empress-Regent Irene, of blessed memory, spent the spring of 784 in touring her northern frontier. It was a felicitous time. Last year her general, Stauracius, had conquered the Slavs of the Greek peninsula, forcing them into obedience to the Empire. Over the frontier everything was quiet; Thrace, devastated by the wars of the last century, was being refilled with a busy population transported from the East, Armenians—heretics indeed, but politically harmless so far away from their kindred. And so the Empress, with music playing, made her Imperial progress along to the town of Berrhoea, rebuilding it and rechristening it Irenupolis, and back to Anchialus.[1]

Her mind was set at rest by what she saw. There could be no danger from Bulgaria. Indeed, two years later, in September 786, when her son, the Emperor Constantine VI, was reaching maturity and appearing dangerously popular with the army, she found it both wise and safe to deplete Thrace of its militia on the plea of an Eastern campaign, so as to have the soldiers, under her friend Stauracius, close by her side in Constantinople.[2]

But early in 789 there came an unpleasant shock. Philetus, strategus of Thrace, was reconnoitring up the River Struma and had, it seems, entered territory which the Bulgars regarded as theirs. He shared the confidence of the government and was marching carelessly. A sudden attack from the Bulgars surprised him at a disadvantage. Many of his soldiers and he himself were killed.[3]

[1] Theophanes, pp. 699, 707. This was the Thracian Berrhoea or Beroe (the modern Stara Zagora), not the Macedonian Berrhoea.

[2] Ibid., pp. 715–6. [3] Ibid., p. 718.

47

The Bulgars, then, were not utterly effete; they might usefully be attacked once more. In April 791 the young Emperor, supreme now and anxious for military glory with which to outshine his mother's popularity, decided to invade Bulgaria. A certain Kardam was on the Bulgar throne. His antecedents and the date of his accession are unknown, but in him the Bulgars found at last a ruler of some competence. However, this campaign was on all sides a fiasco. Constantine advanced as far as a fort called Probatum on the River St. George.[1] There he fell in with the Bulgars; and in the evening a light skirmish began. But during the night the Imperial armies were seized with panic and fled: while the Bulgars, equally frightened, returned hurriedly to their own districts.[2]

Constantine burned to do better, and set out again against Kardam in July next year. An astronomer called Pancrat promised him a glorious victory. But Pancrat was wrong. Constantine marched as far as Marcellae on the frontier and repaired its fortifications; but, as he lay close by, on July 20 Kardam advanced on him with all the armies of his kingdom. The Emperor's youthful ardour and confidence led him to fight without due preparation; and he was heavily defeated. He hastened back to Constantinople in ignominy, leaving his money, his horses, and his equipment in the hands of the enemy, accompanied by shamefaced generals and the false prophet Pancrat.[3]

After this disaster Constantine let the Bulgars alone. Meanwhile Kardam's ambitions rose, and in 796 he sent insolently to the Emperor to demand tribute, threatening otherwise to ravage Thrace right up to the Golden Gate. Constantine replied scornfully that he would not trouble an old man to come so far; he would go to meet him at Marcellae, and God would decide what would happen.

---

[1] The modern Provadia, to the north-east of Adrianople.

[2] Theophanes, p. 723.　　　　　　　　　[3] Ibid., pp. 724–5.

But God was extremely indecisive. Constantine advanced in full force as far as Versinicia, near Adrianople; Kardam, alarmed at the size of his army, hid in the forest of Abroleba.[1] For seventeen days Constantine invited the Bulgars to give battle, in vain; and eventually each monarch returned ineffectually home.[2]

Again a period of peace ensued. Whether a definite treaty was ever concluded is unknown. Modern historians, who unanimously agree in decrying the Empress Irene, are apt to picture her paying tribute to all her neighbours.[3] With regard to the Bulgars, there is no evidence for such an assertion. The Empress certainly desired peace; in 797 she had finally rid herself of her son by blinding him, and such strange maternal conduct lost her her popularity. The army had always been hostile to her, and ecclesiastical support, though it might canonize her, did not help her in foreign campaigns. But Kardam was equally anxious for peace. His timorousness during the wars showed how unsure he felt of his position. Bulgaria was still turbulent and weak; he was probably fully occupied in controlling his *boyars* and reorganizing his kingdom. And so both countries were grateful for a respite, though neither could manage to extract a tribute.

But Bulgaria had recovered marvellously since the days of Constantine Copronymus. Freed from concentrated attack by the discord in the family of its adversaries the Emperors, it had somehow worked out its own salvation. Kardam might be insecure, but apparently he never fell. Had Constantine VI possessed the ability of his grandfather and namesake, again the Bulgars might have lapsed into feeble anarchy. But Kardam's victories must have

---

[1] Places identified by Zlatarṣki (*Istoriya*, pp. 244–5).
[2] Theophanes, pp. 728–9.
[3] e.g. even Bury (*Eastern Roman Empire*, p. 339).

served to strengthen him in his own country, and by
strengthening him to strengthen his whole country. Had
the statesmen of Constantinople turned their eyes to the
north, instead of wondering feverishly who would displace
the heirless Empress, they might well have been alarmed
—terribly alarmed, for far worse was to follow.

Some time after the year 797 the Khan Kardam died,
in the same obscurity in which he had ascended the throne.
The Empress Irene fell in 802; her white horses no longer
drove through the streets of Constantinople. In her place
was her genial, dissimulating *logothete*, now the Emperor
Nicephorus I, eager to display the vigour of a man's rule.
He little guessed whither it would lead him.

Far away to the north, in the plains and foothills of
Pannonia, the Hungary and Transylvania of to-day, the
Avar Empire still lingered, and under Avar domination
there still lived large numbers of Bulgars, the descendants
of those ancient Bulgars whom the Avars carried into
captivity over two centuries before, and of the fourth son
of King Kubrat and his following. But in the closing years
of the eighth century a new power had spread to the
Central European plains; the kingdom of the Franks,
masters of France and Germany, was seeking to safeguard
its eastern frontier by pushing its influence farther and
farther down the Danube. In 791 and again in 795–6
the Frankish King Charles—soon, in 800, to be crowned
Emperor at Rome in defiance of Byzantium—had invaded
the territory of the Avars, supported by their restive Slav
vassals. The Avar resistance was feeble; by the end of
the century the Frankish dominion reached the banks of
the River Theiss.

The Pannonian Bulgars took advantage of the situation.
On the eastern bank of the Theiss they completed the
destruction of the Avars. The details are unknown; but
by about the year 803 the Avar Empire had utterly

disappeared.   Instead, the Franks and the Bulgars met one another at the Theiss.   The Frankish Emperor had even contemplated moving farther eastward and destroying the Pannonian Bulgars; but he desisted, assuming that without Avar help they would not be able to hurt his realm.   He could probably count on the Moravian or the Croatian Slavs acting as buffers for him.

The Bulgar chieftain that conquered the Avars was called Krum.[1]   His origin is unknown.   From his apparent security on the throne throughout his life, it is tempting to see in him the scion of an old-established royal race—for only monarchs of undoubtedly higher birth could long maintain themselves over the jealous Bulgar *boyars*—the royal race of the Bulgars of Pannonia.   He may even have been a descendant of the fourth son of King Kubrat, a child of the House of Attila.   But more important than his birth were his ambitions and his ability.   Krum was not going to remain a Pannonian princeling.   By the year 808 he was firmly placed upon the throne of Pliska, Sublime Khan of Balkan Bulgaria.

How it happened we cannot tell.   Probably the Balkan Bulgars had always kept in touch with their cousins.   Since Asperuch's day the Khan of Pliska had controlled the plains of Wallachia and Moldavia; and the Pannonian Bulgars in Transylvania were not far off; only the Carpathian mountains divided them.   On Kardam's death, the Balkan Bulgars were left without a Khan.   It was probably easy for Krum, the splendid victor of the Avar wars, either by some show of arms or only by persuasion, to transfer himself on to the greater throne, and thus unite

[1] His name appears in various forms, in Greek Κροῦμμος, Κροῦμνος, Κροῦμος, Κνῖμος (once in Leo Grammaticus, probably by error), Κροῦβος, and Κρέμ ; in Latin Crumnus, Crimas, Brimas (both probably miscopied), Crumas, and Crusmas; in early Slavonic translations Kroum, Krâg, Krem, Kreml, Krumel, and Agrum.   On his inscriptions (*Aboba-Pliska*, p. 233—the Shumla inscription) he Graecised his name as Κρουμος.   Krum must therefore approximately represent the original.   See Zlatarski, *Istoriya*, p. 247.

the two Bulgar kingdoms into one great empire, from the
Theiss and the Save to the shores of the Black Sea.[1]

The effect of the union is difficult to gauge. Pannonian
Bulgaria was a Bulgar state, not a Bulgar-Slav state; in
the double kingdom the Bulgar element, the aristocratic
militarist element, must have been proportionately en-
hanced. But Krum was too astute a monarch to allow
the aristocracy to wax too powerful; he probably coun-
tered by subordinating Pannonia to the Balkans and in the
Balkans encouraging the Slav elements. On the whole,
the only important result of the union was to increase
the military strength and temper of the kingdom. The
Balkan Bulgars had made a poor show in the wars of the
eighth century—the Slavs, who formed the bulk of their
armies, were by nature unenthusiastic and disorganized
fighters—but in the ninth century Bulgaria was one of
the great militarist powers of Europe.

Kardam and Irene had both desired peace. Nicephorus
wanted war; and Krum, with his new strength and his
Balkan ambitions, was ready to give him war. It broke
out in 807. Hitherto Nicephorus had been occupied with
wars on his eastern frontier, but that year he had time to
set out against Bulgaria. The campaign was still-born;
when he reached Adrianople he discovered a conspiracy
against him amongst his troops. He put it down with

---

[1] This account of Krum's early career is conjectural. Dvornik (*Les Slaves,
Byzance et Rome*, pp. 34–5) states it categorically, with embroideries and
dates, but for once he gives no references. However, his account is in the
main certainly the only coherent interpretation of the evidence: which is
as follows: (i.) The Avars were utterly conquered by Krum (Suidas,
Lexicon, art. 'Bulgari,' p. 761). (ii.) Charles the Great attacked the Avars in
791 and 795–6 (according to Ekkehard, he first attacked them in 788, and
conquered them in eight years). After they were utterly conquered, he
withheld his hand from the Bulgars as being unlikely to be harmful, *now
that the Avars (Huns) were extinct* (Ekkehard, p. 162). It is only reasonable,
therefore, to assume that Krum's conquest of the Avars was before their
utter extinction. But in 796 Kardam was still Khan of Balkan Bulgaria;
we do not hear of Krum there till 808 (see below). Krum must, therefore,
have been ruler of Pannonian Bulgaria before he ascended the throne of
Pliska. But the date of his accession must remain unknown.

severity, but thought it wise not to proceed farther; and
so he returned to Constantinople.[1] Next year the Bulgars
took the offensive: Nicephorus, suspecting their designs
on Macedonia, had mustered an army in the theme of
Strymon. Late in the winter, so late that no attack seemed
likely, the Bulgars surprised this force, slew the strategus
of the theme and annihilated many of the regiments, and
captured 1,100 lb. of gold destined to pay the soldiers.[2]

In the spring of 809 Krum followed up his victory by
a far more harmful move. There was a strong line of
Imperial fortresses barring the Bulgar advance on the
south and the south-west—Develtus, Adrianople, Philippopolis, and Sardica. They had probably been recon-
ditioned by Constantine Copronymus, who saw their
strategic importance. To the Bulgars they had always
been an irritant, particularly Sardica, lying as it did across
their road to Serbia and to Upper Macedonia. In March
Krum suddenly appeared before Sardica. The fortifications were too strong for him, but somehow his guile won
him an entrance. The garrison, 6,000 strong, was massacred, with numberless civilians, and the fortress dismantled. It does not seem that Krum intended to annex
the district, but merely to make Sardica untenable as an
Imperial fortress.

On the Thursday before Easter (April 3) Nicephorus
heard the news, and left his capital in full strength. By
forced marches he pushed into the enemy country, and on
Easter Day reached the undefended city of Pliska. Pliska
paid the penalty for Sardica; Krum's palace was plundered,
and the Emperor wrote a triumphant letter to Constantinople announcing his arrival in the Bulgar capital. It
had been a triumphant feat of the Imperial armies; the

---

[1] Theophanes, p. 749.

[2] Ibid., p. 752. See Bury (*Eastern Roman Empire*, p. 340) for exact dating.
The amount 1,100 lb. is the equivalent to nearly £50,000.

pious chronicler Theophanes, who strongly disapproved of Nicephorus, decided indeed that he was lying when he claimed to have achieved it. From Pliska, Nicephorus marched on to Sardica, to rebuild the fortress; whether deliberately or by chance, he did not meet Krum's returning army on the way. At Sardica the Emperor had certain difficulties; the soldiers disliked having to work as masons, and were suspicious of his subterfuges to induce them to do so. However, in the end their mutiny was quashed; Sardica was cheaply and quickly rebuilt, and the Emperor returned complacently to Constantinople.[1]

But there had been one more distressing incident. A few officers from the Sardica garrison had escaped Krum's massacre and had come to Nicephorus. He, however, would not promise not to punish them—he probably suspected, with reason, that there had been treason somewhere; so the officers fled to the Bulgar court (thus more definitely hinting at their guilt), where Krum received them gladly. Amongst these refugees was the celebrated engineer Eumathius—a welcome acquisition for the Bulgars, for he taught them all the artifices of up-to-date warfare Later, Theophanes tells us a fuller and quite different tale of Eumathius, who was an Arab; Nicephorus had employed him at Adrianople, but had remunerated him with parsimony—Nicephorus was always anxious to do things inexpensively—and had, further, struck him when he complained; the touchy Arab promptly deserted. Both stories may be true; Eumathius, who was always

---

[1] Theophanes, pp. 752-4: Bury (op. cit., p. 341) assumes that Theophanes was acting from malevolence in casting doubt on Nicephorus's arrival at Pliska; most other historians—e.g. Zlatarski (op. cit., pp. 252-3) or Dvornik (op. cit., p. 36)—believe Theophanes implicitly—Dvornik even adds a successful Bulgar attack. Bury must surely be right. Theophanes took every opportunity for decrying Nicephorus, and, though a saint, he was not above telling lies to discredit Emperors of whom he morally disapproved. Nicephorus, on the other hand, was not a half-wit; he would not have claimed to have penetrated to Pliska when the whole army could have shown him up as an impostor.

employed in repairing fortresses, was working at Sardica at the time of Krum's invasion, and was tempted by his grievance into treachery. Certainly somehow, by his tactlessness, Nicephorus had handed over a valuable asset to the Khan.[1]

The Bulgar ambitions for Macedonia still disquieted the Emperor; and through the next winter he carried out extensive transportations. The Macedonian Slavs were unreliable; he attempted to keep them in control by settling among them colonies of faithful peasants from Asia Minor, the backbone of his Empire. The Anatolian peasants did not appreciate this policy; some even committed suicide rather than leave their homes and the tombs of their fathers. But Nicephorus was inexorable; the situation, he thought, was urgent, and he prided himself on the way in which he dealt with it. The transportations were not, however, on a vast enough scale to be really effective.[2]

But the Emperor had already decided to crush Krum absolutely, for ever. His preparations were long and careful; troops were collected from throughout the Empire. There was no danger from the Saracens at the moment; so the armies of the themes of Asia Minor came with their strategi to swell the host. In May 811 the great expedition left Constantinople, led by the Emperor himself and his son, Stauracius.

At Marcellae, on the frontier, Nicephorus paused for reinforcements to join him. Krum was seriously frightened, and sent an embassy to Marcellae begging humbly for peace. The Emperor dismissed the Bulgar ambassadors; he was distrustful of Bulgar promises and confident of victory. But while he was still at Marcellae one of his household suddenly disappeared, with 100 lb. of gold

---

[1] Theophanes, pp. 753 (he is here called Euthymius), 776.
[2] Ibid., p. 755.

and part of the Imperial wardrobe; they soon heard that he had gone over to Krum. The omen was disquieting —were the rats leaving the sinking ship ?

In July the Imperial armies entered Bulgaria and pushed straight on to Pliska. Krum fled before them, and on July 20[1] they reached the Bulgar capital. Nicephorus was in a fierce mood, and devastated the whole city, massacring and burning, and even passed Bulgar babies through threshing-machines. The Palace of the Khans perished in the flames—it was probably a wooden affair —and on their treasury Nicephorus set the Imperial seal, intending avariciously to reserve the treasure for himself. Again Krum sent to plead for peace, saying: 'Lo, thou hast conquered. Take what thou wilt and depart in peace.' But the triumphant Emperor was proud and obdurate again.

Krum was in despair; but Nicephorus's carelessness gave him another chance. The Bulgar forces fled to the mountains; and Nicephorus followed. On Thursday, July 24 the Imperial army was caught in a narrow mountain defile, and the Bulgars swiftly built wooden palisades at either end. Too late Nicephorus saw the trap into which he had fallen, and knew that destruction was certain. 'Even were we birds,' he said, 'we could not hope to escape.' On the Thursday and Friday the Bulgars worked hard at their fortifications. On Saturday they paused; perhaps they had decided to wait and starve the great army out. But their impatience overcame them; late that night, the 26th, they fell upon the enemy.

It was an unresisting butchery. The Imperial army, taken unawares, allowed itself to be massacred wholesale. The Emperor and almost all his generals and high

---

[1] Theophanes said that Nicephorus only entered Bulgaria on July 20. But, as the great battle took place on the 26th/27th, he must surely have arrived at Pliska not later than the 20th, having journeyed some seventy miles of difficult country since crossing the frontier.

dignitaries perished—some killed in their tents, others burnt to death by the firing of the palisades. The Emperor's son, Stauracius, was wounded, fatally wounded, though he lingered in agony for several months. With his brother-in-law, Michael Rhangabe, one of the few unhurt survivors, and the tiny remnant of the army, he fled headlong to the safety of Adrianople. Nicephorus's head was exposed on a stake for several days, for the delectation of the Bulgars; then Krum hollowed it out and lined it with silver. It made him a fine goblet when he drank with his *boyars*, crying the Slav toast of ' Zdravitza.' [1]

Relics of the battle lasted for many centuries. In 1683 a Serbian patriarch saw at Eskibaba, in Thrace, the tomb of a certain Nicholas who had gone with the army and dreamed a warning dream. The Turks had placed a turban on the head of the corpse. [2]

The news of the disaster came as an appalling shock to the whole Imperial world. Never since the days of Valens, on the field of Adrianople, had an Emperor fallen in battle. It was a stupendous blow to the Imperial prestige—to the legend of the Emperor's sacrosanctity, so carefully fostered to impress the barbarians. Moreover, the Visigoths that slew Valens had been mere nomads, destined soon to pass away to other lands; the Bulgars were barbarians settled at the gate, and determined—more so now

[1] Theophanes, pp. 761–5. He dates the battle July 25; but that was the Friday. The Saturday/Sunday night was the 26th/27th. It is impossible to discover exactly where the battle took place. Shkorpil (*Aboba-Pliska*, p. 564) suggests the Pass of Verbitza, and the defile locally known as the Greek Hollow, where tradition asserts that many Greeks once met their death; and Bury (op. cit., p. 344) follows him. This, I think, is the most convincing location. Jireček assumed that it was in the Pass of Veregava, on Nicephorus's return home (*Geschichte der Bulgaren*, pp. 45–6, and *Die Heerstrasse*, p. 150). But it seems that he took a different route, pursuing Krum rather than retreating. Zlatarski (op. cit., pp. 408–12) does not commit himself definitely, but believes that it took place much nearer to Pliska. But, as he accepts Theophanes's statement (see above) that Nicephorus only entered Bulgaria on July 20, he is very hard up for time, and cannot afford to let Nicephorus march the thirty miles from Pliska to the Pass of Verbitza.

[2] The Patriarch Arsen Cernovič, quoted by Bury (op. cit., p. 345).

than ever—to remain there. The Empire would never live down and forget its shame; and the Bulgars would ever be heartened by the memory of their triumph.

Krum had good reason to be exultant. The whole effect of Constantine Copronymus's long campaigns had been wiped out all at one battle. He could face the Empire now in the position of conqueror of the Emperor, on equal terms, at a height never reached by Asperuch or Tervel. Henceforward he would not have to fight for the existence of his country, but he could fight for conquest and for annexation. Moreover, in his own country his position was assured; no one now would dare dispute the authority of the victorious Khan. He could not have done a more useful deed to strengthen the Bulgar crown. [1]

Sated by their victory, the Bulgars did not at once follow it up with an invasion. Constantinople was given a respite, while the dying Emperor Stauracius made way for his brother-in-law, Michael Rhangabe. [2] But late next spring (812) Krum attacked the Imperial fortress of Develtus, a busy city at the head of the Gulf of Burgas, commanding the coast road to the south. It could not hold out long against the Bulgars. Krum dismantled the fortress, as he had done at Sardica, and transported the inhabitants, with their bishop and all, away into the heart of his kingdom. In June the new Emperor Michael set out to meet the Bulgars; but the news that he was too late to save the city, together with a slight mutiny in his army, made him turn back while he was still in Thrace. [3]

---

[1] The Kadi-Keui inscription given in *Aboba-Pliska*, pp. 228–30, belongs somewhere to Nicephorus's war with Krum. It mentions Nicephorus, Marcellae, Adrianople, and a certain Bulgar called Ekusous ('Εκούσοος) or Ecosus ('Ηκόσος). The text is too badly mutilated for the sense to emerge. Probably it refers to Nicephorus's first campaign, the abortive campaign that never went further than Adrianople. See Bury, op. cit., p. 343.

[2] Michael the Syrian (pp. 25–6) pretends that Stauracius was wounded during a Bulgar invasion after Nicephorus's death. He was clearly misinformed.

[3] Theophanes, p. 772.

His inaction and the Bulgar victories terrified the inhabitants of the frontier cities. They saw the enemy overrunning all the surrounding country, and they determined to save themselves as best they could. The smaller frontier forts, Probatum and Thracian Nicaea, were abandoned by their population; even the population of Anchialus and Thracian Berrhoea, whose defences the Empress Irene had recently repaired, fled to districts out of reach of the heathen hordes. The infection spread to the great metropolis-fortress of Western Thrace, Philippopolis, which was left half-deserted, and thence to the Macedonian cities, Philippi and Strymon. In these last cities it was chiefly the Asiatics transported there by Nicephorus that fled, overjoyed at the opportunity of returning to their homes.[1]

But Krum did not take full advantage of all this. With a caution and forbearance rare in a barbarian conqueror, he sent instead to ask for peace; he wished, it seems, to consolidate carefully his every step. In September 812 his ambassador, Dargomer—the first unmistakably Slav name to appear in Bulgar official circles—came to the Emperor demanding a renewal of the treaty of 716, the treaty made between Tervel and Theodosius III. Bulgaria was to recover the Meleona frontier and the 30 lb. worth of skins and robes; prisoners and deserters were to be returned, and organized trade-intercourse to be reopened.[2] Krum, however, knew that he had the upper hand; he threatened that if the peace was not granted to him he would attack Mesembria. After some consultation the Emperor rejected the peace; he could not bear to give up the Bulgar deserters. It had always been a cardinal point

---

[1] Theophanes, pp. 772–3.

[2] See above, p. 33. As I said there, the name Cormesios is clearly a mistake of Theophanes. Krum would obviously want, and feel able, to return to the state of affairs *before* the disaster of the war with Copronymus. There had probably been some truce with Kormisosh that had distracted Theophanes.

in Byzantine diplomacy to collect and support foreign pretenders and refugee statesmen; and Michael probably hoped to have that clause withdrawn. But Krum was for everything or nothing. Faithful to his threat, he appeared in full force before Mesembria in the middle of October.

Mesembria was one of the wealthiest and most important cities in all South-Eastern Europe. It was not only a salubrious spa, but also a great commercial centre, both as port of embarkation for the produce of Eastern Bulgaria and also as the port of call for all vessels bound from Constantinople to the Danube and the northern shores of the Black Sea. In addition, nature and art alike had made it a magnificent fortress. It occupied a small peninsula, at the northern entrance of the Gulf of Burgas, joined to the mainland only by an isthmus about a quarter of a mile in length, so low and narrow that in storms none of it was out of reach of the foam.[1] This natural stronghold had been further strengthened by huge fortifications.

A vigorous defence could have saved the city. Krum had no ships; he could only attack along the isthmus. The Imperial navy could have poured in reinforcements and food in spite of all the Bulgars. But the Isaurian Emperors had economized on naval armaments; there was now hardly any Imperial navy. The garrison, caught unprepared, had to shift for itself; the Emperor did not even attempt to revictual the city. Krum, on the other hand, was helped by the engineering skill of the deserter Eumathius.

Krum's prompt fulfilment of his threat had alarmed the government at Constantinople. On November 1, Michael summoned a council. He himself was in favour now of peace, but was not strong enough to impose his will on his counsellors: these were sharply divided into two

---

[1] Nowadays the whole isthmus is covered by the waves during bad storms, but then there was probably an efficient causeway.

parties, led, as was characteristic of the times, by clerics
—Theodore, Abbot of Studium, favouring war, and the
Patriarch Nicephorus, the historian, eager for peace. The
war party won, on the same clause about deserters, sup-
porting their policy by talking of the fundamental principles of Christian hospitality, and mocking at the peace
party's readiness to pay tribute. Four days later, their
victory was clinched; news came through of the fall of
Mesembria.

Krum found his capture highly profitable. Not only
was Mesembria well stocked with luxuries and large
quantities of gold and silver, but also the Bulgars discovered some of the most precious and secret of all Byzantine inventions, the liquid 'Greek Fire,' and thirty-six
syphons from which to fire it. Krum removed his spoils,
then, following his usual course, he dismantled the fortifications and retired to his home.[1]

The Emperor was now obliged to plan an expedition
to avenge the disgraceful calamity. Next February two
Christians, who had escaped from Bulgaria, told him that
Krum was making ready to invade Thrace. Michael
busily collected troops from all over his Empire; in May
he set out, with a huge army, chiefly Asiatic. The Empress
Procopia saw the army off, with encouraging messages,
from the aqueduct near Heraclea. But the Empress's
send-off was of little avail. For a month Michael dallied
in Thrace, never attempting to recover and repair Mesembria, while the Asiatic troops grew increasingly restive.
Early in June, Krum crossed the frontier, and the two
armies came face to face at Versinicia. At this spot Kardam had hidden in the woods from Constantine VI; but
Krum was bolder, and prepared for a pitched battle. For
fifteen hot summer days each army waited for the other
to move; at last the general in charge of the Thracian and

[1] Theophanes, pp. 775–8: Theophanes Continuatus, pp. 12–13.

Macedonian troops on the left wing of the Imperial army,
John Aplaces, begged to be allowed to attack. The Imperial army outnumbered the Bulgars by ten to one; and
Imperial troops notoriously could deal with barbarians
when it came to an open fight. Michael gave him permission, and on June 22 John Aplaces began the battle.
The Bulgars fell back in confusion before his attack: when
suddenly he found that he was fighting alone—the rest of
the army had fled in inexplicable panic, led by Anatolic
troops on the right wing. Krum, we are told, was too
astounded and suspicious to pursue at once; but he soon
found that the flight was genuine. After annihilating the
brave, deserted troops of Aplaces, he followed the fugitives
as they ran headlong all the way back to their capital. It
was an amazing battle: the only explanation was treachery
in the Imperial forces—in the Anatolic regiments. The
general of the Anatolic regiments was Leo the Armenian,
and it was Leo that gained most by the battle: Michael
gave up the crown, and it passed to Leo. Under the
circumstances Leo was inevitably suspected, though nothing definite could be proved—he was playing his cards
too cunningly. But Krum also was privy to the plot.
He had taken the risk of a pitched battle against vastly
superior forces in open ground—a risk taken by no Bulgarian before or after for centuries; it is incredible that
on this unique occasion he should have been so rash and
foolish—should have put himself into a position where
only a miracle could save him, had he not been certain
that the miracle would occur. And it was by arrangement rather than from surprise that he did not at once
pursue the fugitives.[1]

[1] Theophanes, pp. 780–3: Scriptor Incertus, pp. 337 ff. Bury (op. cit.,
pp. 351–2) fully discusses Leo's treachery. His conclusion, that Leo was
guilty but too clever to be definitely compromised, is, I think, absolutely
convincing. But it seems to me that, to make the story credible, Krum must
be implicated in the plot.

The victory might be an arranged affair; but Krum had no qualms about following it up. Thrace was denuded of troops, and his progress was easy. Leaving his brother to besiege Adrianople on the way, he pushed on with his army, aiming at nothing else than the Imperial capital itself. On July 17 his army arrived at the city walls.

The huge fortifications daunted him; instead of ordering an assault, he resorted to spectacular displays of his might. Curious and horrified citizens on the walls could watch men and animals being sacrificed on heathen altars, they could see the Sublime Khan washing his feet in the waves of the sea and ceremoniously sprinkling his soldiers, or moving in state through rows of adoring concubines, to the raucous acclamation of his hordes. Having indulged in sufficient barbaric pageantry, he sent to the Emperor demanding to be allowed to affix his lance to the Golden Gate, in token of his triumph. The Emperor, the ambitious traitor Leo the Armenian, refused the insulting request; so Krum set to work more practically. Fortifying his camp with a rampart, he plundered the countryside for several days. Then he sent again to the Emperor, offering peace, probably on the basis of the famous peace of Tervel, but insisting specially on a large tribute of gold and of robes and a selection of young maidens for his personal use. Leo now saw an opportunity for a solution of his troubles.

The episode that followed is deeply distressing to our modern sense of honour, and patriotic Balkan writers have long seen in it an example of the perfidy and degradation of Byzantium. But we live now in a godless age. In the ninth century every true and devoted Christian regarded the heathen either as animals or as devils, according to their capacity for inflicting evil on the faithful. According to these standards Krum, 'the new Sennacherib,'[1]

[1] Theophanes, p. 785.

was a very arch-devil; any means of ridding the Christian world of such a monstrous persecutor would be highly justified. We should remember, too, that Krum himself did not disdain to use guile on more than one occasion; only we have been spared the exact details.

Leo answered Krum's overtures by suggesting a meeting between the two monarchs on the shore of the Golden Horn, just outside the walls; Krum would come by land and Leo by boat, each with a few unarmed followers. Krum accepted, and next morning rode down to the spot, accompanied by his treasurer, by his brother-in-law, a Greek deserter called Constantine Patzicus, and by his nephew, Constantine's son. Leo and his friends arrived in the Imperial barge, and the conversation began, presumably with Constantine as interpreter. Suddenly an Imperial official, Hexabulius, covered his face with his hands. Krum was offended and alarmed, and leapt on to his horse. At that moment three armed men burst out from a neighbouring house and attacked the little group of Bulgars. Krum's followers were on foot; pressing round to defend their master and escape themselves, they were easily disposed of. The treasurer was slain and the two Patzici captured. But Krum, the main object of the stratagem, escaped. Darts were fired at him as he galloped away, but only wounded him lightly. He reached his camp in safety, vowing destruction. The pious citizens of Constantinople were bitterly disappointed. The failure was due to their sins, they said.

The next few days were spent in Krum's fiery vengeance. All the suburbs of the city, not only those close outside the walls, but also the rich towns and villages on the far side of the Golden Horn and up the European shore of the Bosphorus, studded with churches and monasteries and sumptuous villas, all were committed to the flames. The Palace of Saint Mamas, one of the finest of the suburban homes of the Emperor, was utterly destroyed; its ornamented capitals and sculptured animals were packed up in wagons to decorate the Khan's palace at Pliska. Every living creature that they found the Bulgars slew. The devastation spread wider as the Khan began his journey homeward. On the road to Selymbria every town and hamlet was destroyed; Selymbria itself was razed. The dreadful destroyer moved on. Heraclea was saved by its strong walls, but everything outside them perished. The Bulgars had levelled the fort of Daonin; they went on to level the forts of Rhaedestus and Aprus. There they rested ten days, then went south to the hills of Ganus. The miserable inhabitants of the countryside had fled there for refuge; they had to be hunted out, the men to be butchered, the women and children and beasts to be sent to captivity in Bulgaria. Then, after a short destructive excursion to the Hellespont, Krum turned north to Adrianople. The great fortress was still holding out against the Khan's brother. But Krum brought with him machines to apply against the walls. The garrison was starving; it knew that no relief would come now. From necessity it surrendered. The city was destroyed and deserted. All the inhabitants, to the number, it was said, of 10,000, were transported away to the northern shore of the Danube. There they lived in captivity; and Manuel, their Archbishop, and the most steadfast of his flock met with martyrs' crowns. The Imperial government regretted now its obduracy and tricks. It begged the Khan for peace; but Krum was implacable. He had too much to forgive.[1]

[1] Theophanes, pp. 785–6. He closes his history with the capture of Adrianople: Scriptor Incertus, pp. 342–4, giving the most detailed account: Theophanes Continuatus, p. 24: Genesius, p. 13: Ignatius, *Vita Nicephori*, pp. 206–7. The captivity and martyrdom of the Adrianopolitans, is told in the *Vita Basilii* (Theophanes Continuatus, pp. 216–17), *Menologium Basilii Imperatoris*, pp. 276–7, and Georgius Monachus Continuatus, p. 765.

Fᴇ

In these dark days men prayed and hoped in Constantinople that Constantine Copronymus would arise from the
grave, to smite the Bulgars as he had been wont to smite
them. The resurrection was denied them; but the Emperor Leo vowed to be a worthy substitute. He set out
from Constantinople with his army soon after Krum retired, but did not attempt to follow him, taking instead
the road along the Black Sea coast; his object was to rebuild Mesembria. Close to Mesembria he met the Bulgar
forces—probably just a detachment of Krum's army;
Krum was not, apparently, there in person. The district
had been frequently devastated of recent years, and the
Bulgar army was hard up for supplies. Leo, on the other
hand, being in touch with the sea and his ships, was amply
provided for. Finding out the Bulgar difficulties, he re-
solved on a stratagem. He retired secretly with some
picked troops on to a hill. The rest of the army suddenly
saw that he had disappeared and began to be panic-
stricken. The news spread to the Bulgars, who thereupon determined to attack. But Leo warned his army
in time; so that they stood their ground when the Bulgars
came. Leo was then able to swoop down from his hill
and take the Bulgars in the rear. It was a triumph for
the Imperial army; not a Bulgar escaped. Leo was able
to advance into Bulgaria, and devastate the countryside,
sparing adults, but, with sinister foresight, slaying the
children, dashing them against the rocks. The Bulgars
were deeply ashamed by their defeat. The hill where
Leo lay in ambush was long called Leo's hill, and Bulgars passing by would point at it and sadly shake their
heads. [1]

But Leo's success was of little value. During the
following winter, which was unusually mild and dry, a

[1] For discussion of this campaign, whose existence Zlatarski and others
deny, see Appendix VII.

Bulgar army of 30,000 men crossed the low rivers and sacked Arcadiopolis (Lule Burgas). On their return they found that a week's rain had flooded the River Ergenz, and they had to wait till the river subsided and then build a bridge. But during this delay Leo did nothing, so his critics said, to attack them. They returned safely to Bulgaria with their 50,000 captives and their wagon-loads of gold and apparel and Armenian carpets.[1]

Shortly afterwards worse news came to Constantinople. Krum was planning a far greater vengeance on the city that had treated him so treacherously. He was determined to destroy it, beginning his attack on the quarter of Blachernae, whence had been fired the darts that wounded him. The tales of his preparations caused men to gasp with horrified astonishment—tales of the hordes collected by the Khan, Slavs from 'all the Slavonias,' and Avars from the Pannonian plain; of the vast engines that the Khan was constructing, catapults of all sizes, and stones and fire to hurl in them, besides the tortoises and rams and ladders that featured in every big siege; of the thousand oxen feeding in the Khan's great stables, and the five thousand iron-bound wagons waiting there. Leo hastened to put his capital in a fit state of defence, and set about building a new wall outside the Blachernae quarter, where the Bulgar assault was expected and the fortifications were weak.[2] He even sought diplomatic aid. It was perhaps the news that Krum was collecting troops even in Pannonia that reminded the Imperial statesmen that Bulgaria could be attacked in the rear from Germany. In the year 814 ambassadors from Constantinople set out for the court of the Western Emperor Louis, to ask for help against the barbarous Bulgars. They arrived before him in August; but it seems that they met

[1] Scriptor Incertus, pp. 346–7.   [2] Scriptor Incertus, p. 347.

with no response.   Louis had his own barbarians to fight.[1]

But by then the danger was past.   The hand of God had intervened.   On Holy Thursday, the 13th of April, 814, Krum broke a blood-vessel in his head, and died.[2]

Krum had remade Bulgaria.   Kardam had shown that the Bulgars had only been crippled, not conquered, by the wars of Copronymus; but Krum had altered the whole status of his country.   His first achievement, of uniting the Pannonian with the Balkan Bulgars, had given both of them new life.   And then he had embarked on a career of spectacular, terrible triumph.   He had slain two Emperors in battle and caused the fall of a third.   Of the great Imperial fortresses on the frontier he had captured and destroyed four and caused the inhabitants of the two others to flee in terror.[3]   He had even seriously threatened the Imperial capital; and repeatedly he had beaten the best Imperial armies.   Bulgaria, the dying state of half a century before, was now the greatest military power in Eastern Europe.

But Krum had not only asserted so alarmingly the independence of Bulgaria by force of arms; he was also, it seems, a great internal organizer.   The details of his work are lost, but an echo has come down to us in a story given by the tenth-century encyclopaedist Suidas.   Krum, he says, after conquering the Avars, asked his Avar captives the reason of their Empire's fall.   They answered that they had lost their best men through various causes, jealousy and accusations between one another, collusion between thieves and judges, drunkenness, bribery, and dishonesty in their commercial dealings, and a passion

[1] *Annales Laurissenses Minores*, p. 122: the arrival of the Greek embassy immediately follows an event dated August.

[2] Scriptor Incertus, p. 348. Bury (op. cit.) dates it the 14th; but that was a Friday.

[3] Sardica, Develtus, Mesembria, and Adrianople were destroyed, Anchialus and Philippopolis deserted.

for law-suits. Krum was profoundly impressed, and promptly issued laws to prevent such things in Bulgaria: first, when a man accused another of some crime, the accuser had to be well questioned before the trial took place, and, if he were shown to have invented the accusation, he was to be executed; secondly, hospitality to thieves was punishable by confiscation of all the host's goods, while thieves were to have their bones broken; thirdly, all vines were to be rooted up; and finally men were to give sufficiently to the needy poor, under the penalty of the confiscation of their goods.[1] It is highly doubtful that Krum's legislative activity was as simple as Suidas says; but obviously he introduced innovations along these lines. All these laws were simplifications of the paternalist legislation which the Emperor used to give to his people, and very different in their conception from the laws that would occur in an aristocratic state such as Bulgaria had been. Krum, modelling himself, like all progressive Bulgars, on the Empire, was aiming at an almost theocratic supremacy, such as the Emperor enjoyed among his subjects. Krum apparently furthered this policy by encouraging his Slav subjects as opposed to the Bulgars, the aristocracy. It has always been the habit of autocrats to divert their aristocracies from political into military positions; the Byzantine Emperors, when later an aristocracy arose in the Empire, followed that policy; in Western Europe in more modern times it was the policy of statesmen such as Richelieu. So the Bulgars had to confine themselves to the army or to military governorships in the outposts of Empire[2]; they were better fighters than the Slavs, and they were useful there. But for his political work and in the high positions at Court he employed Slavs. His only

[1] Suidas, *Lexicon*, p. 762.

[2] The soldiers whose deaths are commemorated in the tablets found by the Dnieper and the Theiss (see below, pp. 81, 83) have Bulgar names, Onegavon and Okorses.

ambassador whose name we know was a Slav, Dargamer; and the *boyars* with whom the Khan feasted drank to a Slav toast, 'Zdravitza.'[1]

Indeed, it was in this internal organization that Krum was of most service to his country. Contemporary and modern historians have been so dazzled by his startling military triumphs, that they have failed to realize his true significance. Krum's wars were fought for a defensive aim. He was not an ambitious conqueror; in spite of his victories, he never asked for more than the Meleona frontier, the frontier that Tervel had enjoyed. There were tales of his ambitions in Macedonia, but they never amounted to anything. When he captured the great Imperial fortresses he never attempted to hold them; he merely destroyed them and retired. He knew that the Empire would always resent an independent kingdom in the Balkans; he therefore hoped to safeguard his independence by carrying the attack into Imperial territory. But, till his last year, when he was burning for vengeance, he would have welcomed a peace that recognized his freedom and gave him a small tribute (to help both his finances and his prestige) and left him time to organize his country. But in the treaty he must insist on being returned his deserter-subjects; he must have all the unruly elements under his power, so that he could crush them. Barbarian though he was, with his ostentation and craft and cruelty, his concubines, his human sacrifices, and his cup that was an Emperor's head, the Sublime Khan Krum was a very great statesman; and his greatness lies, not in being the conqueror of Emperors, but in being the founder of the splendid Bulgarian autocracy. As it was, his wars distracted him; he did not quite have time enough. The khanate trembled a little and was troubled when the great Khan died.

[1] See above, p. 57.

CHAPTER II

EXCURSION INTO THE WEST

THE sudden disappearance of their terrible ruler took the Bulgars by surprise. Krum left a son, called Omortag; but Omortag was young and inexperienced.[1] It seems that the Bulgar aristocracy took advantage of Krum's death to revolt against his dynasty. We hear of three *boyars* that wore the crown about now: Dukum, who almost at once died, Ditzeng and Tsok, the latter two both cruel men who persecuted the Christian prisoners from Adrianople. But no more than that is known of them. Probably they were only the leaders of rebel factions and parties that for a short while controlled the government at Pliska.[2]

In any case, their rule was brief. Well before the end of 815, Omortag was firmly seated on his father's throne. His first action was to make peace with the Empire. He had not had experience as a warrior himself; it would be wiser to rest upon his father's laurels and to use their

[1] The forms Ὠμορτάγ, Ὠμουρτάγ, Ὠμυρτάγ, and Ὀμουρτὰγ occur in his inscriptions. The Greeks call him Ματράγων, Μοραάγων, and Ομβριτάγος (twice in error Κρυτάγων and Κουτράγων); the Latins, Omortag and Omartag. See Zlatarski, op. cit., pp. 292–3. That Omortag was Krum's son (not brother, as Dvornik (op. cit., p. 39) says) is definitely stated by Theophylact, *Historia XV Martyrum*, p. 192, and implied by Malamir's Shumla inscription (see below, p. 295). Theophylact (loc. cit.) makes Omortag directly succeed Krum; and Theophanes Continuatus (p. 217) implies so.

[2] Tsok is only mentioned in the *Menologium* of Basil II as having succeeded Krum and persecuting Christians (*Menologium*, pp. 276–7); Dukum, who died, and Ditzeng, who persecuted Archbishop Manuel, are only mentioned in a fourteenth-century Slavonic prologue to the *Menologium*, p.392 (see Bibliography). Tsok, however, is probably the Tsuk that appears in a very mutilated inscription found near Aboba dated 823/4 (*Aboba-Pliska*, pp. 226–7)—the sense is undecipherable; it may record Omortag's triumph over the usurper. I am inclined to believe with Loparev (*Dvie Zamietki*, p. 318) that all three were merely military leaders, and not to identify Ditzeng with Tsok (as Bury does, op. cit., p. 359) or Dukum with Tsok (as Zlatarski, op. cit., pp. 424–5).

71

reputation in securing beneficial terms. He appears to have instituted preliminary negotiations that amounted to nothing [1]; the Emperor Leo was contemplating a campaign against the weakened Bulgars—a monk Sabbatius, prompted no doubt by the devil, had promised him a victory against them were he to reintroduce iconoclasm. [2] But this brilliant campaign never took place. Instead, some time in the winter of 815–16 the Khan and the Emperor concluded a Thirty Years' Peace.

The Imperial historians barely noticed the treaty; but the Khan was pleased with his diplomacy, and caused the terms to be inscribed on a column in his palace at Pliska. The column is overturned and chipped now, but it still tells how the Sublime Khan Omortag, wishing for peace with the Greeks, sent an embassy to the Emperor (τὸν βασιλέα), and how the peace was to last thirty years. The frontier was to run from Develtus, between the two rivers, and between Balzene and Agathonice to Constantia and to Macrolivada and to the mountains—the name of the range is mostly erased. Secondly, the Emperor was to keep the Slav tribes that had belonged to him before the war; the others, even though they might have deserted, were to belong to the Khan and be sent back to their various districts. Roman (Imperial) officers were to be bought back at a special tariff according to their rank, common people were to be exchanged man for man, and there was a special arrangement for Imperial soldiers captured in deserted citadels. [3]

[1] If Bury is right (op. cit., p. 360) in placing the much-mutilated Eski Juma inscription (*Aboba-Pliska*, p. 228) here, it vaguely suggests negotiations.

[2] Genesius, p. 13: Theophanes Continuatus, p. 26, and in more detail in the *Epistolae Synodicae Orientalium ad Theophilum*, p. 368. This may refer to Leo's 813 campaign, which was successful, but I think it belongs a little later.

[3] The Suleiman-Keui inscription, which has been the subject of an article by Zlatarski (see Bibliography), gives the reasons for my view of the treaty and the Great Fence in Appendix VI. The Greek historians, Genesius, p. 41, and Theophanes Continuatus, p. 31, mention that a thirty-year peace was concluded—Genesius mentioning Omortag (Motragon) by name.

These latter terms were what might have been expected
—the Bulgars winning on that deserter clause that had
ruined Krum. But the frontier needs elucidation. The
two rivers were probably the Tundzha and the Choban-
Azmak; Baltzene is unknown; but Agathonice has been
identified as the village of Saranti, while Constantia is the
village of Kostuzha, both near Kavalki and the Sakar
mountains. Macrolivada was the present village of Uzund-
zhova, near the junction of the western River Azmak with
the Maritsa.[1] The semi-nameless mountain range was
almost certainly the Haemus; that is to say, at Macrolivada
the frontier turned sharply to the north, to the Haemus and
to the Danube, leaving Philippopolis and Sardica outside
the frontier. This was, as Omortag said, the old frontier,[2]
the frontier which Tervel had won exactly a century ago;
indeed, the whole treaty was in the main a recapitulation of
the famous treaty of 716. But there was a difference.
Omortag had advanced as far as he wished on the side of
Thrace. His main interests were elsewhere; he only wanted
to safeguard this frontier. Accordingly the Bulgars dug a
great ditch and on its northern side built a great rampart all
the way from the neighbourhood of Develtus to Macrolivada. All along this earthen wall, called by the Greeks
the Great Fence, and now known as the Erkesiya, Bulgar
soldiers kept a constant watch.

But so vast a work could not be carried on with hostile
forces just across the frontier. It is almost certain that
some clause in the treaty provided for the erection of such
a 'fence' without interruption from the Imperial forces.
It is noticeable that, of the great Imperial fortresses that
guarded the frontier before the war, only Mesembria and
Adrianople, both of them commercial as well as military

[1] Identified by Zlatarski, *Izviestiya*, pp. 67–8: Shkorpil's identification of
Constantia (*Aboba-Pliska*, loc. cit.) with Kostenets, near Trajan's Gate, is
unlikely and unsupported by any evidence.

[2] 'περὶ τῆς παλαιῆς ἐνορίας ἵνα ἐστίν . . . κτλ.'

metropoles, were re-occupied and rebuilt by the Emperor. The other fortresses—Anchialus, Develtus, Philippopolis and Sardica—though they were not handed over to the Bulgars,[1] were left deserted, and were easily annexed by the Khan a few decades later. Already the Great Fence intercepted the main road from Adrianople to Philippopolis; and the isolation and desertion of the two western fortresses enabled Omortag to dispense with a 'fence' along this western boundary of his Balkan kingdom. Probably even now Bulgar statesmen were contemplating expansion on that side; a 'fence' built to-day, to-morrow would be useless.[2]

To mark the solemnity of the peace-treaty, both the Khan and the Emperor agreed to pledge their word according to the rites of the other's faith. To the scandal of the pious Christians of Constantinople, the Emperor, the Viceroy of God, poured water on to the earth, and swore on a sword and on the entrails of horses and sacrificed dogs to the false idols of the Bulgars. It was almost worse when the heathen ambassadors fouled by their touch the Holy Gospels and called on the name of God. Men were not surprised when plagues and earthquakes followed on the heels of these monstrous impieties.[3]

Omortag, however, was genuinely for peace in the Balkans. Bulgaria's existence had been guaranteed by the weapons of Krum; it was time now to enjoy the gifts of civilization that the nearness of Byzantium would give. Throughout his reign the Thirty Years' Peace was faithfully kept by the Khan. Only once did the Bulgar armies

[1] See Appendix VI.

[2] For about half a mile, near Bakadzhik, there is a second 'fence' a little to the south, curving in front of the other, known as the Gypsy Erkesiya—the legend being that the 'Tsar's' troops were called away and they ordered the gypsies to carry it on; but the gypsies carelessly diverted the direction, which the soldiers corrected when they returned (*Aboba-Pliska*, pp. 542–3).

[3] Ignatius, *Vita Nicephori*, p. 206: Genesius, p. 28: Theophanes Continuatus, p. 31. See Zlatarski, *Istoriya*, pp. 434–4.

march southward from the Great Fence; and that was to help an Emperor.

In the year 823 the Emperor Michael II was beleaguered in Constantinople by the army and the fleet of the arch-rebel Thomas, so desperately that he even was arming the Saracen captives in the city. In his straits he would welcome anyone to help him. It was here that the Khan intervened. Some said that Michael sent to Pliska asking for aid, which was granted him. Others told a longer story; it was Omortag that began the negotiations, asking to be allowed to intervene. Michael refused; he could not, he said, employ heathens to shed Christian blood. But his refusal was put down by gossip to economy; the Bulgars wished to be paid—and, in any case, it would be a violation of the Thirty Years' Peace. But Omortag thought the opportunity for interference and for plunder too good to be missed; he crossed the frontier all the same —and Michael assuredly was privy to it, forgiving the breach of the treaty in return for the help, and granting him freely what booty he could obtain. The Bulgar army crossed the Fence and marched past Adrianople and Arcadiopolis towards the capital. The rebel Thomas learnt of their coming; reluctantly he drew his troops away from the siege and went out to meet the new foe. The Bulgars waited for him at Ceductus, the aqueduct where the Empress Procopia had waved farewell to her hapless husband before the field of Versinicia. At the battle of Ceductus the rebels were badly beaten; the bulk of Thomas's army was destroyed. The Bulgars made their way back to the north laden with spoils. And Michael was saved.[1]

Omortag utilized this rare Balkan peace to create other

---

[1] Georgius Hamartolus, p. 796: he says that Michael asked for Bulgar help. Genesius, pp. 41–2, and Theophanes Continuatus, pp. 64–6, give the longer story, the Continuator adding the touch about Michael's economical motive in refusing aid.

buildings beside the Great Fence. It was probably in the last years of his father's and the first years of his reign that the palace of Pliska, whose ruins we can trace to-day, was built. The great quadrilateral camp some two miles by four, surrounded with its rough rampart and pierced with eleven gates, probably dates from the early years of the Bulgar occupation. But the town had twice been destroyed by the Emperor during the wars of Krum; the present inner citadel probably post-dated these wars. It consisted of a trapezium-shaped fortification, with circular bastions at the four angles, double rectangular bastions guarding the four gates, and eight other bastions. Inside was the dwelling-place of the Khans, a great hall, almost square but trisected with columns, and with an apse for the throne, raised above the ground on a high substructure. It was no doubt in this hall that Krum placed the columns and sculptures that he carried off from the Palace of Saint Mamas. Close to the palace stood the heathen temple of the Khans, later to atone for its past by becoming a Christian church.[1]

But one palace only was insufficient for the glory of the Sublime Khan. At Transmarisca, on the Danube, where the modern Turtukan still guards one of the easiest passages across the river, Omortag made a house of high renown,[2] a strong palatial fortress to watch the northern approach to his capital. He was still living at his old palace at Pliska at the time[3]; and, with morbid symmetry, half-way between his two earthly halls he built a third house where he should lie for eternity—a splendid sepulchre, whose erection he commemorated on an inscribed column, that later builders determined to utilize;

---

[1] *Aboba-Pliska*, pp. 62 ff, 132 ff. This palace was almost certainly built—probably by Greek artisans—in the early ninth century.

[2] ' Ἐπ(οίη)σεν ὑπέρφ(η)μον (οἶ)κο[ν] (εἰ)s τὸν Δανοῦβιν.'

[3] ' (εἰ)s τὸν παλ(αι)ὸν (οἶ)κον αὐτου μέν(ων).'

and now the heathen monarch's sentiments are to be read in one of the churches of Tirnovo.[1]

In the autumn of the year 821 the Khan built another fortress-palace, farther to the south of Pliska, guarding the approaches from the Great Fence. Again he recorded his creation on a column that was found at the village of Chatalar.[2] 'The Sublime Khan Omortag,' it says, 'is divine ruler[3] in the land where he was born. Dwelling in the camp of Pliska[4], he made a palace[5] on the Tutsa and increased his power[6] against the Greeks and the Slavs. And he skilfully made a bridge over the Tutsa.[7] . . . And he set up in his fortress four columns, and between the columns two bronze lions. May God grant the divine ruler that he press down with his foot the Emperor so long as the Tutsa flows and the enemies of the Bulgars are controlled[8]; and may he subdue his foes and live in joy and happiness for a hundred years. The date of the foundation is in Bulgarian *shegor alem*, and in Greek the fifteenth indiction.' The name by which Omortag knew this palace, which he founded in September 821,

[1] For the Tirnovo inscription see *Aboba-Pliska*, p. 553: Uspenski, *O Drevnistyakh Goroda Tyrnova*, pp. 5 ff.: Jireček, op. cit., 148 ff.: Bury, op. cit., pp. 366–7: Zlatarski, *Istoriya*, pp. 325–30, 444–7. Uspenski, Jireček (rather incorrectly), and Zlatarski all give the full text. Uspenski places the tomb at the mound of Mumdzhilar, but Zlatarski, more convincingly, at the village of Ikinli-fount, on the present Roumanian frontier.

[2] For the Chatalar inscription see *Aboba-Pliska*, pp. 546 ff.: Bury, op. cit., pp. 368–9: Zlatarski, op. cit., pp. 319–25, and esp. pp. 441–4.

[3] '$\dot{\epsilon}\kappa$ $\theta\epsilon\omicron\acute{\upsilon}$ $\ddot{\alpha}\rho\chi(\omega)\nu$' [4] '$\tau(\hat{\eta})s$ $\pi\lambda(\acute{\upsilon})\sigma\kappa\alpha s$ $\tau\grave{\omicron}\nu$ $\kappa\acute{\alpha}(\mu)\pi\omicron\nu$' [5] '$\alpha\grave{\upsilon}\lambda(\acute{\eta})\nu$'

[6] Zlatarski's reading, '$M\epsilon\acute{\iota}\zeta\omega$ $\dot{\epsilon}\pi\omicron\acute{\iota}\eta\sigma\epsilon$,' makes much more convincing sense than Uspenski's '$\dot{\epsilon}\pi\hat{\eta}\gamma\epsilon$,' or Bury's '$\ddot{\epsilon}\delta\epsilon\iota\xi\epsilon$.' Zlatarski professes to be able to read the 'M.'

[7] After Tutsa there follows '$M\epsilon\tau$ . . .' Uspenski reads '$\mu\epsilon\tau[\eta\nu\epsilon\gamma\kappa\epsilon$'; Bury accepts it very doubtfully. Zlatarski reads '$\mu\epsilon\tau[\acute{\omicron}\pi\iota\sigma\theta\epsilon\nu$ $\tau\grave{\eta}\nu$ $\alpha\grave{\upsilon}\lambda\grave{\eta}\nu$.' This seems to me to be too long, though better sense.

[8] According to Zlatarski, who reads:

'$\kappa(\alpha\iota)$ $[\dot{\epsilon}]$ $(\omega)s$ $[\dot{\alpha}\nu\tau\iota\sigma\tau\acute{\alpha}$
$\tau\omicron\grave{\upsilon}s$ $\pi\omicron\lambda[\lambda]\omicron\grave{\upsilon}s$ $B\omicron\upsilon\lambda\gamma\acute{\alpha}\rho(\omicron\upsilon)s$ $\dot{\epsilon}\pi\acute{\epsilon}[\kappa\eta$.'

I am doubtful about it, but Uspenski reads even more dubiously:

'$\kappa\alpha\grave{\iota}$ $[\delta]\omega\sigma[\eta$ $\alpha\grave{\iota}\chi\mu\alpha\lambda\acute{\omega}$
$\tau\omicron\grave{\upsilon}s$ $\kappa\tau\lambda$.'

has not come down to us; probably it was some Bulgar
equivalent of the phrase 'of high renown.' But soon it
came to be called by its Slav name, and to feature in
Balkan history as Preslav, Great Preslav, the glorious.[1]
The words of the inscription show clearly that Preslav
was intended to awe the Slavs of the southern frontier
and the Greeks, the Emperor and his subjects, that lived
beyond. Furthermore, they show that the Emperor, despite the Thirty Years' Peace, was still the Khan's traditional foe, the foe whom most he feared and most he longed
to subdue.

At the moment, however, the Khan was at peace with
the Empire—was even borrowing from it the trappings of
his culture. The inscriptions in which he glorified his
works were written in Greek, not the elegant Greek such
as was used by the citizens of Constantinople, but a rough,
ungrammatical language—written no doubt by captives
who had, forcibly or from their own choice, remained on
in the Khan's dominions. Greek was still the only language in Eastern Europe that possessed an alphabet; for
writing, Greeks or natives of the Greek-speaking Empire
had to be employed. These scribes of the Khan, in the
middle of the Bulgar formulae, add to the title the Sublime
Khan, '$\kappa\acute{a}\nu\nu\alpha\varsigma$ $\upsilon\beta\iota\gamma\eta$,' the Imperial formula $\acute{o}$ $\acute{\epsilon}\kappa$ $\theta\epsilon o\hat{\upsilon}$
$\acute{a}\rho\chi\omega\nu$, the divine ruler—though the Khan was far from
approving of the Christian God.[2] The architects of the
new palaces were also probably Greeks. Of the Danubian
palace no traces have been unearthed, and the original
buildings of Preslav are lost beneath the later ruins; but
Pliska shows very markedly the influence of Byzantine

[1] Preslav is a fair translation of the Greek ' $\upsilon\pi\acute{\epsilon}\rho\phi\eta\mu o\varsigma$ ' or ' $\pi\acute{a}\mu\phi\eta\mu o\varsigma$ ' that
occur on the Bulgar inscriptions.

[2] They, of course, only gave him the title of ' $\acute{a}\rho\chi\omega\nu$.' ' $B\alpha\sigma\iota\lambda\epsilon\acute{\upsilon}\varsigma$ ' was
reserved for the Emperor, and ' $\dot{\rho}\acute{\eta}\xi$ ' for Western rulers. The formula does
not mean that the Khan paid any respect to the Christian God; it is purely
a formula.

architecture, suggesting both the Triconchus and the Magnaura in the great Imperial Palace. [1]

But though he encouraged Greek artisans, Omortag firmly discouraged their religion. Christianity was creeping in to Bulgaria in a manner most alarming to him; he could not but regard it as a subtle means of propaganda on the part of the Emperor, the viceroy of the Christian God. It was only later that the Khans realized from their dealings with the West that one could be Christian without necessarily obeying the Basileus. There was another self-appointed viceroy, who dwelt in Italy; and in the north there were Christians who sometimes doubted the viceroyalty of either. Accordingly, Omortag persecuted Christians, as he would have persecuted Imperial spies. The Imperial captives must have propagated Christianity fairly widely, and among the Slavs (though not among the warlike Bulgars) there must have been many converts. Already under Krum and during the brief reigns of the rebel *boyars* the Christians had suffered much. Krum had deported the Christians of Adrianople, with many hardships, to beyond the Danube; though, on the whole, he was fairly tolerant. Ditzeng mutilated the arms of the Archbishop Manuel. Tsok was far more uncompromising; he was said to have ordered the Christian captives, lay as well as clerical, to renounce their faith, and when they refused to have slain them all. Omortag, though less violent, was equally minded. Under his rule the maimed Archbishop Manuel finally met his death [2]; and he was

[1] The rather different, almost Iranian, spirit of the stele of the horseman found at Madara is probably due to an Armenian artist.

[2] Ditzeng's persecution is mentioned in the *Slavonic Prologue* (loc. cit.), Tsok's in the *Menologium* (loc. cit.). The author of the *Menologium* says that Manuel had his arms cut off and was killed by Krum; whereupon the Bulgars, in disgust, strangled their inhuman ruler. This may refer to Ditzeng's mutilation of his arms, and to the sudden fall of Ditzeng or another of the *boyar* Khans, the pious author having muddled and united the stories to give them a moral tone. That Manuel was actually killed by Omortag is stated in Theophanes Continuatus, p. 217.

also probably the Khan who, according to Theodore of Studium, ordered all Christians to eat meat in Lent. Fourteen refused; so Omortag killed one as an example and sold his wife and children into captivity. But the rest remained obdurate, so all were slain.[1] Even a captive called Cinamon, whom Krum had given to Omortag, and to whom Omortag was deeply attached, was thrown into prison for his persistency in remaining Christian, and remained there till Omortag's death.[2]

Both these architectural and these anti-Christian activities were part of the same policy, the aggrandisement of the power and prestige of the Khan. In this Omortag carried on his father's work, and, like Krum, probably furthered it by encouraging the Slavs against the Bulgar aristocracy. There is no more evidence for the internal state of Bulgaria under Omortag; but it seems that in the Balkans the two races were by now mixing. In the lower classes the Slavs were easily able to absorb the few Bulgars; it was only in the upper classes that there was still a distinction. The Bulgar nobility, the almost feudal military caste, was untainted, while the Slav nobility, brought forward by Krum, was a court nobility with no hereditary basis, made or marred by the whim of the Khan. Of the state of affairs beyond the Danube we know even less. Here there was not the same solid Slav background. On the plains of Wallachia and Bessarabia, and in the mountains of Transylvania, there was a conglomeration of mongrel tribes—Slavs, Avars, and Vlachs —clinging in places to the Latin speech and culture left behind by Trajan's Dacian colonists, but wild and disorganized. Over these peoples the Khan ruled, it seems, by a system of military outposts that controlled the districts

---

[1] Theodore Studites, *Parva Catechesis*, pp. 220 ff.
[2] Theophylact, op. cit., pp. 193 ff.

around; and where possible, as in Bessarabia, a Great Fence guarded the frontier.[1]

It was to these northern frontiers that Omortag directed the attention of his diplomacy and his arms. A memorial tablet set up by the Khan tells of his servant the *zhupan* Okorses, of the family of Tzanagares, who met his death in the waters of the Dnieper when proceeding to the Bulgar camp.[2] Things had changed on the Steppes since two centuries ago the sons of Kubrat had spread Bulgarias from the Danube to the Volga and the Kama. The Khazar power was declining, and fierce new tribes were pouring in from the east. About the year 820 the Magyars advanced beyond the River Don, striking for ever a wedge between the two great Bulgar stems. It was against this danger that the army which Okorses never reached went out beyond the Dnieper. It achieved its objects. For a few more years the Magyars stayed outside of the frontier.

But the main scene of Omortag's foreign policy lay further to the west, where the Bulgar frontier ran from the fortress of Belgrade up the River Theiss. Over this frontier lay the struggling kingdom of Croatia, and its oppressor the great power of the West, the Frankish Empire. The rule of the Sublime Khan lay heavily on the tribes that lived in this corner of his dominions, and they determined to search for relief.

In the year 818 the Emperor Louis the Pious was holding his Court at Heristal; and amongst the embassies that waited on his pleasure was one from the Slavs of the Timok (just south of Belgrade) and the Abodriti, a Slav race to the north of the Danube, just opposite. These tribes had

[1] *Aboba-Pliska*, pp. 524–5. Rivers seem to have been able to take the place of fences. Actually in Omortag's day the Theiss and the Dnieper appear to have been the frontiers. In the *Responsa Nicolai*, Chapter xxv., we learn how much the Bulgars valued their entrenchments.

[2] *Aboba-Pliska*, p. 190: Zlatarski, *Edin ot Pravadiiskitie Omortagovi Nadpici*, pp. 94–107.

Gᴇ

revolted from the Khan and wanted help. Louis was
not sure what policy he should adopt in the East; so the
Timocians, in despair, threw in their lot with Liudevit,
the Prince of Pannonian Croatia, who also was represented
at Heristal and who seemed likely for a moment to found
a realm free from Frank and Bulgar alike.[1] But Liudevit's
triumphs were ephemeral; by 823 he had died in exile,
and his country was in the hands of the Franks. Omortag
was alarmed by the growth of Frankish power. He had,
it seems, reconquered the Timocians; but the Abodriti
and the Predenecenti (the Branichevtzi, just across the
Danube to the Abodriti) were airing their independence
and intriguing with the Franks.[2] He decided that he
must free his hands to deal with them by coming to an
arrangement with the Western Emperor. In 824, for the
first time in history, a Bulgarian embassy made its way
to Germany, bringing a letter from the Khan to propose
a delineation of the frontier.[3]

Louis, with his customary caution, sent the embassy
back accompanied by his own legates, including the Bavarian Machelm, to find out more about this country of
Bulgaria. Meanwhile, he received another embassy from
the rebel Slav tribes. Late in the year the Bulgarian ambassadors returned—with Machelm, no doubt, who by
now had informed himself as to the state of Bulgaria. But
Louis was leaning towards the rebels now; he kept the
Bulgars waiting nearly six months before he received them
at Aachen, in May. The audience was unsatisfactory;
the embassy was dismissed with a very ambiguous letter
to the Khan. Omortag patiently tried once more. In
826 a third embassy reached the Emperor, and requested
him either to agree to regulate the frontier at once, or,

[1] Einhard, *Annales*, pp. 205–6. Liudevit was, it seems, secretly supported
by the Eastern Emperors (Dvornik, op. cit., p. 49).

[2] Ibid., p. 209, in 822.   [3] Ibid., p. 212.

anyhow, to come to an undertaking that each Power would keep within its own borders—the Khan was determined that his rebel Slavs should not go flirting with the Franks. But yet again Louis was non-committal. He professed to have heard a rumour that the Khan had died, and sent to the Eastern frontier to find out more about it. But no news was forthcoming; so Louis dismissed the Bulgar ambassador without any answer. [1]

Omortag's patience was exhausted. In 827 he invaded Frankish Croatia. His boats sailed from the Danube up the Drave, spreading destruction. The Slavs and other tribes on its banks were cowed into submission, and agreed to accept Bulgar governors. [2] His attack took the Franks by surprise. In 828 Baldric of Friuli, the governor of the frontier, was deposed for his incompetence in permitting the Bulgar invasion, [3] and that same year the young King Louis, the German, led an expedition against the Bulgars. [4] But he achieved nothing; in 829, as in the previous two years, the Bulgars devastated Pannonia once more. [5] The Khan had asserted his power in a very definite manner; the German court was better informed now. The war dragged till after Omortag's death; peace was concluded in 832, to the satisfaction of the Bulgars. [6] Their frontier was guaranteed, and their position and prestige among the Slavs was assured.

We are only told definitely of the Bulgar campaigns on the Drave; but Bulgar armies had also been operating on land. Another memorial was erected by Omortag for his *tarkan*, Onegavon, of the family of Kubiares, who was on his way to the Bulgar camp when he was drowned in the waters of the Theiss. [7]

[1] Einhard, *Annales*, p. 213: Astronomus, *Vita Hludovici*, pp. 628–9: *Fuldenses Annales*, p. 359.
[2] Einhard, p. 216.   [3] Ibid., loc. cit.   [4] *Fuldenses Annales*, p. 359.
[5] Ibid., p. 360.   [6] *Annalista Saxo*, p. 574.
[7] *Aboba-Pliska*, pp. 190–1.

Omortag did not long survive his *tarkan*. When he built his tomb he caused to be written the words: 'Man dies, even though he lives nobly, and another is born; and let the latest born, seeing this, remember him who made it. The name of the Prince is Omortag, the Sublime Khan. God grant that he live a hundred years.'[1] But God did not grant the Khan so lengthy a life. He died in 831,[2] after a reign of fifteen years—a short reign for a Bulgar ruler; but in its course he had shown the world, the West and the East alike, that Bulgaria was now to be numbered among the great Powers of Europe.

Three sons survived Omortag, called Enravotas, Svinitse, and Malamir. It was the youngest, Malamir, that succeeded to the throne; his mother must have been the Khan's favourite wife.[3] A veil of mystery hangs over Malamir's reign; all its happenings and their dates can only be completed by conjecture. It is even possible that the reign was two reigns, and that Malamir, after five years, gave place to a Khan Presiam.[4] But that is unlikely. It seems, on the other hand, that Malamir reigned for twenty-one years, years of the highest importance in the history of Bulgaria.

Malamir's reign opened in peace. The Thirty Years' Truce with the Empire had still some fifteen more years to run; while in Pannonia the Franks had been awed by Omortag's invasions. Of Bulgarian history during these peaceful years we know nothing. Even inscriptions are very rare. All we learn from them is of the death from illness of a *boyar* called Tsepa, and that the Kavkan

---

[1] The Tirnovo inscription, closing words. See p. 77.

[2] I accept Zlatarski's date for his death—*Istoriya*, p. 317, *Izviestiya*, p. 34. See *Aboba-Pliska*, p. 236.

[3] Theophylact, op. cit., p. 192.

[4] I discuss the Malamir-Presiam problem in Appendix VIII.

Isbules, who appears elsewhere as the Khan's chief general, built for Malamir an aqueduct at his own expense, whereat the Khan gave a series of feasts to his aristocracy. Probably Malamir was engaged in adding to his father's new fortress of Preslav, and the aqueduct was needed to supply the growing city.[1]

This opening peace lasted satisfactorily for five years; but in 835-6 a diplomatic crisis faced Bulgaria and the Empire. The Thirty Years' Peace required, it appears, confirmation at every decade. In 825-6 this had been effected without difficulty; Omortag had been giving his attention then to the middle Danube, while the Emperor Michael II was fully engaged with religious problems at home. But by the end of the second decade certain problems forced themselves on the Khan's and the Emperor's notice. When Krum captured Adrianople in 813 he had transported ten thousand of its inhabitants to a spot beyond the Danube, which soon acquired the name of Macedonia—for Adrianople was the capital of the Macedonian theme.[2] There they still lived, now numbering twelve thousand, enjoying, it seems, a certain degree of self-government and electing their chief magistrate. But they were restive in their exile; its discomforts and periodical persecutions made them long for their old homes. The Khan, however, wished to keep them. No doubt the skilled artisans that must have been amongst them were of great value to him in manufacturing luxuries for his court. It was only with the greatest difficulty that Cordyles, the governor of these Macedonians, made his way to Constantinople, to persuade the Emperor Theophilus to send ships to the Danube to rescue them. They had already once tried to escape across Bulgaria; but

---

[1] *Aboba-Pliska*, pp. 191, 230–1. Uspenski, Zlatarski, and Bury all agree in translating the obscure word ' ἀνάβρυτον ' as aqueduct.

[2] See above, p. 65.

without Imperial help they were doomed to failure. Theophilus, however, waited for the temporary break in the Truce before taking action, but in 836 he sent some ships to the Danube. The 'Macedonians' moved down the river to meet the ships and began to cross one of the northern tributaries of the river—probably the Pruth.[1] The local Bulgar governor determined to check them and crossed over to attack them, but was beaten with great loss; and the Macedonians triumphantly effected their crossing. The Bulgars then called in to their aid the Magyars, whose power now extended to the Bulgar frontier.[2] The Magyars came gladly; numbers of them presented themselves before the Macedonians' camp demanding the surrender of all their belongings. The demand was refused, and in the battle that followed the Macedonians again, by the help of St. Adrian, were victorious. And so they passed on safely to the ships and Constantinople, after more than twenty years in exile.[3]

The Bulgars had played an unimpressive part in this episode. They were too busy elsewhere. Malamir, like Theophilus, intended to get some work done before he renewed the treaty; and his work was of a more drastic

---

[1] Bury, by assuming that this river must be the Danube (op. cit., p. 371), created unnecessary complications that ruin the geography of the story. The fact that no name is given to the river does not necessarily mean that the river must be the same as the last river mentioned.

[2] See above, p. 81.

[3] Leo Grammaticus, p. 232: Logothete (Slavonic version), pp. 101–2: Theophanes Continuatus, p. 216. Bury, loc. cit.: Zlatarski, *Istoriya* i., 1, pp. 339–40. There is some difficulty about the date. The Slavonic version calls the Khan Vladimir, which must be a mistake for Malamir, muddling him with Boris's son Vladimir. Bury and Zlatarski both date the episode 836, Bury to fit his chronology of Basil I's life, and Zlatarski to fit it in before Malamir is succeeded by Presiam. Both reasons seem to me to be invalid; Mr. Brooke (*B. Z.* xx.) has shown Basil to have been born far later, and I do not think that Presiam's reign happened. But, as Bury says (op. cit., p. ix), the tradition given in Basil's life that this exile lasted some twenty-three years is probably reliable, though Basil, like other heroes, has acquired adventures that do not belong to him. Probably it was his father or an elder brother that lived through the captivity.

nature. The treaty of 815-16 had left the great Imperial fortresses of Philippopolis and Sardica isolated and deserted. Malamir now proceeded to annex the latter and the surrounding territory, and to advance even farther, along the road to Thessalonica. The Slavs of Macedonia and the Greek peninsula were too unruly during these years for the Emperor to control, and he had likewise to submit without effective protest to this Bulgar intervention. This advance to Thessalonica was probably not directed against the rich city, but a move to cover work further to the west. The Bulgars were beginning now to settle and set up their rule in the hills of Upper Macedonia, the land that was to be their second cradle—the land for which they sigh so sadly to-day. [1]

Despite these questionable transactions, the truce was renewed and lasted another decade, till its due termination. During these years Malamir kept his attention on his western frontier. On the north-west, in Pannonia, he seems to have lived in peace with the Croats and with his most formidable neighbours, the Franks. But in 845, when the Thirty Years' Truce was drawing to a close, he thought it worth while to send ambassadors to Louis the German's court at Paderborn, to make a permanent peace and alliance that would leave his hands free to deal, when the time came, with the Greeks. [2] Further south he was less peaceful. With the annexation of Sardica, his power had spread into the valley of the Morava.

On the hills beyond the Morava a chieftain called

[1] The Thessalonica expedition is mentioned in the story of Cordyles and his 'Macedonians' (see reference above). The annexation of Sardica is probable, because, while by the peace of 816, Sardica, with Philippopolis, appears to have been left dismantled but not annexed, by the time of the Serbian war, Sardica must have been in Bulgar hands. This is the only date when these annexations can have occurred. It is also probable that some such annexation was the main cause of the Bulgaro-Serbian war. (See below.)

[2] *Annales Fuldenses*, p. 364.

Vlastimer was uniting the tribes around and building the Serbian nation. In his task he was certainly helped by the Bulgarian menace. The Serbs were alarmed by this great empire spreading to their borders and moving to cut off their expansion to the south; they gladly put themselves under Vlastimer's care. Moreover, Vlastimer was encouraged and urged on by his nominal suzerain the Emperor, who was far enough away not to be a menace himself, but who was delighted at the growth of a new thorn in the side of Bulgaria. The loss of the last Imperial outposts beyond Rhodope was amply compensated, if thereby Bulgaria was made a close neighbour of a jealous rival.

Whether Vlastimer or Malamir actually provoked the inevitable war is uncertain: but in 839 the Bulgars invaded Serbia, under Presiam, probably a scion of the royal house. But the Serbs knew how to fight among their hills. After three years Presiam had achieved nothing, but had lost large numbers of his men. In 842 the Bulgars returned to their country defeated.[1]

But Malamir did not let this set-back interfere with his Macedonian policy. Soon after the year 846, when the Thirty Years' Truce was ended, he sent his general, the Kavkan Isbules, to invade the regions of the Struma and the Nestos, again probably to cover the Bulgar penetration farther to the west. The Imperial troops in those themes were probably engaged in fighting rebel Slavs in the Peloponnese, and could not oppose him. But to create diversion the Empress-Regent Theodora strengthened her garrisons in Thrace and began systematically to devastate Thracian Bulgaria. This drew Isbules back, but not before the Bulgars had annexed Philippopolis and advanced to Philippi. A truce seems to have followed this campaign. Of its terms we know nothing; probably

---

[1] *De Administrando Imperio*, p. 154. See Appendix VIII. I follow Zlatarski's dates (op. cit., p. 346), but certainty is impossible.

the Bulgars were authorized to proceed with their penetration of the Macedonian hinterland—a work which the
Empire was powerless to prevent.[1]

Malamir lived some five years longer; but his latter
days were clouded. Probably his health was poor—he
never led his armies in person—and he was troubled with
domestic problems; Christianity was spreading even into
his own family. The trouble was due to a Greek called
Cinamon. As a young man Cinamon had been captured
at Adrianople by Krum and had been assigned as a slave
to Omortag. He was a very able slave, but obstinately
remained a Christian; which so annoyed Omortag that
eventually he put him in prison. After Omortag's death
Enravotas, desirous of possessing the perverse paragon,
asked his brother Malamir to release him and give him
to him. Unfortunately Cinamon acquired a great influence over his new master, and gradually Enravotas
became a convert to the Christian faith. This was very
awkward; Enravotas, besides being a prince, held some
high position in the army—the Greek martyrologist calls
him also Boïnos, a Greek transliteration of the Slavonic
for a warrior. But Christianity was inevitably associated
with Greek propaganda; the Empire was the only Christian
State with whom Bulgaria had had intimate dealings, and
the Emperors were fond of using missionaries for political
purposes. Enravotas's conversion smelled strongly of
treachery. Besides, Christianity was probably spreading
among the humbler classes, and to have a prince on their
side would encourage far too much subjects whose loyalty
was inevitably doubtful, but who were negligible so long

---

[1] Georgius Continuatus, p. 821: Logothete (Slavonic version), p. 103: I
follow Bury (op. cit., pp. 372–3) and Zlatarski (op. cit., p. 350) in assuming
that the Philippi (Villoison's) and the Shumla inscriptions both belong to
this campaign (*Aboba-Pliska*, p. 233). The latter inscription indicates
clearly that it was now that the Bulgars annexed Philippopolis; it also
mentions Probatum and Burdizus in terms that would imply that they
were the forts mentioned vaguely by the Logothete.

as they remained humble and fairly scattered. Malamir begged his brother to come back and worship the sun and moon, as all good Bulgars did. But the glory of being the first Bulgarian martyr was too much for Enravotas; he remained obdurate. The Khan was obliged to put him to death.[1]

Three years later, in 852, Malamir himself died. He was succeeded by his nephew, the son of Svinitse, Boris.[2]

The new Khan Boris was young, and full of the impetuous audacity of youth. He longed to restore the military prestige of Bulgaria and her Khans, that had lain dormant during his uncle's reign. His first move was to collect his forces on the southern frontier, with the intent of breaking Malamir's treaty. But the Empress-Regent Theodora was, we are told, a match for him. She sent to him saying that, if he invaded the Empire, she would lead its forces against him in person: so that if he won he would have no glory in defeating a woman, and if he lost he would be ridiculous. The young Khan was gallantly abashed; but the Empress supplemented her feminine diplomacy by offering to revise the frontier— moving it southward to run south for some twenty-five miles from the neighbourhood of Develtus to the Iron Gate in the Stranya Planina, and then due west to join the Great Fence at the Sakar Planina. It was not a great sacrifice on the Empress's part; the ceded territory included Anchialus and Develtus, but, like the other fortresses that Krum destroyed, they had lain dismantled and

[1] Theophylact, Archbishop of Bulgaria, pp. 192 ff. He dates Enravotas's death three years before Malamir's. I think it was the aspect of treachery rather than the religious aspect that caused Malamir to kill his brother. It appears as an isolated case of martyrdom.

[2] I follow Zlatarski's date (*Izviestiya*, pp. 45–7) for Boris's succession. It is made probable by the embassy to Germany known to have taken place that year, and fits with the date given by Theophylact (p. 201). His name appears in the Greek writers variously as Βώγωρις, Βόγαρις, Βωρίσης, and Βορίσης (miswritten also once as Γόβορις and once as Βορώσης), in early Slavonic translations as Borish and Boris. On his inscriptions he is Βόρης.

half-deserted ever since that day, and the whole district
had been waste land since the war. But its cession achieved
Theodora's object; she could not then have afforded a
war. Her persecution of the Paulicians on her eastern
frontier was causing her more trouble than so pious a
policy deserved.[1]

Boris then turned his attention to the north-west. In
852 he had sent an embassy to Mainz to Louis the German, to announce his accession and renew his uncle's
treaty. But next year, encouraged no doubt by his own
bloodless triumphs in the south and instigated by Louis's
rival, Charles the Bald of the Western Franks, he invaded
Frankish territory. But, despite the support of local Slavs,
he was defeated and obliged to retire; and peace was soon
re-made. It is probable that his aim had been the annexation of Pannonian Croatia, which at the time was a vassal-
state of the Franks; indeed, the victory that the Frankish
chroniclers claimed may really have been the victory of
the Croats. We know that he invaded Croatia without
success, and at last had to retire and make a peace, at
which he received many handsome presents. But the
Croats never became his vassals nor paid him any tribute.[2]

---

[1] Genesius (pp. 85–6) tells the story of Theodora's message, but does not
name the Bulgar Khan. Theophanes Continuatus (pp. 162–5) reproduces
it, calling the Khan Boris (Βώγωρις) and connecting it with Boris's conversion, owing to which Theodora ceded the territory. But Theodora had
fallen in 856—seven years before Boris was converted. The Imperial
records would more probably be accurate about which Emperor or Empress
ceded territory than about Bulgarian semi-internal affairs. Besides, Theodora's message, though it makes a pretty anecdote and probably is not
entirely apocryphal, would hardly by itself deter an ambitious Bulgar.
The talk about the treaty implies that the incident took place soon after
Boris's accession, when Malamir's treaty probably needed renewing. I
therefore follow Zlatarski (*Izviestiya*, pp. 54 ff.: *Istoriya*, i. 2, pp. 2 ff.) in
isolating these incidents from the conversion, and dating them early in the
reign—probably 852. I accept Zlatarski's geography of the ceded territory
(*Izviestiya*, loc. cit.); the old identification of the Σιδηρᾶ Pass with Veregava
is clearly impossible.

[2] *Annales Bertiniani*, p. 448: *De Administrando Imperio*, pp. 150–1. I believe
that these refer to the same war, which was an attempt by Boris to wrest
Pannonian Croatia from the Franks: hence the Franks recorded it as a
war against them. The Croatia must be Pannonian Croatia, not Dalmatian

There were other enemies on that western frontier.
Boris was eager to avenge Presiam's defeats at the hands
of the Serbs; and he realized that a strong Serbia would
necessarily make difficult his expansion both in Croatia
and in Upper Macedonia.   The latter question probably
caused him to declare war.   It seems that throughout
his first decade Boris was busily continuing the work of
Malamir's reign and pushing his frontier right to the
mountains of Albania, and even the northernmost peaks
of Pindus.   In 860 he sent an embassy to Constantinople.
We know neither the cause nor the achievements of this
embassy save that its audiences kept the Arab ambassador
waiting.[1]   Probably Boris was asking for recognition of
his Macedonian annexations and for the neutrality of the
Imperial government before his attack on the Serbs.   But
he was no more successful than Presiam.   Since Vlastimer's
death his sons Muntimer, Stroëmer, and Goïnic had
shared the Serbian throne.   They united to meet the invader, and caught him in the treacherous valleys, defeating him utterly and capturing his son Vladimir and twelve
Great Boyars.   To ransom them Boris was forced to make
peace.   He agreed to evacuate the country, and on his
humiliating retreat Muntimer's two sons acted as his escort
as far as Rase on the frontier (Račka, near Novi-Bazar),
where they exchanged presents, the Serbian princes giving
the Khan two slaves, two falcons, two hounds, and ninety
skins.   This friendship with Muntimer's family later bore
fruit, when the Serbian princes quarrelled amongst

Croatia—Ratimir's kingdom, not Tirpimir's, as Zlatarski (*Istoriya*, i, 2,
pp. 8–9) and Dvornik (p. 54) say; to reach Dalmatian Croatia, Boris would
have had to operate either through Serbia or through Pannonian Croatia.
Nor is it necessary to identify the Slavs mentioned as Boris's auxiliaries as
Moravians, as Zlatarski (op. cit., p. 7) and Bury (op. cit., p. 383) do.   The
Moravians were well enough known to the Frankish annalists by now to
be called by name, not generically as Slavs.   The Φράγγων νέφος, which
Theophylact (loc. cit.) says covered Bulgaria at the time of Boris's acces-
sion, probably means the Frankish victories in this war.

[1] Tabari, in Vasiliev, *Vizantiya i Araby*, i., Prilozheniya, p. 57.

themselves. Muntimer, who emerged victorious, sent his brothers and their families to prison in Bulgaria, and thus gave the Bulgars many excuses for intervening among the Serbs. So, finally, Boris recovered from the consequences of his defeat.[1]

This Serbian war was the last episode in the history of the heathen Empire. Already the drama was opening that would change the fate of Bulgaria and of half Europe. Of the internal aspect of the land in the last days of its old life we have little more information than in its earlier history. The Slav element in the country by now was displaying its predominance. The Slavonic language was in general use. Greek might still be needed for public inscriptions, there being no Slavonic alphabet; but the old Bulgar tongue had utterly or almost utterly disappeared.[2] The Khans since Krum had encouraged the Slavs, inviting Slavs to their Court; Omortag's sons had even borne Slavonic names, and Boris's likewise.[3] In the vast Bulgar lands beyond the Danube the proportion of races was probably fairly even, though both Slavs and Bulgars were leavened by the remnants of innumerable tribes that had lingered in the Eastern Carpathians. But south of the Danube, in what was now the centre of the empire, the Slavs far outnumbered the Bulgars, particularly in the new Macedonian provinces on which the Khans were spending so much attention. It was only the military

---

[1] *De Administrando Imperio*, pp. 154–5. The date of the war is doubtful, some writers—e.g. Rambaud (p. 462)—placing it as late as 887. But Constantine implies that it took place fairly soon after Vlastimer's death (about 845–50), and it cannot have happened during the years immediately following the Conversion (863), as we are fairly well informed about those years. On the other hand, Boris was old enough to have a son fighting (Vlastimer is Constantine's misprint for Vladimir); considering that he only died in 907, this cannot have been much before 863. I think it best to connect the war with the mysterious embassy of 860. Bulgaria has always had to try to prevent an alliance between Constantinople and the Serbs.

[2] Titles and proper names only survived. There was never an attempt to create an alphabet for the Bulgar language.

[3] e.g. Malamir and Vladimir.

aristocracy that remained purely Bulgar. For several
more generations their names remained without a trace
of Slav in them, and their old Bulgar titles lasted till the
fall of the Empire, whereas the title of Khan was, as soon
as men learnt to write Slavonic, superseded by the Slavonic
Knyaz. The power of this nobility had been curtailed
by Krum, but under the weaker control of Malamir it
had revived. The Kavkan Isbules, who could give the
Khan an aqueduct, showed by his very munificence what
a formidable subject he was. It seems that the Khan
was engaged in a perpetual struggle with the Bulgar
nobles, he wishing to rule like the Emperor, autocratically,
through a non-hereditary bureaucracy, and they, probably
with constitutional justification, aiming at reducing him
to be the president of a council of *boyars*. The Khans'
favourization of the Slavs, the middle and lower classes,
was obviously directed against this aristocracy—they even
created a rival Slav nobility. Probably Krum and Omortag sought to deal with the constitutional difficulty by
appointing Slavs on the council of *boyars*, who necessarily
became their creatures, and somehow breaking down the
hereditary principle: while Malamir, who was weaker, let
in the Bulgars again, and thus had to suffer the patronage
of magnates such as Isbules; and the young Boris inherited the difficulty. It was probably from among
these *boyars* that provincial governors were chosen, who
ruled the ten provinces by military force from fortified
camps. [1]

The vast bulk of the population was engaged in agriculture, living in free peasant communities and following
the simple pastoral methods that have lasted almost un-
changed in the Balkans to this day. But by now a small

---

[1] The number of the provinces into which Bulgaria was divided (ten) is
known from the story of the revolt of the nobility at the time of the Conversion (see below, p. 105).

commercial middle-class was rising. The annexation of cities such as Develtus and Anchialus included in the Bulgar dominions a certain number of Greeks and Armenians who had lingered in the dismantled towns, and who no doubt eagerly took advantage of the new trade conditions: while round the inland fortresses, such as Sardica, there remained a population claiming Roman descent. Moreover, Bulgaria herself enjoyed commercial activities; Bulgarian salt from the Transylvanian provinces was exported to saltless countries like Moravia; while the Byzantine exports to Central Europe passed most of them through Bulgar territory, either by the great Constantinople–Adrianople–Philippopolis–Sardica–Belgrade road or by the road from Thessalonica that joined it at Naissus (Nish). Most of this carrying trade was done, probably, by Greeks and Armenians; but the native inhabitants must sometimes have shared in it. It is unlikely that the Bulgarians were yet working the mines that so enriched later Balkan monarchs; and such crafts as building were in the hands of Greeks, captives, or newly made subjects.

Indeed, the culture was all in foreign hands. Lack of an alphabet forbade any native literature; the few official inscriptions had to be written in Greek. The arts, too, were practised only by Greeks; it was Greek artists that the Khan employed to paint him frescoes in the palaces that Greek architects had built for him. Thus the arts did not flourish there, save perhaps primitively among the peasants. Even architecture was seldom needed. The peasants lived in their huts and hovels, the small middle-class lived in the old Greek cities; only the nobility and the Khans required proper edifices. The Bulgarians were adept at constructing earthworks and rough fortifications; but probably the nobles were following the Khans' examples, and wanted halls and chambers built inside their rectangular castle walls, all bravely modelled on the fine palaces of Constantinople.[1]

Of the personal habits of the dwellers in these halls we know little. They were polygamous, they wore turbans and trousers, and, contrary to expectation, they liked to wash themselves quite often.[2] Domestic slavery was common there, as everywhere else in the Near East. Their religion was apparently a crude worship of the sun and moon and stars and other natural phenomena, whom they adored with human sacrifice and the sacrifice of horses and dogs. A horse's tail was their standard, and they swore by their swords.[3] But none of their old temples and altars has survived, save a rectangular building at Pliska, which later ages converted into a church.[4] It was a religion without much ethical background; the Bulgars remained cruel in their practices, torture and the death penalty playing a part in all their legal processes, with mutilation as a new-fangled humanity.[5]

This state of affairs was hardly worthy of a magnificent empire. Boris began to wonder whether some change might not be made. But before he could act himself, his hand was forced.

Far away to the north-west, in the valleys between Bohemia and the Western Carpathians, there lived some Slav tribes known collectively as the Moravians. In about the second decade of the century the Moravians were united under the rule of a prince called Moïmir, who in

[1] Pliska is the only palace to have been systematically excavated, save for the early Preslav in the Dobrudja, which is too early to have much remains of interest. Great Preslav is only now being excavated as far as the earliest layer, but almost certainly was built on the same lines.

[2] Nicolaus I Papa, *Responsa*, cap. vi., p. 572.

[3] Theophylact, Archbishop of Bulgaria, p. 189: Nicolaus I Papa, op. cit., cap. xxxiii, p. 580: see above, p. 74, and reff.

[4] *Aboba-Pliska*, pp. 104 ff.

[5] Nicolaus I Papa, op. cit., cap. lxxxvi., p. 595.

the years 833 to 836 conquered the Prince Pribina of Nitra and extended his power to the east along the northern bank of the Danube as far as its sharp bend southward by Esztergom. This expansion alarmed the Franks. The Margrave of the Eastern Mark and the Bishop of Passau regarded Moravia as a legitimate field for their enterprises, political and religious, and they disliked this show of native vigour. They waited till Moïmir's death (845); then Louis the German intervened and forced on the Moravians Moïmir's nephew, Rostislav, little thinking that Rostislav would show both ability and ingratitude. Louis was soon undeceived. Rostislav first established himself firmly in Moravia, and then began to extend his influence over the neighbouring tribes. The Czechs became his firm allies and probably his vassals; he annexed the country of the Avars, who lingered on the middle Danube, and thus became a neighbour to the Bulgars on the Theiss; and he began to threaten the Slav principalities that clustered under Frankish suzerainty round the River Drave and Lake Balaton. Louis the German had been powerless to check him. His great expedition of 855 had come back having achieved nothing; even his campaigns against the Czechs were ineffectual. Rostislav even intervened to encourage Carloman in the revolt against Louis, though he wisely refrained from helping the rebel son too far. By the year 862, Rostislav was ruler of an empire stretching from the Theiss and Lake Balaton to the neighbourhood of Vienna and to the upper waters of the Oder and the Vistula and the middle Carpathians, with Bohemia loyally guarding his flank. The German chroniclers showed their awe by calling him a king, a title they reserved only for great independent sovereigns.[1]

There were now four great Powers in Europe, the two

---

[1] See Dvornik, pp. 150 ff., who gives references. The history of Moravia before 862 is chiefly to be found in the *Annales Fuldenses*, pp. 364 ff., *passim*.

He

Christian Empires on the east and on the west[1] and the two barbarian States in between. The situation was too simple, too delicately balanced to last. It was Rostislav that made the first move. He had long coquetted with Christianity; but he was faced with much the same problem as the Bulgarians. To the Moravians, Christianity was connected with Frankish influence; the missionaries that overran the country were the minions of the Bishop of Passau and of Louis the German. And yet Christianity was desirable; it would raise his prestige and improve his culture, and it might be made to mould his empire into a firmer unity. But it must be a national Church, not a German or a Latin affair. Rostislav's restless mind sought out a new solution.

Early in the year 862 an embassy travelled from Moravia to Constantinople, asking of the Emperor that he should send a master to teach the True Faith in the language of the Slavs.[2]

---

[1] The Carolingians were by now subdivided; but, on the whole, Louis the German and the sons of Lothair in Lorraine and Italy acted together.

[2] *Vita Constantini*, pp. 199 ff.

CHAPTER III

THE AUCTION OF SOULS

A WAR was raging in Christendom, a spiritual struggle that was moulding the destinies of Europe. The caprice of Providence had brought contemporaneously into the world two of the greatest statesmen of ecclesiastical history, two whose ambitions and conceptions would inevitably lead to conflict. In April 858, through the influence of the unsuspecting Western Emperor Louis II, a certain Nicholas ascended the Papal throne at Rome. Eight months later, on Christmas Day, the Caesar Bardas, regent of the East, having somewhat roughly dispossessed the former Patriarch of Constantinople, Ignatius, appointed in his stead his friend, the First Secretary Photius.

Pope Nicholas I was possessed of boundless vigour and resolution, bold and far-sighted, praised by his followers as a man of deeds not words; and all his talents were directed at one splendid aim, the world-supremacy of the Roman see. Christendom was still one, save in the distant south and east, where Copts, Armenians, or Nestorians indulged in their various heresies; and its spiritual pinnacles were occupied by five Patriarchal thrones—those of Rome, Antioch, Alexandria, Jerusalem, and Constantinople. Of these patriarchates the Roman bishopric, the see of St. Peter, had always enjoyed the first place. Its jurisdiction extended over all Christian Europe north and west of the Adriatic (save for Sicily and Calabria), an area vastly increased in recent centuries by the spread of civilization along the Baltic and North Seas. Compared to his Roman rival, the Patriarch of Constantinople was a parvenu, the last to be created; but he had always enjoyed great power through his association with the Eastern

Empire, over all of whose provinces he was spiritual governor. The other patriarchates were of little importance now; their sees were in territories controlled by the infidel. Though the patriarchates had their order of precedence, except at Rome, none was considered supreme over any of the others; the only supreme office or body in the Church was a general Oecumenical Council to which all sent their representatives; and such representatives were even invited to the less important synods and councils in any one patriarchate—but save at Constantinople they were seldom held; the other patriarchs, freer from secular control, regarded them as a challenge to their authority.[1]

Nicholas wished to alter this. He was the first bishop of the world; he intended to be supreme bishop. He experienced difficulty even among his own subjects. The German Church had always been closely influenced by the secular powers, and pandered to the whims of the German monarchs. But Nicholas was a match for it. A climax came in 863 over the matrimonial high-handedness of Lothair of Lorraine: when the Pope triumphantly asserted his jurisdiction and defied the whole great Carolingian clan. At the same time he was turning his attention to the East, to the rival Empire, where the irregularity in Photius's election to the patriarchate gave a splendid loophole for intervention.

But Nicholas little knew the man with whom he had to deal. Photius was prodigiously learned—too learned, some said, whispering of sorcery; he was as determined and courageous as the Roman, and far more subtle,

---

[1] I cannot here go into the highly controversial details of Romano-Byzantine ecclesiastical relations, which Roman historians have almost always befogged by confusing 'primacy' with 'supremacy,' and by regarding the various settlements that favoured Rome as final and the others as ephemeral. Actually all attempts to settle the question once and for all had been equally ephemeral, and were to be so till the ultimate schism in the eleventh century. Here I have merely stated the general view held in the East in the ninth century.

far more imaginative, with far more knowledge of his audiences. The battle began in 860. Nicholas had at first attempted to bargain, to recognize Photius in return for the ecclesiastical provinces of Calabria and Illyricum, which had belonged to Rome till the reign of the Emperor Leo III; but Photius outwitted the Papal legates and wrote to Nicholas letters of perfect courtesy, but letters as from an equal to an equal. Things steadily worsened. Nicholas grew more and more outraged and furious, and the Patriarch, sure of secular support at home, more and more serenely independent. At last, in April 863, the Pope solemnly excommunicated Photius, and Photius made the superb retort of excommunicating the Pope.

It was in the midst of this storm that Rostislav's ambassadors arrived at Constantinople. Rostislav well knew what was happening, and he had learnt his lesson. He, like the Basileus, must have a Church under his secular power. Neither Germany nor Rome would give it to him; but Constantinople, in theory the champion of spiritual independence, in practice too distant to control such a Church, would help him now. Moreover, the goodwill of the Empire would be useful in case he had trouble with his new powerful neighbour, the Bulgarian Khan.

The Emperor Michael received the embassy gladly. His uncle, the Caesar Bardas, who governed in his name, and the Patriarch thought of their mutual friend Constantine the Philosopher, a Greek from Thessalonica, better known by the name that he assumed on his deathbed, Cyril, a missionary of previous experience and a linguist and philologist of renown. Accordingly Cyril and his elder brother Methodius set off for Moravia, armed with an alphabet by means of which they would translate the holy writings into the Slavonic tongue.[1]

---

[1] I deal with the question of the Cyrillic and Glagolitic alphabets in Appendix IX.

The news of the embassy and the mission stirred the European Courts. Boris of Bulgaria at once suspected a political significance. He took the obvious measures for safeguarding himself, and entered into negotiations with Louis the German. Later in the year (862), when Louis's son Carloman, governor of the East Mark, revolted with Moravian help against his father, the Bulgarians appeared as the close allies of the German king.[1] We do not know the clauses of this treaty, but there was apparently one amongst them that roused the government at Constantinople to action. Boris, like Rostislav, was toying with the idea of Christianity; he now was undertaking to receive it from the German Court.[2]

Various stories were related of the cause of the Khan's conversion. Some told of a Greek slave, a monk called Theodore Cupharas, who had long laboured to convert his royal master. After some time, Cupharas was ransomed by the Empress Theodora in exchange for the Khan's own sister, an honoured captive in Constantinople. But the princess had embraced Christianity, and she too used her influence to persuade the Khan. Nevertheless, Boris was obdurate, till at last a dreadful famine visited the country, and the old heathen deities could give no help. In despair the Khan turned to the God of his sister and of his slave, and there he met with help. In gratitude he became a Christian.[3] A second story was simpler. A Greek painter called Methodius had been commissioned to paint hunting-scenes round the walls of the royal palace; when Boris, moved by a sudden whim, told him instead to paint something terrible, no matter what. Methodius, who was a monk, piously considered that nothing would be more terrible than the Last Judgement; and so he

---

[1] *Annales Fuldenses*, p. 367 (?).

[2] *Annales Bertiniani* (Hincmar), p. 465; Nicolaus I Papa, *Epistolae*, p. 293.

[3] Theophanes Continuatus, pp. 162–3.

depicted with ghastly realism the punishment meted out to
the wicked, and the righteous being rewarded. The Khan
was deeply awed, and in terror joined the ranks of the
righteous.¹ Others told merely of the True Faith being
forced upon Bulgaria by Imperial arms and diplomacy.²

The story of Methodius is probably apocryphal, despite
the handsome tribute that it pays to the potency of art.
It has too suspicious an air of monkish naïveté. But the
story of Cupharas may well be mainly true. The influence
that these educated slaves had on their masters has been
shown in the case of the Prince Enravotas, while it is very
likely that some Bulgar princess should have been a hostage and been converted at Constantinople, and have used
her powers of persuasion on her return. But the Emperor's
armies were the final decisive factor.

The idea of Carolingian influence spreading to the
Balkans by means of religion was seriously alarming to
Constantinople. Carolingian influence meant in the end
the spiritual control of Rome. At the moment, it is true,
the German bishops were rebellious against the stern rule
of the Papacy, but it was a pitiably poor rebellion that
hardly could be hoped to succeed. At any time the Emperor would have regretted Roman intervention so close to
his capital; now, with Nicholas and Photius at the height of
their contest, the thing was unthinkable. But there was one
way out, one way of turning it all to the profit of the Empire.
The Emperor Michael brought his army to the frontier and
dispatched his fleet along the Black Sea coast.

It was a good moment to strike. The Bulgar armies were
away far in the north, campaigning against Carloman and
the Moravians. Moreover, by what, surely, seemed the
direct interference of Heaven, Bulgaria was being visited by

¹ Theophanes Continuatus, pp. 162-3.
² Georgius Monachus Continuatus, p. 824: Logothete (Slavonic version),
p. 104.

a peculiarly severe famine.   Boris was powerless, and wisely made no resistance.   At the first news of the invasion, he sent to ask the Emperor's conditions of peace.[1]

Michael and his advisers were eager to be propitiatory. As a sop to the Khan it seems that they recognized his jurisdiction over Upper Macedonia as far as a frontier line drawn roughly from the Rivers Black Drina, Devol, Ozum, and Voiusa, and round Mount Grammus up the Lake Ostrovo, thus including all the land round Lake Ochrida and Lake Prespa.[2]   But in return Boris must give up his offensive alliance with the Germans and indulge in nothing closer than an ordinary treaty of peace.   And, most important of all, Boris and his people must accept Christianity, and accept it from Constantinople.   To all of this Boris agreed, even surprising the Greeks by his readiness to change his faith.   His ambassadors at Constantinople were baptized there, as a guarantee of their master's intentions.   Finally, early in September 865,[3] with the Emperor standing sponsor, the Khan himself was baptized, and rechristened by his godfather's name of Michael.[4]

In this great revolution, Boris had been guided, not only by a spiritual impulse and by the diplomatic needs of the moment, but also by a wise foresight of the political effect

[1] Georgius Monachus Continuatus, loc. cit.: Logothete (Slavonic version), loc. cit.   In Theophanes Continuatus (pp. 165 ff.) this is muddled up with Theodora's Bulgar treaty (see above, p. 90).

[2] Ochrida and Prespa were definitely Bulgar later in Boris's reign.   It was probably a formal cession of such territory now that muddled the Continuator of Theophanes and made him connect the whole Conversion with Theodora's cession of Develtus.   I accept Zlatarski's rough frontier-line (*Izviestiya*, pp. 70 ff.).

[3] The date of Boris's baptism has been fixed by Zlatarski (*Istoriya*, i., 2, pp. 29 ff.) as between September 1 and 19, 865. Photius (*Epistolae*, p. 742) and the *Vita S. Clementis*, p. 1201, give rough dates, but Zlatarski's ingenious arithmetic is based on Tudor Doksov's *Poslieslovie* (p. 98) and on an Albanian inscription.

[4] Georgius Monachus Continuatus, loc. cit.: Logothete (Slavonic version) loc. cit.   Henceforward the chroniclers usually call him Michael.   I shall however, for the sake of simplicity, continue to call him Boris.

within his dominions. Hitherto the State religion had been the old Bulgar idolatry, a crude worship of the heavenly bodies and the forces of nature; and the Slavs had had to join as best they could in the devotions of the masters. Christianity would be a common religion for them all, a religion that welcomed Bulgar and Slav alike. Moreover, the old heathenism was probably bound up with the old Bulgar institutions, with the clan-system that the Khans had so long tried to break down; possibly many of the clans claimed a divine origin, and so would never recognize in the Khan more than a mere primacy. But Christianity gave the Emperor in Constantinople a sacrosanctity removing him far above all his subjects. Boris, too, sought such a halo; he too would be a viceroy of God, in altitudes that his noblest subjects could never reach.

Boris began the process of evangelization on a very large scale; all his subjects had to undergo the rite of baptism. But the country could not be converted quite so simply. The Bulgar nobility, too, appreciated the position. Some of the *boyars* may have been attached to their old religion; all were certainly attached to their rights. In their anger they incited the people of all the ten provinces of the kingdom against the Khan, and Boris was soon surrounded in his palace at Pliska by a huge and seething mob. That the Khan, helped as he was only by a few faithful followers, should have escaped at all seemed miraculous; people talked of divine intervention, and by the time that this story reached Western Europe this intervention had grown to fine proportions. Boris, so they said in France, had only forty-eight Christian friends with him.[1] With the bravery of despair he led them out to face the multitudes,

---

[1] *Annales Bertiniani* (Hincmar of Reims), pp. 473–4, supply the details. Theophanes Continuatus (p. 164) says briefly that Boris had few followers, and that he emerged from the palace bearing a cross and was victorious. Nicolaus I Papa (*Responsa*, cap. xvii., p. 577) refers to the victory over the great rebellion being due to divine aid.

calling on Christ's name and bearing a cross on his breast;
but, as the gates opened, seven priests, each with lighted
taper in his hand, appeared marching before him.   Then,
as they gazed, the angry crowds saw strange sights.   Behind, the palace seemed to be on fire and like to fall down
on their heads; in front, the horses of the royal party were
walking on their hind-legs and with their forelegs kicking
at the rebels.   Terror rushed over them; unable to fight
or to flee, they fell to the ground and lay prostrate.

Be that as it may, the rebellion was crushed, and Boris
was able to take a revenge shocking in so new a devotee
of Christian meekness, but salutary for his country.   Fifty-
two nobles, the ringleaders of the revolt, were put to death,
and with them their children.   The leaders of the clans,
the rivals of the monarch, were thus wiped out for ever.
The rebels belonging to middle and lower classes he spared
and pardoned; their opposition had been genuinely religious, not political; they would have no social prejudices
against their ultimate conversion.

But, even though the *boyars* were crushed, the Conversion did not at once have the effect that Boris hoped from
it.   The Emperor had firmly ordained in the treaty that
the new Church must be spiritually dependent upon the
see of Constantinople.   Accordingly, Bulgaria was flooded
with Greek priests, come to organize its structure and
teach it true doctrines: while the Patriarch himself wrote
a letter to the Bulgar monarch, to 'my beloved son,
Michael the archon of Bulgaria . . . the fair ornament of
my labours.'   It was an extremely long letter.   First it
contained a full account of the articles of faith as laid
down in all seven of the Oecumenical Councils.   Then,
after touching on the general principles of morality,
showing how they arise out of the two New Testament
commandments, the Patriarch went on to delineate the
duties of the good prince, in almost a hundred polished

aphorisms and shrewd comments derived from all the wisdom of the Hebrews and the Greek philosophers.[1] Historians ever since have gaped at this torrent of patronizing culture and metaphysical sensibility that was poured over a simple barbarian, who sought only to have far simpler problems solved for him—whether trousers were indecent and turbans counted as hats. But Photius knew his business. The high authorities of the Church should not trouble about details; it was their work to impress, not to conciliate. The mysteries of the True Faith were in the keeping of the Patriarch. It showed the Khan better the relative status of his country and the Emperor's, that he should understand not one word of those subjects that were apparently the common talk of Constantinople. Photius took a long view; he kept his dignity intact even at the expense of the needs of the moment.

Boris, the beloved son Michael, was impressed, but dissatisfied. It was more difficult than he had thought to be a Christian. The inrushing Greek clergy sought to teach in Greek, a method that was being successful among the Slavs of the Empire, but one that the Bulgarian government somewhat resented. Moreover, many of these Greeks were of inferior quality; some were of those who had not the ability to secure good posts in the Church within the Empire, and so had to seek their fortunes abroad. And missionaries of other tenets joined in the invasion. With the Greeks came Armenians; some perhaps were mere monophysite heretics, but there were others of a far more sinister and pregnant brand, Paulicians, to sow the seed of the fatally attractive creed of Dualism.[2] Meanwhile, in the north, the Carolingians, safeguarded

---

[1] Photius, *Epistolae*, viii., pp. 628 ff.

[2] Nicolaus I Papa (*Responsa*, cap. cvi., p. 599) mentions the Armenians, probably Paulician heretics. It was a growing Imperial custom to settle such heretics in colonies in provinces such as Thrace, whence they could easily spread to Bulgaria.

by a new alliance with Constantinople, sent in their German missionaries to acquire what influence they could; and all the time Pope Nicholas was waiting to intervene. So many creeds and nations were anxious to help; but none would give the Khan the simple guidance necessary to enable him to provide his country with a Church not too disturbing for its traditions and well under his secular control.

After a year of Christianity, Boris was a wiser man. He was in a stronger position now, with peace on his northern frontier, and no turbulent *boyars* and no famine at home. And he was angry with the Greeks. The authorities at Constantinople were treating him as a poor barbarian, and were attempting to keep the Church tightly under their control, not letting it pass into his—denying him even a bishop. So Boris looked elsewhere. The struggle between the Pope and Photius was reaching its climax; Photius, to his scandalized glee, had found the Pope subscribing to the monstrous and indefensible heresy of the Dual Procession of the Holy Ghost and was preparing denunciations to rouse the indignation of all true Christians.[1] Boris had no strict views about the mystical symmetry of the triangle. On the other hand, he realized that he could be a useful factor in the struggle. In August 866, Bulgar ambassadors, the Khan's cousin Peter, John, and Martin, arrived in Rome with rich and holy gifts and asked the Pope in Boris's name for a bishop and for priests. They also submitted to him a list of 106 questions on which their master desired his opinions.[2] Boris also, lest Rome should fail him, sent a similar request for a

[1] Photius did not actually denounce the Roman heresy in public till 867, but already the Churches were mutually excommunicated and the Patriarch had discovered the heresy.

[2] Johannes VIII Papa, *Epistolae*, p. 159: Anastasius Bibliothecarius, pp. 1373-4. The presents included the arms wearing which Boris had defeated the heathen rebels. Louis the German promptly demanded them from the Pope (*Annales Bertiniani*, p. 474).

bishop and priests to Ratisbon to Louis the German.
Louis complied, but when his clergy arrived they found
their places already filled, and went back promptly to
Germany.[1]

Nicholas was overjoyed at this unexpected support. At
once he dispatched a consignment of his clergy to Bulgaria,
supplying them fully with books and vessels and robes
and all the trappings of his faith, and placed at their head
two of his ablest legates—Paul, the Bishop of Populonia,
and Formosus, Bishop of Porto. At the same time he
sent detailed answers to all the questions, however trivial,
that the Khan had submitted to him.

Nicholas's answers made a document vastly different
from the polished, subtle, theological sermon sent by
Photius. It was simply written, helpful and very conciliatory. Boris had asked almost entirely about matters
of religious practice, when to fast and what to wear in
church, and whether the stricter forms of abstinence
demanded by the Greek priests were really obligatory.
There were also one or two special cases, particularly to
do with a Greek who pretended to be a priest and baptized
huge numbers of innocent Bulgars; need they all be re-
baptized ? But Boris even asked advice about matters
more properly concerning civil law, such as the penalties
for murder, and matters entirely social: should he continue
to eat his meals in solitude, and what did the Pope really
think about his costume ? Nicholas was deeply concerned
not to lay too heavy a yoke on a people as yet rude and
untrained. As regards abstinence, though strict, he condemned many of the complications introduced by the
Greeks; it was not necessary to fast every Wednesday as
well as Friday, nor to abstain from bathing on both days,
nor to refuse to eat food killed by eunuchs: though one
should not eat food hunted by a Christian but killed by

[1] *Annales Fuldenses*, p. 379.

a heathen, or vice versa.[1]   Trousers were permissible; but
the Greeks were right in insisting that turbans, like other
forms of headgear, should be removed in churches, and
women should, of course, enter churches veiled.[2]   He
denounced the Greek habit of *sortes biblicae* as well as a
long list of pagan superstitions.[3]   As for the Khan refusing
to eat in company, this was bad manners, but not actually
impious.[4]   With regard to murder, the civil law should
see to that, but the right of sanctuary in churches should
be upheld.[5]   Polygamy, which is the same as adultery,
was a far worse crime; the surplus wives must firmly be
discarded, and the priest must impose a suitable penance.[6]
Nicholas also wished the Khan to mitigate the severity
of his punishments.[7]   He showed up the uselessness as
well as the barbarity of extracting evidence by torture;
he censured Boris's treatment of the rebels.   He even considered that the Khan had been too severe in cutting the
nose off the Greek who had pretended to be a priest.[8]
Even resolute heathens were to be wooed by persuasion,
though socially shunned by the faithful.   One class of
criminals alone must be punished without mercy—the
apostate, who had sworn fidelity to the Christian creed
and had fallen back into heathendom.   That was the
one unforgivable sin.[9]

Boris had also asked whether his country might some
time have a Patriarch.   Nicholas had to answer carefully.
The Western Church over which he ruled was suspicious
of Patriarchs.   Boris's request was due to his simple, hopeful longing to be the equal of the Eastern Emperor.   The
Pope was non-committal.   Boris should have bishops,
and later, when the Bulgarian Church was larger, an

---

[1] Nicolaus I Papa, *Responsa*, cap. iv., v., lvii., xci., pp. 570–2, 588, 596.

[2] Ibid., cap. lviii., lxvi., pp. 588, 590–1.   [3] Ibid., cap. lxvii., p. 593.

[4] Ibid., cap. xlii., p. 583.   [5] Ibid., cap. lxxxiii., p. 595.

[6] Ibid., cap. li., p. 586.   [7] Ibid., cap. lxxxiii.–lxxxvi., p.595.

[8] Ibid., cap. xiv.–xvii., p. 575–7.   [9] Ibid., cap. xli., pp. 582–3.

archbishop; and then they would consider about a Patriarch. Constantinople had grudged him even his bishops; so he had to be content for the while with the promise of an archbishop from Rome.[1]

Certainly the Roman clergy started their work with the most ingratiating zeal. Boris gave them the monopoly within his dominions, dismissing all other priests and missionaries. Latin replaced Greek as the sacred tongue. The Romans built churches and organized congregations, bringing the light of Christian doctrine into the darkest homes and teaching at the same time the beauties of obedience to the civil powers. Boris was overjoyed. Taking hold of his hair, in the old Bulgar manner, he swore that he would always remain faithful to the see of Saint Peter.[2] The Papal Court, too, was delighted, and spread the Khan's praises throughout the Western world. Save in Constantinople, everyone was happy.

This triumph was due chiefly to the tact and affability of one man, Formosus, Bishop of Porto. He won entirely the Khan's affections and trust; and Boris destined him for the patriarchate that he still hoped to receive from Rome. After a year, in 867, he sent to Rome demanding that Formosus should be made archbishop at least.[3] But Nicholas was unaccustomed to dictation: Boris had to learn now what the Roman Church was. Possibly, had Boris asked for anyone but Formosus, his request might have been granted. But Formosus was beginning to be regarded with suspicion at the Papal Court. He had been thought suitable to go to Bulgaria in the first place from his known hatred of Greeks. But he was wildly ambitious; perhaps he was encouraging Boris in his dreams of an autonomous Bulgar Church, that he might be its

[1] Nicolaus Papa I, *Responsa*, cap. lxxii., pp. 592–3.

[2] Anastasius Bibliothecarius, *Preface to the Eighth Oecumenical Council*, Mansi, vol. xvi., p. 11

[3] Anastasius Bibliothecarius, *Vita Nicolai*, pp. 1375–6.

independent Patriarch. Certainly Boris was said to have
undertaken solemnly always to press forward Formosus's
claims.[1] Nicholas was suspicious: Formosus, he reminded
the Khan, was Bishop of Porto, and his diocese needed
him back after so long an absence. He recalled the
previous envoys, and instead sent to Bulgaria two new
bishops, Grimoald of Polimarti and Dominic of Treviso.[2]

The Bulgars might be angry, but the Pope thought that
he could afford it now. The European situation had
altered. In September 867 the Emperor Michael was
murdered by the stable-boy that he had so extravagantly
befriended, and Basil the Macedonian was installed in
his victim's place. Basil wished for popularity: he also
had designs in Italy and Illyricum that would be helped
by an understanding with Rome. Photius had enemies
even in Constantinople who had never forgiven him his
treatment of Ignatius. Basil promptly declared Photius
deposed, and reinstalled Ignatius. He then wrote to the
Pope to ask him to send legates to a council at which the
past should be forgotten, the Roman precedence stated
and supremacy hinted, and no one should mention the
word 'Filioque.'[3] Nicholas saw in this the utter triumph
of Rome, and his conciliatory movements decreased. He
little knew the monarchs with whom he had to deal, the
parvenu Basil, and Boris the ex-barbarian.

And he never was to find out the truth about them.
On November 13, 867, still victorious, he died.[4]

His successor, Hadrian II, was a personal enemy of
Formosus. More than ever the Papacy was stern in its
refusal of the Bulgar request. Grimoald and Dominic
continued on their journey; and Formosus and Paul of

[1] Johannes VIII Papa, *Epistolae, passim collectae*, p. 327.
[2] Anastasius Bibliothecarius, op. cit., pp. 1376-7.
[3] For the Eighth Oecumenical Council, see below, pp. 113-4.
[4] Anastasius Bibliothecarius, op. cit., p. 1378. Ignatius was not actually
reinstated till November 23.

Populonia had to return to their shepherdless congregations. But Boris clung to the hope of having an archbishop
of his own choice—if not Formosus, at least someone personally acceptable to him. There was a deacon Marinus,
whom Nicholas had once sent on a mission to Constantinople at the height of the Photian war. The Emperor
had refused to admit him into the Empire, and he had
taken refuge at the Bulgar Court, where he had won the
Khan's friendship. He had no diocese calling for his care;
could he not be the Bulgar archbishop? A second embassy, again led by Peter, travelled to Rome, in company
with the returning bishops. But Hadrian II was inexorable. Boris must be taught once and for all that the Pope
intended always to appoint whomsoever he chose all over
his spiritual dominions.[1]

Towards the close of 869 a council, known proudly as
the Eighth Oecumenical Council, with legates from all
the Patriarchs, assembled at Constantinople. The Papal
legates—Stephen, Bishop of Nepi, Donatus, Bishop of
Ostia, and Marinus, Boris's friend—attended with all the
smugness of certain victory. Things did not go altogether
smoothly; the Emperor Basil took a different view to them
with regard to the procedure for the trial of Photius. But
they adhered to their instructions, and finally emerged
triumphant. On February 28, 870, the council was dismissed, with a growing feeling of hostility on all sides;
but the Papal legates were well satisfied with their
achievements. Three days later the indefatigable Peter,
ambassador of his cousin the Khan,[2] arrived at Constantinople, to ask the Oecumenical Council to which patriarchate Bulgaria belonged. Basil summoned the assembly
to meet again. The legates of the Eastern Patriarchs, well
entertained by Basil and at one with the Greeks in disliking

[1] Anastasius Bibliothecarius, *Vita Adriani*, pp. 1393–6.
[2] For the curious list of the Bulgar ambassadors, see Appendix V.
IE

the pretentions of Rome, gladly concurred with the
Greek bishops and with historical truth in answering that
it was to Constantinople. The Pope's representatives were
in a tiny minority; they could only record their protest.
Then they returned, crestfallen, to their master; a mocking
providence detained them on the way for nine months,
spent chiefly as the prisoners of Dalmatian pirates. Hardly
were the Papal legates gone, before Ignatius on March 4
consecrated an archbishop and bishops for Bulgaria—
presumably persons of Boris's choice.[1]

The reversal was complete. The frontier now was closed
to Roman priests; the Roman bishops were sent back in
ignominy to Rome.[2] In the place of Latin, Greek was
heard once more in the churches. Boris was well satisfied.
He had taught the great hierarchs to treat him with respect, and the Greeks, more adaptable than the Latins,
had learnt the lesson. The Bulgarian Church was still
under the Constantinopolitan patriarchate; but the yoke
weighed lightly. The Archbishop of Bulgaria ranked
next after the Patriarch; and the Bulgar monarch was
tacitly allowed similar powers to the Emperor's in his high
ecclesiastic officials. Thus Boris's dream of an autonomous
Church was practically realized; but Constantinople kept
a nominal control, lest in the distant future it might be
useful.

The news came as an appalling shock to Rome; the
Pope had never contemplated such insubordination, such
ingratitude in a barbarian, nor such wiliness and presumption in the gentle old Patriarch, in whom, as the
victim of Photius, he had condescended to place such
trust. He wrote in a tone of hurt surprise to Basil, asking what all this meant.[3] But Basil, though very friendly,

[1] Theophanes Continuatus, p. 242: Anastasius Bibliothecarius, *Vita
Adriani*, pp. 1395–6: Idem, *Praefatio in Synodum VIII.*, p. 148; ibid., pp. 20 ff.
[2] Idem, *Vita Adriani*, loc. cit.   [3] Hadrian II Papa, *Epistolae*, p. 1310.

was quite unyielding. When Hadrian died, in December 872, the check had been in no way recovered.

Rome, however, still hoped. She could not believe that this triumph, this extension of her realm almost to the very gates of the hateful Patriarch's city, had been so very ephemeral. All her energies were devoted to winning back the vaunted land. Even in the north were felt the reverberations of the struggle. A decade now had passed since the Macedonian brothers had set out to convert Moravia. With the help of their Slavonic liturgy and the goodwill of the Moravian monarchs—the great King Rosti-slav, and Kocel, prince of the country round Lake Balaton— their work had been crowned with success; but, to ensure its permanence, Cyril had decided, with remarkable broad-mindedness for a friend of Photius, that it must be con-firmed by Rome. Constantinople was too far away, with the bulk of Bulgaria in between, to be able always to watch and to protect. Cyril's overtures, however, somewhat embarrassed the Papal Court. The Popes could not whole-heartedly approve of missionary enterprise that was not conducted in the Latin tongue. But, in the desperation of his struggle against Photius, Pope Nicholas had been eager to accept so great a prize, even at the price of recog-nizing the Slavonic liturgy. To make sure of the future, he summoned the brothers to Rome. He died before they arrived, and his successor, Hadrian, was a more uncom-promising statesman. But, in view of the support given them by the Moravian lay powers and with Constanti-nople in the background, Hadrian could not do other-wise than receive them with honour[1] and set his approval upon all that they had done. To silence opposition he had their disciples consecrated by that notorious anti-Greek, Formosus. While they were at Rome, Cyril, the

---

[1] The honourable reception was largely due to the fact that St. Cyril brought with him the relics of St. Clement.

younger but more brilliant of the brothers, died, and
Methodius was left to carry on the work alone.

Methodius was sent back to Moravia, authorized to use
the Slavonic liturgy whersoever he chose. Hadrian had
determined to found him a diocese, but was still uncertain
of the details when news came through of the terrible de-
fection of the Bulgars. At once Hadrian subordinated his
Moravian to his Bulgarian policy. Hoping to use the
weapon of the Slavonic liturgy to capture the Bulgars,
he revived for Methodius the old diocese of Sirmium,
whose seat was on the very edge of their dominions and
whose jurisdiction spread along the length of their north-
western frontier. But this seductive scheme was never
given a fair trial; Methodius on his return found his patron
Rostislav fallen; his nephew and successor Svatopulk,
though he attained to independence and dominions even
exceeding his uncle's, was, all the same, deeply attracted
by German culture and despised the Slavonic liturgy as
plebeian and unimpressive. Under his patronage the
German bishops were able to imprison the valiant missionary as an impertinent impostor. Before his protests
could reach Rome, Pope Hadrian was dead and John VIII
was installed in his place.[1]

John VIII had not come under the influence of the
Bulgar disappointment. The tradition of Nicholas was
forgotten; Rome went back to the thunder of intran-
sigeance. John thought he could terrify the Bulgars into
obedience. One of his first actions was to write Boris a
letter in which he threatened the Bulgars and all the
Greek clergy with excommunication, 'that thus they may
join the Devil, whom they have imitated.'[2] Meanwhile,
careless of Methodius's persuasive influence, and trusting

---

[1] For the history of Methodius in Moravia, see Dvornik, op. cit.,
pp. 209 ff.

[2] Johannes VIII Papa, *Fragmenta, Ep.* 7, p. 277.

on Svatopulk's fondness for the Latin tongue, he released
Methodius from his German prison, but forbade him the
use of the Slavonic liturgy. Methodius was in despair; to
save Christianity he ignored the order; but the situation
was not one that would help him to win his neighbours
for Rome.

Boris remained unmoved by the Pope's fulminations,
particularly as in Croatia and along the Dalmatian coast
Latin influence was dying, and the local States were airing
their independence or falling under the suzerainty of the
Eastern Emperor. Experience taught John that he must
employ milder methods. In February 875 he wrote again
to the Bulgarian Court, still sternly forbidding the Bulgars
to receive the sacrament from Greek priests, under the
penalty of being considered schismatic.[1] Boris in reply
sent an embassy to Rome to pay his respects there, and
continued to encourage the Greek clergy. A simultaneous
letter from the Pope to the Emperor asking for Ignatius
to face his trial at Rome produced even less effect.[2]

But John was indefatigable. In April 878 his legates—
Eugenius, Bishop of Ostia, and Paul, Bishop of Ancona—
set out for Constantinople, with instructions to call on the
way at the Khan's Court. John was now trying a new
method. The legates brought four letters with them for
Bulgaria. The first was addressed to the Greek bishops
in Bulgaria, categorically ordering them to leave within
thirty days a diocese that belonged to Illyricum and so
to Rome.[3] The second letter was to Boris. Here John
captured the tone of Nicholas. Boris was greeted with
great cordiality; the Pope only wished to warn him of
the dangers of adhering to Constantinople, the birthplace
of so much schism and heresy. He reminded the Khan
of the fate of the Goths, baptized by the Greeks and soon

[1] Johannes VIII Papa, *Fragmenta, Ep.* 37, pp. 294–5.
[2] Ibid., *Fragmenta, Ep.* 40, p. 296.   [3] Ibid., *Ep.* 71, pp. 66–7.

the victims of that dreadful Arianism.[1] The third letter
was to Peter of Bulgaria, that relative of Boris's who twice
had figured in embassies to Rome. John addresses him
as an intimate friend and begs him to use his influence
on the Khan to bring him back to the see of Saint Peter.[2]
The fourth was to another Bulgar notable, apparently
Boris's own brother, probably the monk Duks, urging him
too to do what he could to further the cause of Rome.[3]
Having delivered the Bulgarian letters, the bishops proceeded to Constantinople with a letter to Ignatius, ordering him, in the same severe language as the Greek bishops
in Bulgaria had received, to remove his clergy from Bulgaria within thirty days, under the definite penalty of
excommunication.[4] A letter to the Emperor Basil required
him to aid the Papal legates in their work.[5] But all these
letters were written too late. On October 23, 877, the
aged Patriarch Ignatius had died. No sooner was he dead
than Basil made the whole world gasp by appointing in
his stead his rival, the ex-Patriarch Photius.[6]

In Rome and in Constantinople the situation was entirely altered. But, in Bulgaria, things went on just the
same. Neither the Khan nor his nobles answered the
Papal letters; nor did the Greek clergy leave Bulgaria.
Yet the Pope could not abandon his hopes. He had to
evolve a new policy with regard to Constantinople. To
recapture Bulgaria first would help him so much. Once
more in 879 he wrote to Boris and to his *boyars*, to Peter,
Zergobul, and Sondok. This time the letters were sent
by the hand of John the Presbyter, his legate to Dalmatia

[1] Johannes VIII Papa, *Ep.* 66, pp. 58 ff. In this letter he complained
also about the interference of George, the (Greek) Bishop of Belgrade, in
Serbia or Pannonian Croatia.

[2] Ibid., *Ep.* 67, pp. 60 ff.

[3] Ibid., *Ep.* 70, pp. 65–6 ff. For the identity of the recipient, see Zlatarski,
Istoriya, i., 2, pp. 168–70.

[4] Ibid., *Ep.* 68, pp. 62–3.   [5] Ibid., *Ep.* 69, pp. 63–5.

[6] Theophanes Continuatus, p. 276.

and Croatia. There, even as he wrote, the sky was brightening; Zdeslav, the Byzantine-made prince of Croatia, had just been deposed by Branimir, an adherent of the Roman faction. Branimir would see to it that John the Presbyter reached Bulgaria safely. The Pope's tone to Boris was even more pleading and conciliatory; he apologized if the Khan had been displeased by anything in his former embassy. [1]

Meanwhile, he was vastly cheered by his dealings with the Patriarch. Photius brazenly and illogically, to please the Emperor, had sought Papal approval of his appointment. John, with that unhappy passion for bargaining, known as realism at Rome, offered his consent on one condition, a condition showing the greatest longing of his heart—that Constantinople would give up the Church of Bulgaria. To his delighted surprise the Patriarch promptly agreed. Once again Papal legates journeyed to Constantinople to take part in a peace-bringing council.

The council opened in November 879, and sat without a hitch. The Emperor Basil, in mourning for his eldest son, did not attend; Photius managed it all as he chose. The Roman legates, ignorant of the Greek language, were unaware that Photius's self-justification, so enthusiastically received by the 383 bishops present, had been facilitated by slight mistranslations of the Papal letter; they also failed to realize that they subscribed to a resolution refusing the Pope's wish to prohibit the nomination of laymen to the episcopate, and to an anathema against all who added to the Nicene creed—that is to say against all the Western Church guilty of the interpolation of 'Filioque.' The question of the Bulgarian Church was referred to the Emperor, who condescended to decide in favour of Rome. Rome in its satisfaction would not, so

[1] Johannes VIII Papa, *Ep.* 182, p. 146; 183, p. 147. He wrote again a month later (June 879) in an equally friendly tone (*Ep.* 192, p. 153).

Photius calculated, challenge the authority of the decision: whereas, by establishing the Emperor's right to decide, Constantinople was safeguarded against the future.[1]

The legates returned in happy innocence to Rome, and Rome rejoiced at her victory. But the Pope had carelessly forgotten that the persons most concerned in the transaction were the Bulgarians themselves. Early in 880 an embassy arrived from Boris to the Papal Court. John was full of hope, but the Bulgarian ambassador, a *boyar* called Frunticus, merely paid his master's respects and announced that everything was going very pleasantly in Bulgaria; and that was all. However, John could not but regard it as a favourable sign; he sent back a letter teeming with eager expectation,[2] and wrote, too, to the Emperor Basil to announce his contentment.[3] But there was no reply from Bulgaria. John was puzzled and distressed. He wrote again at the close of 880, to ask by what mischance no further embassy had been sent; the Croatian bishop, Theodosius of Nona, had given him to understand that one was forthcoming. But again there was silence; and silence greeted his next letter, written in 881.[4] John could not understand what had happened. At last, towards the close of that year, the Bishop Marinus, Boris's former friend, returned from an embassy to Constantinople and opened his eyes to what had really happened at the council of 879. In his fury, John deposed the two legates that had attended the council, and excommunicated Photius.[5] But, as he wrote, the truth was dawning over him; he began to understand why Photius had so smilingly given up his rights over Bulgaria. Photius had not forgotten the Bulgarians. Photius realized that

---

[1] Council of 879 in Mansi, xvii., pp. 365–530.

[2] Johannes VIII Papa, *Ep.* 198, pp. 158–9.

[3] Ibid., *Ep.* 259, pp. 228 ff.   [4] Ibid., *Ep.* 298, p. 260; 308, pp. 266–7.

[5] Stephanus V Papa, *Ep.* I, pp. 786–9: Hergenröther, *Photius, Patriarch von Konstantinopel*, ii., pp. 576–8.

Boris could not wish to go back to Roman bondage; the ways of the Eastern Church suited him far better. And Boris was well able to look after himself.

Rome was defeated. John had been cheated of his victory, outwitted by the Patriarch. Bulgaria, the land for which Saint Peter's successors had striven so hard, had eluded their grasp for ever. But Pope John was not given long on earth in which to brood upon his bitter humiliation. On December 15, 882, he died, poisoned, men said, by his enemies. The Bishop Marinus stepped into his place—but there was something mysterious, something sinister, about the whole affair.[1]

Boris had chosen the East rather than the West; and his choice was almost inevitable. At first sight there might be some advantage in preferring the distant rule of Rome to the near-by rule of Constantinople; but Rome could not really give him what he wanted, nor had it the same attractions for him. In Constantinople the Emperor was supreme, and his supremacy was sanctioned by the Church. He was not only Caesar, but also the viceroy of God, and therefore all things, Caesar's and God's alike, could rightly be rendered unto him. In the West, on the other hand, there was always a dual allegiance. The Roman Church refused to recognize its dependence on any temporal power. Its ambitions were international, and its sole autocrat was the Roman Pontiff; and he not only forbade the interference of any lay ruler, but aimed at controlling even their unspiritual actions. Whatever Boris's motives may have been in first adopting Christianity, he certainly intended to use the conversion for his own ends in unifying his country and perfecting his autocracy. His model was the Emperor; the Empire's Caesaropapism should be copied in Bulgaria. It was because Constantinople had been unwilling to allow him the independence that he

[1] *Annales Fuldenses*, pp. 395, 398.

wished that he had turned to Rome; but he soon learnt that Rome always aimed at a far stricter control. It was only useful to him as a threat to hold over the head of Constantinople.

Then, apart from practical considerations, Constantinople would certainly impress the Bulgars infinitely more than Rome. Their memories did not stretch as far back as the days when Rome was mistress of the world and Constantinople was only still Byzantium, obscure in its distant province. They saw Rome as she was in their time, a dirty town on a yellow river, rich only in churches and prelates and vast, crumbling ruins. How could it compare with the wealthiest city in all the universe, Constantinople, the home of art and of learning, with towers and gleaming domes and never-ending walls, the merchant ships crowding in the harbours, the palaces teeming with mosaics and tapestries, and the Emperor seated on his golden throne? All this glory had been since first they crossed the Danube. Why should they cross the bleak Albanian mountains and the windy sea to do obeisance in a dying town, when so much splendid life was at their gates? Rome could not compete with Constantinople in the vigour and perfection of her civilization; and already the Bulgars had come under the influence of the Greeks. Greeks had built them palaces in Pliska and Preslav, had given them a written tongue in which to keep their records, had painted them pictures and woven them stuffs. The Romans had done nothing for them save to talk to them in unintelligible Latin and to issue them peremptory commands. It was both natural and wise for Boris to make the decision that he made.

Had Boris been allowed to retain Formosus or Marinus, history might have been different: though probably they, like him, would have grown to resent Papal interference. But destiny forbade those ambitious prelates to side-track

their careers in Bulgaria. Both attained to the heights
of the Papal throne, Marinus over a poisoned corpse, and
Formosus amid a storm and turmoil that tore him even
from his grave.

Meanwhile, Greek was all the fashion in Bulgaria; Greek
artisans came with Greek priests, to build churches and
houses suitable for Christian gentlemen. The Bulgars
even strove to obtain some part of the famous learning
of the Greeks. The nobles hastened to send their sons
to Constantinople in order to perfect their education.[1]
Thither among them came the Prince Symeon, younger
son of the Khan himself. Boris was well informed about
events in the Imperial Palace. He knew that growing up
there was a prince, the youngest son of the Emperor Basil,
whom his father designed for the Patriarchal throne. Boris
thought the idea excellent; it smacked of true Caesaropapism. His younger son should go to Constantinople,
and should come back in due course, stocked with Greek
lore, to become Archbishop and Primate of Bulgaria.[2]

Fashions, however, change. Bulgaria was not to become a mere provincial annexe of Byzantium. Thanks
largely to their great Khans, the Bulgarian subjects had
too strong a national feeling to suffer absorption; and the
Imperial statesmen, far-sighted in their moderation, and
haunted by the spectre of Rome, decided not to press
Bulgaria too far. Their one aim now was to advance
Christianity in Bulgaria along lines that would most help
Christianity, not the Empire. It was an altruistic policy,
originating largely in genuine missionary zeal; but also, like
most altruistic policies, it would probably pay in the end.

Towards the close of 881, while the Pope and the Patriarch were still officially friends, a distinguished visitor

[1] Photius, *Ep.* xcv., pp. 904–5. He put the Bulgar nobles under the charge
of the Higumene Arsenius.
[2] Liudprand, *Antapodosis*, p. 87.

arrived in Constantinople—Methodius, the surviving
apostle of the Slavs.[1] He had long wished to revisit his
fatherland; and Emperor Basil and Photius, his old friend,
had much to discuss with him. He returned to Moravia
next spring,[2] but Basil kept back a Slavonic priest and a
deacon and certain liturgical books which the brothers
had written in the Slavonic language. The Imperial
Government had learnt from the great missionary's own
lips of his experiences; they were encouraged to emulate
his methods. Rome had long profited by the work of the
Macedonian brothers; but Constantinople had sent them
forth; she would profit now. And she had one great advantage over Rome. The Romans could hardly bear to
admit a liturgy in a tongue other than Latin. The Greeks
had no such prejudices; they saw the Georgians worship-
ping God in Georgian, the Abasgians in Abasgian; and
both the Georgian and the Abasgian Churches recognized
themselves, and were welcomed, as being under the Constantinopolitan Patriarch. Basil and Photius decided
to make use themselves of Saint Cyril's liturgy. A Slavonic
school was founded at Constantinople, possibly with the
idea of using it as a training-ground for the conversion of
the Russians, and certainly to aid in the good work in
Bulgaria.[3]

The year 885 was a turning-point in the history of Slavonic Christianity. That year Methodius died in Moravia,

[1] This visit of Methodius is only recorded in the *Vita Methodii* (Pastrnek, pp. 234 ff.), but it is useless to regard it either as apocryphal or as marking a revolution in Methodius's career. (See Dvornik, op. cit., pp. 271 ff.) Zlatarski (op. cit., p. 219) follows Malyshevski (*Kiryll i Methodi*, pp. 279 ff.), in dating it 883–4, but it must have occurred before the schism with Rome.

[2] It is most unlikely that Methodius visited Boris of Bulgaria on his return, as Zlatarski (loc. cit.) says. The *only* authority for saying so is the sentence in the *Life of Saint Clement* (p. 1201), which says that Boris was specially favoured of Methodius. This need not mean more than that Methodius was pleased with Boris's career and had high hopes of him.

[3] The existence of this school is nowhere stated, but it is distinctly implied by such stories as that of the slaves in Venice. It was probably under the Higumene Arsenius, as Photius's letter to him (cit. above) implies.

his whole work on the brink of failure. John VIII had
in the end supported him, but Marinus threw him over,
and Hadrian III and Stephen V continued against him,
urged on by the wholesale forgeries of Wiching, Latin
bishop of Nitra, and by Methodius's refusal to join Rome
in heresy and tamper with the Nicene Creed. Methodius's
death meant the end of the Slavonic liturgy in Central
Europe. He had named his ablest disciple, Gorazd, as
his successor; but Gorazd's abilities were powerless against
the torrent of Latin and German intrigue, reinforced by
the lay powers, by King Svatopulk. The leaders of the
Slavonic Church—Gorazd, Clement, Nahum, Angelarius,
Laurentius, and Sabbas—were seized and imprisoned with
their followers. As they lay in prison sentence was passed.
Many of the minor clergy were kept in captivity; the more
prominent were condemned to perpetual exile. One day
that winter a little group of the faithful, headed by Clement, Nahum, and Angelarius, was brought under guard
to the Danube, and there left to find its own fortune.[1]

That same winter an embassy from the Emperor Basil
was visiting Venice. As he passed one day the booths of
the Jewish merchants the ambassador's notice was struck
by some slaves. On inquiring, he discovered that they
were Slavonic clergy sold by the Moravian lay powers as
heretics. He knew his master's interest in such persons,
so he bought them and brought them with him to Constantinople. Basil was delighted, and received them with
honour, and even provided them with benefices.[2] Some
went on soon, probably at the Emperor's behest, into
Bulgaria, equipped with the Slavonic liturgy.[3]

But they were not the only newcomers to Bulgaria.
Clement and his following came down the Danube, longing to reach that country that seemed to them the Promised

[1] *Vita S. Clementis*, pp. 1220–1.
[2] *Zhitiya Sv. Naum*, ed. Lavrov, pp. 4–5.   [3] Ibid., p. 5.

Land of the true orthodox faith.   In time they came to Belgrade, the great frontier fortress, where the governor, the Tarkan Boris, [1] welcomed them gladly and sent them on to the Court at Pliska.   The Khan's welcome was even warmer than the *tarkan's*; Boris was delighted to see experienced and distinguished Slavonic missionaries, who would make him less dependent on Greek clergy: while the Imperial Government, pursuing its altruistic policy, could make no objection.   The Court nobility followed its master's lead; the officers of state hastened to offer hospitality to the holy visitors.   Ekhatch, the *sampses*, entertained Clement and Nahum, while Angelarius lodged with a certain Tcheslav. [2]

The Greek clergy in Bulgaria were a little less pleased. They were not in a very strong position; Basil and Photius were encouraging the Slavs.   But it was always probable that Basil and Photius would protest and take measures if things became too bad.   The Greek clergy were, however, to be robbed of that potential support.   On August 29, 886, the Emperor died.   His successor, Leo V, detested Photius and at once deposed him; a youth of eighteen, the Emperor's brother Stephen, followed him on the Patriarchal throne.   Leo, his youth embittered by a doubtful parentage and a miserable marriage, was an apathetic, indolent statesman; he would never go out of his way to intervene abroad.   And the Patriarch, in his youthful inexperience, was an equally broken reed.   But the Greek clergy had one support; Boris himself was uncomfortable at rousing their displeasure.   The situation was a little difficult for him.   The lower classes, the Slav peasants, were, it seems, taking to Christianity willingly, if not enthusiastically; but the Bulgar nobility, thinned though it

---

[1] Βοριτακάνῳ τῷ τότε φυλάσσοντι.   Boritacanus must, I think, be the Tarkan (provincial governor) Boris.

[2] *Vita S. Clementis*, pp. 1221, 1225.

had been by Boris's treatment after its revolt, was growing up again. These Bulgar nobles, naturally contemptuous of the new religion, were not likely to be impressed by Slavonic clergy. They could be overawed by the Greek ecclesiastics with their majestic background of culture and self-confidence, hierarchs whose mode of life was filled with refinement and whose minds saw niceties that the crude Bulgar intelligence could never grasp. He took the only way out; the Greek clergy remained at the Court, and the Slavonic clergy were sent to missionize the provinces. Soon, probably in 886, Clement set off to take up his residence in Macedonia.

The Macedonian Slavs were the most recent of the Khan's subjects; but they apparently had accepted his rule with pleasure. They were, however, difficult to govern; they had joined Bulgaria as being the great Slav State, and so they might resent the rule of *governors* drawn from the old Bulgar nobility. Boris determined to bind them to his rule by means of Slavonic Christianity. Christianity had barely as yet reached their lonely valleys, but a desire for conversion was animating the whole Slavonic world. Boris was bidding for their souls against the Empire, his one political rival in the south-west, which only gave them Greek Christianity, wishing always to strengthen the Greek sections of the population. Then, the Slavonic Christianity firmly established in Macedonia, it could in time be introduced all over the Bulgar dominions; the Greek clergy, at present so useful, should one by one be replaced by Slavs, till at last the Khans' old dream should be realized. The Bulgar lords would be swamped in a sea of Slavdom, and the Khan would rival the Emperor in Byzantium, and should rule a great Empire bound, like his, with two strong bonds—a common faith and a common language.

Thus it was as the prelude of a vast new policy that

Clement was dispatched. In pursuit of it, Boris altered
the government of Macedonia. Hitherto it was one
province, known as the 'Colony'[1]; Boris detached from it
the districts farthest to the south-west (where the nationalist propaganda and the missionary work would be most
useful), known as Kutmitchevitza and Devol,[2] and, re-
calling the local Bulgar governor,[3] sent to administer it
a lay official called Dometa[4]—probably a Slav;—at the
same time he sent Clement with Dometa, to act as spiritual
adviser, and apparently as Dometa's superior.[5] Clement
was given three residences in the Devol district and houses
at Ochrida and at Glavenitza.[6] Clement set to work in
earnest in his civilizing mission; and Boris had the satisfaction of seeing his scheme well started on its first
important phase.

A year or two later, Boris showed his hand more openly.
Nicephorus I, during the transportations that he had
made to bolster up the Greek or Anatolian element in
Macedonia, had moved, amongst others, many citizens
from Tiberiupolis in Bithynia; and they brought with
them to their new Tiberiupolis, a town near the present

[1] 'τοῦ κοτοκίου': I think this must be an adaptation of the Greek word
'κατοικία,' a colony.

[2] Devol must be the district between Lake Ochrida, the River Devol, and
the River Ozum; Kutmitchevitza extended probably to the east and
slightly to the south of Devol—the extreme south-west of Boris's dominion.
See above, p. 104.

[3] 'παραλύσας τὸν οὔτρον τῆς διοικήσεως,' Vita S. Clementis MS.:
'παραλύσας ἑαυτον κτλ,' Moscow MS.: 'παραλύσας αὐτὸν κτλ,' text in
the Patrologia Graeca (p. 1224). The first reading makes best sense, if we
assume 'οὔτρον' to be a Bulgar proper name. I cannot, however, follow
Zlatarski in saying emphatically that it is the same as Kurt (Zlatarski, op.
cit., p. 229).

[4] 'Δομεταν' in Ochrida MS.; 'Δοβεταν' in Moscow MS.; and printed in
text in the Patrologia. It seems to be a Slav name.

[5] Vita S. Clementis, loc. cit. The hagiographer's eloquence slightly obscures
the exact relationship, but it seems that Dometa was subordinate to Clement.

[6] Ibid., loc. cit. Glavenitza has been identified by Zlatarski (Izviestiya,
pp. 70 ff.) as being between the upper waters of the Voiusa and the
Ozum, near Mount Tomor.

Strumitsa, some sixty miles north of Thessalonica,[1] many of their holiest relics, those of Saint Germanus and other saints martyred by Julian the Apostate. Now Tiberiupolis was part of the Khan's dominions. About this time miracles were reported; visions of Saint Germanus and his followers were seen in the streets of Tiberiupolis, and their bones performed wonders. Boris came to hear of it, and at once ordered the local governor, the Bulgar 'Count' Taridin, to build a church for the relics in the diocese of Bregalnitsa and to move them to this new home. Probably the church was to adorn the town of Bregalnitsa itself, a growing Slavonic village that was the seat of a Bulgarian bishopric. The citizens of Tiberiupolis were furious at being robbed of possessions so revered and so useful; they rioted and would not let them go. Taridin had to use all his industry and tact to prevent the outbreak spreading. At last a compromise was agreed upon. Saint Germanus was allowed to remain in peace at Tiberiupolis; three only of his saintly comrades were taken —Timothy, Comasius, and Eusebius. Their relics were conveyed with honour to Bregalnitsa, performing miracles as they journeyed. There they were received into the new church, and clergy were appointed for them to hold the liturgy in the Slavonic tongue.[2] The new Christianity was creeping over Bulgaria.

Boris was well pleased. He had seen his country through the vastest revolution in its history; he had inherited it as a great power, he had made it a great civilized power. He could vie now on equal terms with the Frankish monarchs, even with the Emperor himself. And his country's Church was his to control; he had made the world realize that. The versatile bargaining and the dogged persistence

[1] See above, p. 55. Tiberiupolis is located by Zlatarski (*Istoriya*, i., 2, p. 236).

[2] Theophylact, Archbishop of Bulgaria, *Historia Martyrii XV Martyrum*, pp. 201–8.

KE

had triumphed in the end. And now his schemes were leaping higher, and still successfully. Soon Bulgaria would have one national Church, to bind it together and to enhance the glory of the Khan. Boris could rest now. His conversion had been sincere; it was from genuine piety even more than from policy that he had built so many churches and monasteries, and the purity and austerity of his life had long been admired throughout the Christian world. Now, ill and weary, he decided to retire from the world, to give himself up utterly to a life of devotion. In 889 he abdicated in favour of his eldest son, Vladimir, and entered into a monastery, probably into Nahum's great foundation, the monastery of Saint Panteleimon by Preslav. [1] All Christendom was edified by this renunciation; men told of good King Boris in Germany and Italy. [2]

But Boris had done more than convert his country; he had shaped its destinies for ever. Since the days of Krum Bulgaria had faced two fronts. Was she to expand on the West on the middle Danube, where German culture came filtering through and where there was no lasting power to oppose her, only the ephemeral principalities of the Slavs? Or was she to remain in the Balkans, looking to the East and battling against the eternal walls of New Rome? Omortag had leaned on the West, and Boris, toying with the Roman Church, had almost made himself a Central European potentate. But in the end he chose the Christianity of Byzantium, the Christianity best suited to his country. And by so doing he anchored Bulgaria for ever in the Balkans.

[1] For the monastery of Saint Panteleimon, the ruins of which are now called Patleina, see Zlatarski in *Izviestiya na Bulgarskiya Archeol. Institut*, vol. i., pp. 146–62. I incline to think that Symeon's movement of the capital to Preslav (see below, p. 136) was due to his father's presence close by.

[2] Theophylact, Archbishop of Bulgaria, op. cit., p. 201: Regino, p. 580: Manegold of Lautenbach, p. 364: Sigebert, p. 341.

Book III
THE TWO EAGLES

CHAPTER I

EMPEROR OF THE BULGARS AND THE ROMANS

BY his wife, christened Maria, Boris had six children
—Vladimir, Gabriel, Symeon, Jacob, Eupraxia,
and Anna.[1] Gabriel probably died young, and possibly
Jacob also; Eupraxia became a nun, and Anna no doubt
married—it may be, into the Moravian royal house[2];
Symeon had entered the church; and Vladimir was to
succeed his father on the throne.

Vladimir had been a crown prince for too long. He
must now have been nearing his fortieth year, for he had
accompanied his father to the Serbian war in the old heathen days. And, like all impatient crown princes, he was
filled with the spirit of opposition to his father's policy.
Of the inward history of his reign we know little, save
that he received an embassy from King Arnulf of Germany in 892.[3] It seems that no sooner was Boris safely
hidden from the world in his monastery than the new
Khan upset all his reforms. The old Bulgar aristocracy,
that Boris had so firmly cut down, had grown up again
to an effective height; and Vladimir fell under its influence.
The *boyars* had disliked Boris's Christianity, with its austere

---

[1] The names of the royal family are given in the marginal notes to the
Cividale gospel as patronising some monastery (Rački, *Documenta Historiae Chroaticae*, pp. 382–3). Vladimir is called there Rosate, probably his
pre-Christian name.

[2] The Anonymous Hungarian historian says that King Salanus (Svatopulk
II) of Moravia was connected by marriage with the Bulgar king (at that
time Symeon). Such a statement from him must naturally be taken with
reserve; but if, as is quite likely, there was such a connection, it would
almost certainly be through one of Symeon's sisters marrying the Moravian
King. It is unlikely that Symeon's first wife could have been a Moravian
princess (*Anonymi Historia Ducum Hungariae*, p. xli.).

[3] *Annales Fuldenses*, p. 408. The envoys entered Bulgaria down the River
Save. Vladimir is called Landimir or Laodimir.

and autocratic tendencies. In contrast, Court life became extravagant and debauched, and there was even an official attempt to reintroduce the old pagan rites and idolatries.

But Vladimir and his *boyars* had reckoned without Boris. Immured though he was in his monastery, he knew what was going on outside. For four years he let them be; then, when he saw his life-work being too seriously endangered, he emerged. His prestige as a terrible saint was enormous; with the help of a few older statesmen he easily took possession of the Government. Once again in power, he sacrificed his paternal feelings for the good of his country. Vladimir was summarily deposed and blinded, and so passes out of history. [1]

This was the last attempt of a pagan revival—its dying throe. It was doomed to fail; no one could expect the lower and middle classes to revert to a cruder and more oppressive religion at the behest of semi-alien overlords, and the overlords themselves were guided more by political than by spiritual motives. Boris had only to reappear to cause the whole business to collapse. But it was rather a delicate situation for Boris. In dethroning his son he had saved Christianity, but he had endangered its corollary. He acted warily. Summoning a congress from all his kingdom (how it was composed we cannot tell—probably of the Court nobility, the provincial governors or their representatives, the ecclesiastical authorities, and any other outstanding citizen), he justified his interference on the grounds of religion, and then bade them accept as their monarch his younger son, the monk Symeon. [2]

---

[1] Regino, p. 580: Manegold, p. 364: Sigebert, p. 341: Theophylact, Archbishop of Bulgaria, *Historia XV Martyrum*, p. 213; *Chudo Sv. Georgiya*, pp. 19–20.

[2] Regino, loc. cit. Boris threatened Symeon that he would treat him similarly should he relapse—a needless threat to a pious monk, but one probably calculated to show that only on religious grounds could the monarch be deposed, and only Boris as an ex-monarch could effect the deposition.

At the same time, he took the opportunity of the presence
of the congress to complete his last great reform. The
seed that Clement was sowing in Macedonia—work
uninterrupted, it seems, by Vladimir's reign—and that
Nahum was sowing nearer to the capital, had taken root
sufficiently; it was time to replace the Greek tongue by
the Slavonic throughout the Bulgarian Church.[1] There
were several reasons for doing this now; it is probable
that there was a vacancy in the Bulgarian archiepisco-
pate; it is possible that the Greek clergy was too closely
connected with the Court aristocracy; and certainly it
was a good moment for a measure that might displease
the Empire—Basil and Photius were dead, and the Emperor Leo and his brother the Patriarch were too indifferent and weak to oppose the fulfilment of a movement that
even their great predecessors had regarded as inevitable.
Moreover, Boris calculated, the enforcing of Slavonic as
the one national language of Bulgaria would submerge
for ever the conscious exclusiveness and superiority of the
old Bulgars. The Children of the Huns were to lose their
identity; Bulgarian was to mean now Slav and Bulgar alike,
any subject of the Bulgarian monarch—who was the Sublime Khan no longer, but the Knyaz, the Slavonic Prince.

With the change in the language, it is probable that the
organization of the Bulgar Church was completed, to fit
the new state of things. Some time about now the country
was divided up between seven metropolitans under the
Archbishop of Bulgaria—the metropolitans of Dristra,
Philippopolis, Sardica, Provadia, Margum (or Morava),
Bregalnitsa, and Ochrida.[2] Most of their dioceses had

---

[1] See Zlatarski, *Istoriya* i., 2, pp. 254 ff. It is inherently probable that
the change was effected now and his arguments are, I think, conclusive,
though I think that the process was more gradual than he allows; the
Greek language did not fall entirely into disuse.

[2] Zlatarski, op. cit., pp. 207 ff., dates their creation in 864; but it seems
obvious from Saint Clement's career that Ochrida at least dates from later.

been organized before, particularly those in Eastern
Bulgaria; the diocese of Bregalnitsa was being organized
in 889.[1]   The diocese of Ochrida had probably not yet
come into being—Macedonia was still too wild.   But
Clement's missionary work had advanced now far enough
for a bishopric to be created for him.   He became bishop
of the dual see of Debritsa (Drembitsa) and Belitsa, two
small towns between Ochrida and Prilep.[2]   Later their
importance was overshadowed by Ochrida.

In connection with these ecclesiastical reforms another
great change was made.   Joseph, the new Archbishop of
Bulgaria, had his archiepiscopal seat not at Pliska, but at
Preslav.[3]   The capital was being moved.[4]   Pliska, the
Hunnish capital, with its memories of the great heathen
Khans, was no longer suitable.   The Christian Prince
should dwell at Preslav, close by the monastery of the
Panteleimon and the Christian college of Nahum.

When all this was done, Boris returned to his cloister.
His work was really finished now.   Before, he had rested
too soon; Vladimir had been a broken reed.   But this
time he was certain.   He could devote himself for ever
now to religion; nor would he help his country ever again
save by his prayers.   He had helped it enough already—
enough to have his name everlastingly revered as the
greatest of all its benefactors.

[1] See above, p. 129. Boris's transference of relics from the Greek town of
Tiberiupolis to Bregalnitsa was clearly incidental to the founding of the new
diocese.

[2] *Vita S. Clementis*, p. 1228.   Zlatarski (op. cit., pp. 269 ff.) identifies
Drembitsa and Belitsa.   The *Vita S. Clementis* says that Clement was appointed by Symeon (who succeeds Vladimir on Vladimir's death, which is
mentioned without comment), but that he was the first Slav bishop—i.e.
his was probably the first appointment made after the change of language,
or else the Archbishop Joseph was of Greek origin.

[3] His name is supplied in the *Sinodik Tsaria Borisa* (ed. Popruzhenko,
Odessa 1899), pp. 74–5, and in the *Chudo Sv. Georgiya*, loc. cit.   For the
whole question see Zlatarski, *Bulgarski Arkhiepiscopi Patriarsi, passim.*

[4] A note to a copy of the Book of Isaiah informs us that Symeon moved
the capital.

The new Prince, Symeon, was a far better son than Vladimir. He was about thirty years of age.[1] Much of his life had been spent at Constantinople, living, it seems, in the precincts of the Palace and studying probably not only at Photius's Slavonic college but also at the University. Certainly he became a proficient Greek scholar, with a taste for the works of Aristotle and Demosthenes. Indeed, he was sometimes known as Hemi-Argus, the half-Greek.[2] Of recent years he had taken monastic orders, being, it may be, designed by his father for a Bulgar patriarchate, and was living in a Bulgarian monastery, probably with his father in the Panteleimon. His Christian zeal was undoubted. Nevertheless, there were some unfavourable comments when he renounced his vows and resumed a very secular life in order to ascend the throne.[3]

If the statesmen at Constantinople had hoped that the accession of the 'half-Greek' meant the revival of their influence in Bulgaria, they were sadly disappointed. Symeon's devotion to Greek literature only had the effect of making him wish for it to be translated into the vernacular. The decade following the official adoption of the Slavonic language and alphabet bore an amazing crop of literature. The Bulgarian people, long restricted in their writing to Greek characters and language or perhaps a few runic signs,[4] suddenly had found a means of expression. But the blossoming was not altogether spontaneous; a heathen illiterate empire, however great, will not at once turn into a vigorous bed of flowering culture. Bulgarian

---

[1] Nicholas Mysticus (*Ep.* xxix., p. 181) calculated in 923 that Symeon was then over 60.

[2] Liudprand, *Antapodosis*, p. 87.

[3] Liudprand (loc. cit.) speaks of the incident with disapproval; but he gathered his material about Symeon in Constantinople, after Symeon's wars against the Empire.

[4] Khrabr implies that the Slavs employed such signs, but certainly no traces of them survive in the Balkans.

literature only became a natural growth a century later, when Christianity and letters had had time to permeate through.[1]   At present it was called into being by the active patronage of the Prince. Symeon wished his people to enjoy the treasures of Byzantine civilization; he encouraged translations to be made not only of holy and patristic works, but also of suitable romances. Consequently the first Bulgarian writers were mainly translators; and their work has that somewhat artificial air given when the matter is more sophisticated than the language.

Nevertheless, it was a creditable beginning for any literature. Already, ever since he had settled in Macedonia, Clement had been busily translating. He had found himself greatly handicapped by the prevalent ignorance of Greek; and the people were very stupid.[2] The only hope lay in copious translations. But Clement was indefatigable. He could draw on the works of his great masters, Cyril and Methodius, and he supplemented them as best he could. By the end of the century he had made Ochrida one of the most renowned centres for the dissemination of Christianity and culture; and when he began to retire from active life his work was amply carried on by his old fellow-disciple, Nahum, who came over from Preslav to take on the bishopric of Ochrida.[3]

But at present Clement's Macedonian school was overshadowed by the royal school of Preslav. There translations were being made on all sides. Symeon himself even superintended a collection of explanatory extracts from the Fathers; and the preface paid a flattering tribute to

[1] The Bogomil legends really represent the first spontaneous Bulgarian literature.

[2] *Vita S. Clementis*, p. 1229.

[3] *Vita S. Clementis*, loc. cit. and ff.: *Zhitiya Sv. Naum*, pp. 4–5: Zlatarski, *Istoriya*, i., 2, pp. 351 ff.

his patronage, calling him the 'new Ptolemy, who like the industrious bee gathers the juice of all the flowers, to spread it over the *boyars*.'[1] A Bishop Constantine translated some homilies for holy days and the works of Saint Athanasius[2]; the Presbyter Gregory translated the chronicle of John Malalas, and also a romantic tale of Troy for the 'book-loving Prince.'[3] John the Exarch, at the behest of the royal monk Duks, brother of Boris, translated John Damascene and wrote a *Shestodniev*, an adaptation of Saint Basil's *Hexameron*. John, writing probably a little later than the others, was more adventurous, and wrote chapters of his own composition. To his John Damascene he wrote a preface that gave a short history of Slavonic letters and discoursed on the difficulties of a translator—what is one to do when the words are of different genders in Greek and in Slavonic?—and to his *Shestodniev* he added an epilogue praising the glories of Symeon's Court at Preslav.[4] Even the royal family produced an author, Tudor (or Theodore), son of Duks; but only a small prologue of his survives.[5]

But all these translations were valueless unless the public could be persuaded that Slavonic was a suitable medium for literature. It was to justify its use that the first original Bulgarian work was written. Shortly after the adoption of the Slavonic liturgy the monk Khrabr wrote a little apologia on the Slavonic alphabet, in which he pointed out that though Hebrew, Greek, and Latin

[1] *Sbornik na Tsar Simeona*, preface.

[2] Given in Archbishop Antony's *Ep. Konstantin Preslavski*. I do not think that Constantine's see can be identified; it cannot have been Preslav, which had other occupants.

[3] Kalaïdovitch, *Ioann Eksarkh*, pp. 138 ff.

[4] Idem, op. cit., p. 138: John the Exarch, *Shestodniev*, which gives full text.

[5] Given in *Pripiskato na Tudora Chernorizets Doksov*, by Gorky i Nevostruev, pp. 32–3. His relationship to Symeon has been worked out by Zlatarski, *Koi e bil Tudor Chernorizets Doksov* (see Bibliography).

were the languages sanctified by their use in the Scriptures
and by the Fathers, that did not exclude the permissibility
of Slavonic; for, after all, the Greeks once used the
Phoenician alphabet, and, anyhow, the Greek alphabet
was created by a heathen, whereas the Slavonic was
created by that Christian saint, Constantine or Cyril.
The treatise is a conscientious piece of polemic writing,
occasionally naïve in style and argument, and just
occasionally bearing the mark of one who felt that the
ice was thin. But it must have served its purpose well,
making the advocates of the new alphabet feel that they
had divine sanction in adopting it. [1]

There was, however, one more difficulty about the new
alphabet; but it seems to have died a natural death.
Saint Cyril's ingenious brain had evolved two alphabets,
those known to-day as Cyrillic and Glagolitic. The
former was based on the Greek alphabet supplemented
by the Hebrew, and probably represented his first
attempt, destined for the Balkan Slavs near his home at
Thessalonica. But when he arrived in Moravia, where
anything suggesting Greek propaganda was deeply suspect, he found his alphabet a liability, and began again,
arbitrarily distorting the Greek letters, to disguise their
origin, and generally elaborating the whole affair. This
was the alphabet to which Clement had been educated;
he brought it to Bulgaria with him, and in it some of the
earliest Bulgarian manuscripts were written. But in a
land where Greek culture was not suspect, but, on the
contrary, highly fashionable, there was no reason for the
existence of Glagolitic. Cyrillic, the alphabet that was no

---

[1] Khrabr, in Kalaïdovitch, op. cit. pp. 190–2 *passim*. Zlatarski, *Istoriya*,
i., 2, pp. 853 ff. discusses his identity, deciding that he was neither John the
Exarch (Ilinsky's theory) nor a disciple of the school of Ochrida (Mazon's
theory). But his suggestion that he was Symeon in his monastic days (ibid.,
p. 860) seems to me too fanciful. Also I think he is wrong in dating the
work *before* 893. It seems to me to have the unmistakable air of an apologia
after the event.

doubt taught at the Slavonic college at Constantinople, was far simpler and far more practical. Glagolitic inevitably gave way before it; but whether the victory of Cyrillic was in any way hastened by official action we cannot tell.[1]

The literary richness was balanced by a growth of the arts and luxuries. Symeon had seen in Constantinople the aureole of splendour that surrounded the Emperor and emphasized his sanctity as the Viceroy of God; he understood its value for the cause of autocracy. In his new capital of Preslav, Great Preslav, the renowned,[2] he attempted to magnify himself likewise. The city began to blossom with churches and with the palaces built by the courtiers who followed the prince's lead. But the royal palace was the centre of it all; the glory radiated from Symeon. The effect was the more overwhelming in that it was so suddenly created; nothing had ever been seen like it in Bulgaria before. John the Exarch, in the dedicatory chapter of the *Shestodniev*, attempted to describe the sensations of a visitor from the provinces, how he would be overcome by the sight of all the great buildings, with their marbles and their frescoes— 'the sights of heaven adorned with stars, sun, and moon, earth with the grass and trees, and the fishes of the sea of all sorts, come upon him, and his mind is lost. He comes back despising his own home and wishes to build himself as high as heaven.'[3] In the midst of it all sat Symeon, 'in a garment studded with pearls, a chain of medals round his neck and bracelets on his wrists, girt with a purple girdle, and a golden sword by his side.'[4] John's eloquence breaks down under the strain of describing it

[1] For the Cyrillic-Glagolitic question, see Appendix IX.

[2] Preslav means renowned. The name was frequently given to cities all over the Slav world.

[3] John Exarch, *Shestodniev*, p. 47.   [4] Ibid., p. 46.

all; he can only complain that he is guilty of understatement. His visitor departs to exclaim to his friends that 'it is impossible to tell of the splendour, beauty, and orderliness, and each of you must see it for yourselves.'[1] Symeon's object seems, therefore, to have been achieved; but it is doubtful if beneath this surface gorgeousness there was what to the eyes of Constantinople would have seemed a respectable standard of civilization and comfort.[2] Moreover, outside the capital there were no luxuries to be found; John the Exarch's visitor lived in a house of straw.[3] Even in Ochrida the oldest stone-built churches date from a century later.[4] But that perhaps was not unintended. Symeon wished Preslav to be the centre of Bulgaria, even as Constantinople was of the Empire. His hope was forlorn; his capital, like his literature, had been artificially forced. Geography, that had made Constantinople the greatest port and market of the mediaeval world, had given no such lasting advantages to the little inland valley among the low mountains where Preslav lay. To-day of that great city, which even three centuries later[5] covered an area far greater than any other Balkan town, only a few meaningless ruins remain.

Indeed, though the traveller to-day may still marvel at the greatness of the site,[6] it is hard for him to envisage its past glory. Of Symeon's vast palace little has been

[1] John Exarch, *Shestodniev*, p. 46.

[2] Certainly in 927 Maria Lecapena took all her furniture, etc., with her to Bulgaria. See below, p. 179.

[3] John Exarch, op. cit., p. 46.

[4] Probably coastal towns such as Anchialus or Develtus, built and still largely inhabited by Greeks and Armenians, had higher standards; and the formerly Imperial fortresses inland probably retained a few buildings; the Red Church at Philippopolis seems to date at least from the early ninth century. The first Ochridian churches date from Samuel's reign.

[5] In the days of Nicetas Acominatus (p. 486).

[6] It was shaped roughly as a solid pentagon, its sides averaging some 2 kms. in length. The Great Palace or Inner City occupied about ⅓th of the whole area. The walls of both cities can be traced, the latter's still in part standing.

unearthed, but what is bare reveals only foundations and
a few marble columns. The city has for centuries been
a quarry for the Turks, just as it itself was probably built
from old Roman cities, such as Marcianopolis.[1] The
churches that have been excavated—Symeon's in the
outer city[2] and Boris's at Patleïna—bear greater traces
of splendour. To anyone coming from Constantinople,
their size is unimpressive and their decoration must have
seemed coarse. It consisted of marble slabs and mosaics,
applied, as far as can be judged, without much delicacy;
but its main characteristic was the copious use of ceramic
tiles, some plain, others ornamented with simple patterns
singularly free from Byzantine influence, resembling
rather peasant art as it is found throughout the world.
But at Patleïna a ceramic icon of St. Theodore has been
found, quite Byzantine in feeling and showing a high
state of technique. To-day it stands unique, but whether
it was always a unique climax of the art of Symeon's
Golden Age, we cannot now know.[3]

Though literature and refinement might need an
artificial stimulus, Bulgarian trade and commerce were
flourishing naturally. The main industry of the country
was agriculture, and probably Bulgarian cereals and
beasts helped to feed the Imperial cities of the coast and
Constantinople itself. Mines were worked, and their
produce swelled the royal revenues. Moreover, the Bulgarian dominions lay across great trade routes. The
busy trade that passed between the Steppes of Russia and
Constantinople went as a rule by the sea along the
western shore of the Black Sea; but some of it must have

[1] The marble is certainly from Asia Minor. Symeon may have added
to his stores in his raids on the suburbs of Constantinople.

[2] Built, according to a MS. at Moscow, in 907.

[3] Now in the museum at Preslav. The workmanship seems to me to be
certainly native. The circumstances of its discovery clearly indicate that
it dates from the first monastery on the site, i.e. before A.D. 900.

travelled overland through Preslav and Adrianople or by
a coast road, and some through Dristra to Thessalonica.
There was another trade route, almost equally important,
which could not avoid Bulgaria; this was the route from
Central Europe, which entered the Balkan peninsula at
Belgrade and, like the railway to-day, forked at Nish, one
branch leading through Sardica (Sofia) and Philippopolis to Adrianople and Constantinople, the other cutting due south across to Thessalonica. This meant a
steady flow of merchandise passing through Bulgaria, and
enriching on its way the Bulgarian traders or the Greek
and Armenian subjects of the Prince.[1]

Symeon watched with care over his country's commercial welfare; and, early in his reign, his intervention
in its interests set going a train of circumstances which for
a moment seemed likely to destroy Bulgaria and all its
new-born culture, and which in the end served to confirm
for ever the Balkan destiny that Boris had planned for his
country.   Ever since Tervel's day trade between Bulgaria
and the Empire had been carefully organized, and by
now the Bulgarians had their counters at Constantinople
(probably in the Saint Mamas quarter, along with the
Russian counters) where they took their merchandise to
distribute it to the Imperial merchants.   In the year 894[2]
an intrigue in the Imperial Court resulted in two Greek
merchants, Stauracius and Cosmas, securing the monopoly of the Bulgarian trade.   They thereupon not only
put heavy duties on the goods, but also insisted on moving
the counters to Thessalonica—corruption was easier to
manage at some distance from the capital.   All this
naturally upset the Bulgarians, and they complained to
Symeon.   He at once made representations before the

---

[1] The trade routes are given by Constantine Porphyrogennetus, *De Administrando Imperio*, pp. 79, 177.   The Thessalonican routes must, however, be
considered in connection with the episode related below.

[2] I discuss the date below.

Emperor.   But the dishonest Greek merchants were under the protection of Zaützes, the Basileopator, the all-powerful father-in-law of the Emperor; Leo therefore ignored Symeon's embassy and the scandal went on. Symeon thereupon decided to have recourse to arms, and prepared to invade Thrace.   The main Imperial armies, under Nicephorus Phocas, the hero of the Italian wars, were away in the East fighting the Saracens; Leo could only send against the invaders unseasoned troops, under Procopius Crenites and an Armenian, Curticius.   These, in spite of their numbers, Symeon had no difficulty in routing; the two generals were slain in battle, and the captives had their noses slit.   The Bulgars then advanced through Thrace up to the capital itself.

Leo next tried diplomacy.   He had sent that year an embassy to Ratisbon to King Arnulf—probably before the war broke out, as a counterblast to Arnulf's embassy to Vladimir in 892—but his ambassador was not well received.[1]   But now he had a far better plan.   Ever since the days of Omortag the wild Magyars had been established on the Steppes right up to the Bulgarian frontier on the River Dniester, if not by now to the Pruth.   In 895 he sent the patrician Nicetas Sclerus to the Magyar settlements and proposed to the Magyar chieftains, Arpad and Kurson, that they should invade Bulgaria; he promised that ships should be sent to convey them across the Danube.   The Magyars gladly agreed, especially as they were feeling somewhat pressed on their eastern borders by an even wilder nation, the Petchenegs; they gave hostages and the treaty was concluded.   Leo then summoned Nicephorus Phocas from Asia and fitted out the Imperial fleet under the Admiral Eustathius.   These

---

[1] *Annales Fuldenses*, p. 410.   The ambassador had only one audience, and left the same day.   There was a second and more successful embassy in 896, but it is doubtful if it had any great bearing on the Bulgarian war (ibid., p. 413).

Le

latter preparations were really intended just to overawe
the Bulgarians.   Now that Symeon was going to have the
Magyars to deal with, Leo would have preferred not to
fight; he had no wish to magnify Magyar power at the
expense of Bulgarian, and, besides, his tender Christian
conscience made him dislike to fight fellow-believers. He
sent the Quaestor Constantinacius to warn Symeon of
the coming Magyar invasion and to suggest a peace
treaty.   But Symeon was suspicious and truculent; he had
learnt in Constantinople how subtle Imperial diplomacy
could be, and probably he disbelieved in the story about
the Magyars.   Constantinacius was put in custody, and
no answer was returned.

Symeon was soon disillusioned. As he prepared to
meet Nicephorus Phocas in Thrace, news came to him
that the Magyars had arrived.   He hurried north to meet
them, but was defeated.   In despair he retreated to the
strong fortress of Dristra.[1]   The Magyars advanced, pillaging and destroying.   At the gates of Preslav they met
Nicephorus Phocas, to whom they sold Bulgarian captives
in thousands. The Bulgarians were in despair. They
sent to Boris in his monastery to ask for advice; but
he could only suggest a three days' fast and offered
to pray for his country. The situation was saved by
far less reputable means—by Symeon's diplomatic
trickery.

When he realized the seriousness of his state, he sent
through Eustathius to ask the Emperor for peace. Leo
was glad to comply.   He ordered Phocas and Eustathius
to retire, and sent the Magister Leo Choerosphactus to
discuss terms. This was exactly what Symeon had
wished. When the Magister Leo arrived he was detained
under guard at the fortress of Mundraga: while Symeon,
free of the embarrassment of half of his enemies, set out to

[1] Dorostolum, the modern Silistria.

attack the remainder, the Magyars. In a great battle he
succeeded in defeating them and driving them back
across the Danube. The struggle was so bloodthirsty
that even the Bulgarians were said to have lost 20,000
knights. Victorious over the Magyars, Symeon informed
the Magister Leo that his terms now included the release
of all Bulgarian captives recently bought by Phocas from
the Magyars. The unhappy ambassador, who had not
been able meanwhile to communicate with his Government, returned to Constantinople, along with a certain
Theodore, a familiar of Symeon's, to see what could be
done.

Leo wished for peace, and was prepared to give up the
prisoners. He had never regarded the war with enthusiasm, and just recently he had lost the services of
Nicephorus Phocas, another victim to his evil genius,
Zaützes. Symeon, discovering this, determined to fight
on. He waited until all the prisoners were returned to
him, then, declaring that some had been kept back, he
appeared again in full force on the Thracian frontier.
The new Imperial commander, Catacalon, lacked Phocas's
ability. He came with the main Imperial army upon
Symeon at Bulgarophygon, and was utterly routed. His
second-in-command, the Protovestiarius Theodosius, was
killed; he himself barely escaped with a few refugees. The
battle had been so ghastly that one of the Imperial soldiers
determined thereupon to renounce the world, and retired
to receive beatitude later under the name of Luke the
Stylite.[1] It was now the year 897.

Symeon was again master of the situation; and Leo
Choerosphactus again set out to make the best peace that
he could. It was a thankless task. Much of his correspondence with Symeon and with his own Government
survives, and shows the trials that he had to face. Symeon

[1] *Vie de Luc le Stylite*, pp. 200–1.

was in turns cunning, arrogant, and suspicious; he felt, it
seems, that his adversaries were his mental superiors, and
so he mistrusted their every gesture lest it should hold
some sinister further meaning that he did not see. His
letters would contain phrases on the verge of being offensive; he declared that 'neither your Emperor nor his
meteorologist can know the future'—a remark very
galling to a monarch who prided himself on his prophecies. [1]
The chief difficulty was that Symeon was unwilling to give
up, even at a price, the prisoners, estimated at 120,000,
that he had recently taken. 'O Magister Leo,' he wrote,
'I promised nothing about the prisoners. I never said
so to you. I shall not send them back, particularly as I
don't clearly see the future.' [2] But the prisoners were
eventually returned, and the ambassador secured a
better peace than might have been expected. The
Emperor agreed to pay a yearly subsidy, probably
not large, but we do not know its size, to the Bulgarian
Court [3]; but Symeon, so far from making any new annexation of territory, gave back thirty fortresses that his lieutenants had captured in the theme of Dyrrhachium [4]; and
the Bulgarian counters apparently remained at Thessalonica. [5]

The reason for this moderation was not far to seek. The
contemporary Arab historian Tabari told a story of how
the 'Greeks' were at war with the 'Slavs,' and the Greek

---

[1] Leo Choerosphactus, *Ep*. iii. (Symeon to Leo), p. 381. The Emperor
Leo prophesied correctly his brother's reign, and had a great reputation
for his predictions, whence came his surname 'The Wise.'

[2] Ibid., *Ep*. v. (Symeon to Leo), p. 382. This was the complete letter.

[3] That this tribute existed we know from Alexander's refusal to continue
the arrangement made by Leo (Theophanes Continuatus, p. 378, and
Nicholas Mysticus, *Ep*. vii., p. 57). He suggests that the arrears should be
paid up.

[4] Leo Choerosphactus, *Ep*. xviii. (to the Emperor Leo), p. 396.

[5] In the *De Administrando* (loc. cit.) the trade routes are calculated from
Thessalonica.

Emperor was reduced to the expedient of arming his Moslem captives, who defeated the Slavs, but were thereupon promptly disarmed again.[1] The story is obviously fanciful; at most the Emperor may have provided arms for the duration of the emergency to the settlements of Asiatics in Thrace. Symeon was held in restraint by events from a very different quarter. When the Emperor called in the Magyars against him, Symeon decided that he too would draw on diplomacy, and he bribed the Petchenegs that lay beyond to attack the Magyars in the rear. The result was not altogether what he had wished. When the Magyars, defeated in Bulgaria, returned to their homes—the lands across the Dniester that they called Atelkuz—they found them occupied by the Petchenegs, the one race of which they were mortally afraid. They had to migrate; and so with all their families and all their belongings they crossed the rivers once more and then moved to the west, over the Carpathian mountains into the Central Danubian plain, to the banks of the Theiss, the frontier between the Bulgarian and Moravian dominions. It was a suitable time for them. The great King Svatopulk had died in 894, and his successors were effete and quarrelsome. Their opposition was easily overcome. By the year 906 the Magyars were lords of the whole plain, from Croatia to the Austrian marches and Bohemia.[2]

Symeon could not let this pass unchallenged. Transylvania and the valley of the Theiss were of no great importance to him, save for their salt-mines, whose produce was a great Bulgarian export. But no proud king can

---

[1] Tabari in Vasiliev, *Vizantiya i Araby*, vol. ii., Prilozheniya, p. 11. Dvornik (op. cit., pp. 304–5) places credence in this story and follows Marquart (*Osteuropäische Streifzüge*, pp. 517 ff.) in doubting the account given in the *De Administrando* of the Petchenegs—Dvornik doing so on the grounds that the *Annals* of Fulda do not mention it. But on diplomatic matters Constantine Porphyrogennetus is by far the most reliable writer of the time.

[2] Constantine Porphyrogennetus, *De Administrando Imperio*, pp. 168 ff.

endure to lose vast provinces without striking a blow. But, though we know that his troops fought the Magyars, of the extent of the fighting we know nothing. According to the Magyars, the Greeks helped the Bulgarians, but they were both defeated.[1] Probably after a few unsuccessful skirmishes Symeon cut his losses and evacuated the land. His vast trans-Danubian Empire was reduced to the plain of Wallachia.[2]

The coming of the Magyars had far-reaching effects on Bulgaria and the whole of Europe. At the moment and for nearly a century their presence seemed to their neighbours—Slav, Frank, and Greek alike—an unmitigated nuisance; they were chiefly remarkable for their efficient and incorrigible raiding. But far-sighted Frankish and Greek statesmen could see them as a deliverance and a blessing. Hitherto there had been a solid and prolific mass of Slavs spreading from Greece and Italy to the Baltic. Were they ever to unite—and that was not inconceivable—their predominance in Europe was assured. But now a wedge had been driven right in the midst of them; the Northern and the Southern Slavs were separated for ever. They would each go their own way now. With this new enemy in their midst, they could not expand further. The neighbouring races were saved.

But though the Slav world in the end was to lose by it, on Bulgaria the effect of the Magyars was as a stimulant. Boris had laid down that Bulgaria should be an Eastern Power. Now there was no alternative. She was cut off entirely from the middle Danube and the West; it was

---

[1] *Anonymi Historia Ducum Hungariae*, p. xli.

[2] In the absence of any definitive statement, it seems best to assume that Symeon only retained Wallachia, which he lost a few years later to the Petchenegs. The Magyars certainly acquired Bulgarian Transylvania and Pannonia; Moldavia, over which Symeon's hold was weak, probably fell to the Petchenegs.

useless to sigh over hopeless ambitions there. Bulgarian ambassadors were no more to journey to Aachen or to Ratisbon; the road was blocked, and so they would forget it. Symeon's longings for greater power must be realized now in the Balkans. He turned his eyes hungrily on Serbia and Croatia, and most of all upon the Eastern Empire. And certainly strange things were happening there.

The years immediately following the war were spent peacefully enough, in the adorning of Preslav and the literary blossoming that Symeon patronized; but the relations between Bulgaria and the Empire were at times somewhat strained. This was chiefly due to minor acts of Bulgar aggression in Macedonia. The Bulgarians obliged the Greek cities of the Macedonian plain to pay them tribute, and were accustomed to pillage the countryside if this was not forthcoming.[1] In the year 904 the Arab pirate, Leo of Tripoli, already famous for his raids on the coasts of the Aegean, suddenly descended upon the great city of Thessalonica. There was no time to organize a proper resistance; the city was taken and sacked, and vast numbers of the population killed or made prisoners. It so happened that at the time there were two officials passing through Thessalonica, the one the Cubicularius Rhodophyles, a eunuch, carrying gold to the troops in Sicily, the other the Asecretis Symeon, carrying gold destined for the Bulgarians, the tribute sent on behalf of the Macedonian cities. During the disaster they hid their gold. Rhodophyles was captured by the Saracens and ordered to reveal the hiding-place; but refusing to betray his trust, he suffered a martyr's death. Symeon was less heroic, but wiser. He offered the whole of the hoard to Leo of Tripoli on condition that he destroyed the city no further and sailed away. The bargain

---

[1] John Cameniates, *De Excidio Thessalonicae*, p. 496.

was successfully struck and kept, and the *asecretis* was rewarded by the Emperor.[1]

But the Bulgarians in Macedonia forwent their tribute. In revenge they moved down into the plain and began to settle. The Greek population had been enfeebled and reduced by its terrible experience; it appealed to Constantinople. The ambassador Leo Choerosphactus set out once more to the Bulgarian Court to protest. Symeon did not want a war just then, so he agreed to withdraw his people.[2]   But he insisted on a fresh delineation of the frontier; the new line ran within fifteen miles of Thessalonica itself.[3]

This restraint on Symeon's part may have been due to his father's influence; but Symeon was soon to lose his advice for ever. On May 2nd, 907, Boris died.[4]   Outside Bulgaria no one noticed it; he had retired so long ago, and Germany, where men had told of him with awe, was far too far away now that the Magyars roamed between, and in Constantinople the busy Greeks thought of other things. Yet it was the end of one of the greatest lives in history. Clement survived his great patron for

---

[1] John Cameniates, op. cit., pp. 569 ff., 574 ff. *Vita Euthymii*, pp. 53–4: Theophanes Continuatus, p. 368: Cedrenus ii., pp. 262–3. The story is a little muddled; only the *Vita Euthymii* (which is, however, one of the most reliable authorities) mentions that Symeon was bearing tribute to the Bulgars—he calls it 'φιλικὴν δεξίωσιν'—the others merely connect Symeon with Rhodophyles, who was bound for Sicily. It seems clear that the two officials were travelling together. The fact the Symeon was at Thessalonica shows that this was not the yearly tribute to Preslav, but a local tribute which was, however, paid from Constantinople.

[2] Leo Choerosphactus, *Ep.* xviii. (to Emperor Leo), p. 396.

[3] This is proved by two columns, dated A.M. 6142 (A.D. 904), found on the river Narish (22 Km. from Thessalonica). The columns were placed by the Olgu Tarkan Theodore. (Uspenski, in *Izviestiya Russk. Arkhaeolog. Inst. v Konstantinopolie*, vol. iii., pp. 184 ff.). Zlatarski (*Istoriya*, i., 2, pp. 340 ff.) gives a rough frontier-line, but bases it on the list of bishoprics in Leo VI's reign: which is not conclusive—e.g. Develtus is at this time included as an Imperial bishopric, though it was certainly a Bulgarian town. Probably its Greek population used the Greek rite and so did not depend on the Bulgarian archbishop, but directly on the Patriarch.

[4] Tudor Doksov, pp. 32–3.

nine years, dying in harness in 916. Nahum, who left
Preslav to retire to a monastery that he founded at Ochrida, had died in 906.[1]

Peace lasted a few years more, varied only by a small
Magyar raid through the west of Bulgaria to Dyrrhachium[2]; but meanwhile Symeon was watching with eager
interest the curious happenings at the Court of Constantinople. The Emperor Leo the Wise was most unfortunate
in his marriages. His first wife, a saint whom he disliked,
had died without surviving issue; his second wife, the
daughter of Zaützes and his mistress for many previous
years, died leaving only a daughter. Of his two brothers,
one, the Patriarch Stephen, had died in 893, the other,
the co-Emperor Alexander, was childless and debauched.
A third marriage was against ecclesiastical law, and Leo
himself had denounced it in his codification; but under
the circumstances he felt justified in considering himself
above the law. But his third wife also died leaving no
child behind; and soon, it seems, his only daughter followed to the grave. Leo, in despair, might have then
resigned himself to the extinction of his dynasty—a judgement on its bloodstained, adulterous origin; but suddenly
a new factor arose. He fell in love with a dark-eyed lady,
Zoe Carbopsina, of the family of Saint Theophanes. At
first he only took her to the Palace as his acknowledged
mistress; but late in the year 905 she bore him a son, Constantine surnamed Porphyrogennetus. Leo found it now
imperative to marry Zoe and so legitimize his heir. But
in Nicholas Mysticus, the friend that he had placed on
the Patriarchal throne, he met unbending opposition;
Nicholas as Patriarch could not condone anything so
outrageous as a fourth marriage. At last he suggested a

[1] *Vita S. Clementis*, p. 1236. *Zhitie Sv. Naüma*, ed. Lavrov, p. 41.
[2] The Magyar leaders lost their way and never returned (*Anonymi Historia Ducum Hungariae*, p. 46). Nestor, p. 19, mentions this raid as having
reached the neighbourhood of Thessalonica.

compromise. His terms, offering to baptize and recognize
the boy on condition that the mother left the Court, were
accepted, but broken by the Emperor. Three days after
the baptism, in January 906, Leo quietly married his
mistress and crowned her Augusta. This was a direct
challenge; and Nicholas—proud, domineering, and fearless—took it up. All attempts to patch a peace failed.
Leo secured the support of the Pope and of the other
Eastern Patriarchs, all of them jealous of the see of Constantinople; but Nicholas remained obdurate, and on
Christmas Day closed the doors of Saint Sophia in the
Emperor's face. Leo retorted a few weeks later by arresting
him and sending him into exile. His place was taken by a
gentler, more subservient monk, Euthymius the Syncellus.

Leo had triumphed, but by force, in the face of pious
opinion. There were many that believed that God's
viceroy the Emperor was above all law, but many others
believed that even he was bound by the laws of God's
Church. Once more the whole question of Church and
State was raised, and Constantinople was rent with controversy. Leo's triumph was ephemeral and superficial.
Nicholas's exile to half the city was martyrdom, and his
party was thereby heartened. Besides, Leo's health was
poor; he would die soon. Alexander, his brother, hated
him and all his ways. But he was sunk in dissipation; he
too would die soon. Even the little boy on whom the
future hung was very delicate. Wherever men looked,
the sky was overcast; a storm was blowing up.[1]

Symeon, in the new-made glories of his palace at Preslav, was well informed of what was happening. He
waited for the waters to be troubled; and schemes and
ambitions flitted through his mind.

[1] Theophanes Continuatus, pp. 360 ff.: Nicholas Mysticus, *Ep.* xxxii.,
pp. 197 ff.: *Vita Euthymii, passim.* I have dealt more fully with the episode
in my *Emperor Romanus Lecapenus*, pp. 40 ff.

On May 11, 912, the Emperor Leo the Wise died, and the Emperor Alexander took over the government of the Empire. Everything at once was reversed. Nicholas came back from exile and Euthymius was sent out in his place; a new martyrdom succeeded to the old, and embittered the conflict. The Empress Zoe retired from the Palace; her son was only saved from castration by friends insisting on the poorness of his health. All the ministers of the old régime were dismissed, some to die in prison. Meanwhile Alexander enjoyed himself, with drink and idolatry and gaming and his favourites. [1]

A few months after Alexander's accession a Bulgarian embassy arrived in Constantinople. Symeon, very correctly, was sending to congratulate the new Emperor and to ask for a renewal of the treaty concluded with Leo. Alexander received them immediately after indulging in an orgy, and, with drunken bravado, he sent them away, curtly refusing to pay any tribute. The ambassadors returned to Symeon to tell of their reception. He can hardly have been distressed; he had an excellent reason now to break the peace, and the Empire, under this dying drunkard, would never be able to withstand him. He prepared for war. [2]

There was no need to hurry; the Empire was going from bad to worse. Alexander died on June 4, 913, leaving the government in the hands of a Regency Council, dominated by the Patriarch Nicholas. [3] This was all to Symeon's advantage. Nicholas, fearless foe though he was to the Emperor, was always anxious to conciliate Symeon; he never forgot that he was Oecumenical Patriarch, spiritual father of the Bulgarian Church; he was determined to leave the patriarchate no weaker

[1] Theophanes Continuatus, pp. 377 ff. : *Vita Euthymii*, pp. 61 ff.
[2] Theophanes Continuatus, p. 378.
[3] Ibid., p. 380: *Vita Euthymii*, pp. 69, 70.

than he had found it.   Clearly he would have therefore
to pacify the Bulgar monarch and keep him from the
temptations of independence or of Rome.   It was to this
anxiety that we owe the long series of letters, sometimes
reproachful, but almost all pleading, that he addressed
to the Court of Preslav—letters whose delicately varying
temper form the main source of the history of these years.

In August 913, Symeon in full force invaded the Empire.
Nicholas, in vain, had tried to dissuade him, appealing
to his better nature not to attack a little child, and to his
worse nature by offering to send the arrears of the tribute
at once to Develtus.[1]   But neither appeal could move the
Bulgar.   His aims were far higher.

His invasion followed on the heels of a military rebellion,[2] and the Imperial Government was in no position
to oppose him.   Marching quickly through Thrace, he
appeared before Constantinople and stretched his great
army along the line of the land walls from the Golden
Horn to the Marmora.   But the sight of the city's huge
fortifications daunted him; it was the first time that he
had seen them with the eyes of an enemy, and he realised
how impregnable they were.   He decided to negotiate.

Nicholas was delighted.   There followed a series of
friendly interviews.   First Symeon sent his ambassador
Theodore into the city to see the Regents; then the Regents
and the young Emperor in person entertained Symeon's
sons at a feast at Blachernae[3]; and finally Nicholas went
out to visit Symeon himself, and was received with marked

---

[1] Nicholas Mysticus, *Ep.* v.–vii., pp. 45–60, esp. pp. 53, 57.

[2] The revolt of Constantine Ducas, Domestic of the Schools.

[3] Scylitzes (Cedrenus, ii., p. 282) says that Symeon himself was entertained at this feast, but the earlier chronicles agree that only Symeon's sons
came (see references below).   Byzantine etiquette rarely permitted foreign
monarchs to enter Constantinople.   Even Peter of Bulgaria, who married
Maria Lecapena, was only allowed inside the city for one brief interview
(see below, p. 179), and then only to the Blachernae Palace, adjoining the
walls.

respect. Meanwhile terms were discussed. Symeon was moderate in his demands; he received the arrears of the tribute and a great many presents, and a promise that the Emperor should marry one of his daughters. With these he returned to Bulgaria.[1]

These terms require a little explanation. Their key lies in the fact that it was now, I think, that Symeon first definitely formulated to himself the ambition that soon came to dominate him. He aimed at nothing less than becoming Emperor. Already his refusal to be contented with the usual tribute showed that he was hoping for greater things; and now, through this marriage, he was going to get a legitimate foothold in the Palace. The idea was not so fantastic as it might seem. The Empire was still a universal international conception; men of many diverse races had climbed on to the throne. None, it is true, had been already seated upon foreign thrones; but that surely would act to their advantage. And the present was so hopeful a time. With the Imperial family reduced to one delicate boy, the future seemed to lie with the strongest person at hand. And no one would be stronger than Symeon, with a daughter established in the Palace, the Patriarch as his friend, and his huge armies ready at any moment to descend upon Thrace; and, once Constantinople was his, the Empire would be his, for Constantinople was the Empire. His was by no means an impossible ambition. Fortune, however, did not favour him: though thereby Bulgaria was fortunate. For these dreams were a betrayal of Boris's policy. Boris's Bulgaria, with its national language and national Church, was too immature as yet to stand absorption with the Empire. A century later it was different; Bulgaria was an established

---

[1] Theophanes Continuatus, p. 385. Logothete (Slavonic version), p. 126. I discuss the marriage question (which certainly dates from these negotiations) below in Appendix X.

nation. But now the various Slav tribes and the Bulgars would have fallen apart, and the Greek Imperial spirit would have triumphed. Boris's work would have been undone.

But these speculations are idle; for Symeon made a miscalculation. He did not realize how precarious the Patriarch's Government was. Nicholas was regent for a child whose legitimacy he could scarcely recognize, and, Patriarch though he was, he was only a party leader. The other party had a leader whose claim to the regency was far stronger and far more logical. The Empress Zoe, mother of the Emperor, though now she was temporarily in unwilling retirement as a nun, had a large following; and soon Nicholas's fellow-regents, tired of his domination, came round to her side. Hardly had Symeon arrived back in Bulgaria, when Zoe emerged from her retreat and took charge of the Government.[1]

Zoe had none of Nicholas's preoccupations. It mattered nothing to her if he lost his titular headship over the Bulgarian Church. And she was determined that her boy should not marry a barbarian. Nicholas remained on in the patriarchal chair, but he had no voice now in the Government. All Symeon's moderation and cajolery were wasted. He had recourse to arms once more. In vain Nicholas wrote to him reminding him of his promise of peace. Symeon considered himself released from his obligations; the new Imperial Government carefully forgot the clause about the marriage.[2]

In September, 914, Bulgarian forces appeared before Adrianople; and the Armenian governor of the fortress was induced to betray it into their hands. But the Empress was a vigorous ruler. At once she sent men and

---

[1] Theophanes Continuatus, p. 383: *Vita Euthymii*, p. 73.

[2] Nicholas never mentions it in his letters to Symeon till after Romanus's accession, when we hear that Symeon had been demanding it for a long time before.

money to recover it; and the Bulgarians found it more
prudent to retire.[1]   After this essay of the Empress's temper, Symeon waited a little.   The history of the next two
years is very obscure.   Symeon made no move against
Constantinople; but, in 916, if not in 915, his troops were
actively engaged in raiding the provinces farther to the
west, by Dyrrhachium and Thessalonica.[2]   In 916 they
even penetrated as far as the Gulf of Corinth, and inter-
mittently remained in the neighbouring districts for about
ten years.   Their presence did not tend for comfort; even
Saint Luke the Less, famed for his asceticism and mortifi-
cation of the flesh, migrated for that period to Patras.[3]

But Constantinople was Symeon's real objective.   By
917 he was again amassing an army on the Thracian
frontier.[4]   He even attempted to win the support of the
Petchenegs, his friends of the previous war; but his ambassadors were outbid by the Imperial agent, John Bogas,
whose financial resources were no doubt larger.   Under
the circumstances the Empress decided to strike first.
The time seemed well chosen; she was flushed with the
triumphs of her troops in Armenia and Italy; and now
there came the news that the Petchenegs were prepared
to invade Bulgaria from the north.   Her fleet sailed to the
Danube to carry them across, and the full Imperial army
marched up through Thrace to the frontier.[5]

Symeon was caught.   The Petchenegs were far worse

[1] Theophanes Continuatus, p. 384.   The governor was abetted by the
Archbishop Stephen Bees, *Epidromai Boulgaron*, pp. 368–9.

[2] Nicholas Mysticus, *Ep.* ix., p. 76.

[3] *Vita S. Lucae Minoris*, p. 449.   Saint Luke lived ten years in Patras, and
only returned after Symeon's death.   But I do not think that the ten years
should be taken too literally; for Bulgarian armies were busy elsewhere in
917 (when Diehl, in *Choses et Gens de Byzance*, pp. 3–4, dates this invasion)
over the Achelous campaign, and in 918 in Serbia. It seems better to connect
the invasion with the acts of aggression reported in 916 from Thessalonica.

[4] Nicholas Mysticus, loc. cit., p. 672.

[5] Theophanes Continuatus, p. 387.   For Zoe's successful foreign policy
see my *Emperor Romanus Lecapenus*, p. 53, and elsewhere.

than the Magyars, and he could scarcely hope to repeat his cunning diplomacy of twenty years ago.   But fortune favoured him, so unexpectedly that we can hardly doubt that he supplemented fortune by bribery.   John Bogas arrived at the Danube, guiding the Petcheneg hordes; but there he quarrelled with the Imperial admiral, Romanus Lecapenus, and Romanus refused to transport the barbarians.   They, weary of the delay, would not wait; after devastating and probably half-occupying Wallachia, they returned to their homes.   Contemporary opinion suspected Romanus of some sort of double-dealing.   Nothing was proved.   Romanus was certainly ambitious and unscrupulous in his ambitions; one must suspect that Symeon's gold also affected his actions.[1]

Saved from the Petchenegs, Symeon could face the future more confidently.   He had probably, it is true, lost his last province across the Danube, but the loss was of very little consequence; the Danube made a far better frontier.   Still, the whole main army of the Empire was nothing negligible.   But fortune was kind to Symeon once more.   The Empress was a poor judge of a soldier.   Her commander-in-chief, the Domestic of the Schools, was Leo Phocas, son of the great soldier Nicephorus, but quite without his father's ability.   His campaign was well enough planned.   After the fiasco on the Danube, the Imperial fleet had come down the coast to Mesembria, the peninsula-port beyond the frontier-line, still held by the Empire.   Thither Phocas directed his army, hoping probably for reinforcements before he struck inland to Preslav.

Symeon waited on the hills, watching for an opportunity.   It came as the Imperial troops rounded the head of the Gulf of Burgas, and turned north-west towards

[1] Theophanes Continuatus, loc. cit., and ff.   There is no means of telling definitely when Bulgaria lost Wallachia, but it seems to have been overrun by Petchenegs well before Symeon's death, probably from now; in 917 the Petchenegs had, one gathers, to come some distance to the Danube.

Mesembria. There was a little stream called the Achelous, close to Anchialus. On August 20, Phocas halted there, leaving his troops carelessly disposed. Suddenly Symeon swept down from the hills on to the unsuspecting army. What exactly happened no one knew, save that there was a panic and almost the whole Imperial army was slaughtered. The bones lay bleaching on the field for half a century. Only Phocas and a few miserable fugitives ever reached Mesembria. Many of the soldiers had fled to the coast; but the fleet which should have been at hand to rescue them had sailed already for the Bosphorus.[1]

The triumph revived all Symeon's ambitions. He came marching down through Thrace towards the capital. Zoe gathered together another army, but again she put it under Leo Phocas. Again Phocas led it to disaster. As it lay at Catasyrtae, in the suburbs of the city, the Bulgarians attacked it by night, and destroyed it.[2]

After this second victory Symeon might almost have attacked the city successfully, but he did not dare; and even the Greeks had confidence that their walls were impregnable. Negotiations were impossible; Symeon demanded what Zoe could not possibly give. And Nicholas, though for the sake of the patriarchate he dissociated himself from Zoe's policy, seems to have regarded Symeon's terms as being unthinkable.[3] But no further attacks were

[1] Theophanes Continuatus, pp. 388 ff.: Cedrenus, ii., p. 286: Zonaras, iii., p. 465. Scylitzes (Cedrenus) says that Leo Phocas was bathing at the time, and his riderless horse took fright and caused a panic among the troops, who thought their general dead. This is quite possibly true. It is clear that the army was taken utterly by surprise. Leo Diaconus (p. 124) tells that the bones were still to be seen in his day. The Slavonic version of the Logothete (p. 12) calls the river the Tutkhonestia. It is foolish to assume that Achelous must be a mistake for Anchialus, just because there is a river Achelous in Greece.

[2] Ibid., p. 390. No date is given for the battle, but it apparently followed close on the Achelous.

[3] Nicholas Mysticus, Ep. ix., p. 69. He says that he was not consulted about the campaign, but he claims that it was justified. However, he seems to regard any prospect of arriving at terms as impossible and is very despondent in tone.

ME

made just yet.   It was very late in the year; and Symeon retired to winter in Bulgaria.

The year 918 passed sadly and wildly in Constantinople. Zoe was falling from power. She had always had enemies, and now her disasters had cost her the love of the populace. There was a scramble to take her place. It would have been an excellent opportunity for Symeon to appear before the city; and in the atmosphere of disloyalty and intrigue he might easily have won admittance inside the walls. But Symeon never came. Zoe, despite her failures, had achieved one great triumph; she had entangled Symeon elsewhere. For over half a century Bulgaria had lived peacefully with her Serbian neighbours. During these years Serbia acquired the benefits of Christianity, and looked to Bulgaria as the source of her culture. Of late, under her Prince Peter, she had increased her territory in Bosnia and had reached a certain standard of prosperity. In 917, just after the Achelous, an embassy from the Empress reached Peter's Court and pointed out to him the dangers of too great a Bulgaria. Peter was convinced by the argument, and undertook to attack Symeon unexpectedly in the rear. But Peter had rivals; Serbia's growth alarmed the cognate maritime principalities, now under the hegemony of Michael, Prince of Zachlumia, an unscrupulous pirate and brigand whose territory stretched along the coast to the north of Ragusa. Michael already once had shown his enmity to the Empire by capturing the son of the Venetian doge on his return from a visit of respect to Constantinople, and sending him to Symeon, from whom the Venetians had to ransom him.[1] Now he heard of the alliance, and at once passed the information on to Symeon. Symeon determined to strike first; accordingly, in 918, his Generals Marmaëm and Sigritze invaded Serbia. They succeeded

[1] Dandolo, *Chronicum Venetum*, p. 198.

in overrunning the country; and when Peter came to make
peace with them they treacherously seized him and carried him off to Bulgaria.   In his place they set up his
cousin Paul, a prince who had long been a hostage at the
Bulgarian Court.¹

How long this Serbian war lasted we cannot tell; but
apparently it occupied the whole campaigning season of
918.   Symeon, with his troops engaged in the west, could
do nothing against Constantinople.   Possibly, also, he
was being troubled by the Petchenegs; possibly he was ill-
informed about the true, desperate state of affairs at the
Imperial Court.   Certainly it was not till the next year
that he was able to march his armies southward again.
And then it was too late.   Romanus Lecapenus had won
the race for power.   In March 919 he took possession of
the Imperial Palace; in April his daughter Helena was
married to the young Emperor.   He called himself
Basileopator; later, in September, he would take the title
of Caesar; and before the year was out he would be
Emperor.

The war was lost.   All Symeon's victories availed him
nothing.   Romanus Lecapenus, a discredited admiral of
peasant origin, had climbed on to the throne by the very
steps that Symeon had hoped to use.²   It would have

¹ Constantine Porphyrogennetus, *De Administrando Imperio*, pp. 156–7.
Constantine does not date the war, but says that the Imperial negotiations
with Peter took place at the time of the Achelous.   The negotiations may
have been begun previous to the disaster, but it seems to me impossible to
explain Symeon's inaction against Constantinople in 918, save by a Serbian
war.   And even though Symeon did not go to Serbia himself (he never
went campaigning in the west in person), I do not think he could have sent
an expedition to Serbia big enough to overrun the country in 917.   The
three years' intervals that Constantine gives between the Serbo-Bulgarian
wars need not, I think, all be taken as infallibly accurate.

² Zlatarski (*Istoriya*, i., 2, pp. 399 ff.) says that in 918 Symeon took an
Imperial title and raised the Bulgarian archbishopric to a patriarchate.
I cannot discover on what he bases this.   It is incredible that we should have
no reference to such an action in Nicholas's voluminous correspondence.
Romanus's letters to Symeon protesting against his Imperial title date from
after the two monarchs' interview (924, see below, p. 172); and it is clear

been well for Bulgaria had Symeon admitted his failure and sought to make the best peace possible. Romanus would gladly have given very favourable terms; he eagerly wished for peace, so as to consolidate his own position. But Symeon no longer showed the moderation of his youth. Ambition, fed by his victories, dominated him now, and blunted his statecraft. He was very angry, and determined to revenge himself on the usurper; and so the war went on.

In the late summer of 919 Symeon invaded Thrace once more, and penetrated to the Hellespont, encamping opposite to Lampsacus. Nicholas wrote offering, if his health permitted, to come out and interview Symeon; but the suggestion was not accepted. The Bulgarians met with no opposition; after wasting the countryside, they returned to winter in Bulgaria.[1]

All through 920 Nicholas wrote anxious letters to the Court at Preslav, not only to Symeon, but also to the Bulgarian Archbishop and to Symeon's chief Minister, urging a peace. In July he wrote to tell Symeon of the end of the schism caused by Leo's fourth marriage—he tactfully assumed that Symeon would be delighted to hear of this triumph of Romanus's Government—and to point out that Romanus had no connection with the previous Government (Zoe's) and was not responsible for its follies.[2] Next he reverted to Symeon's old desire for a marriage-alliance; Romanus, he said, was very willing for such a

from Symeon's offensive joke at the interview (see below, p. 170) that he still regarded Nicholas as the official spiritual father of Bulgaria. It is quite possible, as Zlatarski suggests, that the Archbishop Joseph died in 918, and the Archbishop Leontius succeeded him; but, even though Leontius was created Patriarch by Symeon, we need not assume that that happened the very moment of his installation. Leo Diaconus's words about Symeon taking the title of Autocrat (pp. 122–3) provide no chronological data.

[1] Nicholas Mysticus, *Ep.* xcv., p. 301, written to Romanus when he was Caesar (Sept. to Dec. 919): *Ep.* xi., p. 84, written to Symeon.

[2] Ibid., *Ep.* xiv., p. 100.

union. He affected to ignore the fact that the only marriage that Symeon desired was now impossible.[1] Symeon
returned no answer. Nevertheless, he did not invade
Thrace that year. His troops were engaged in Serbia
once more. Romanus had sent the Serbian Prince,
Zacharias, a refugee at Constantinople, to stir up trouble
against the Bulgarian client, Prince Paul. Zacharias was
defeated, owing to the intervention of the Bulgarians, and
was carried off captive to Bulgaria, to be used against
Paul, should he be insubordinate.[2] Encouraged by
Symeon's preoccupation with Serbia, Romanus talked of
himself leading an expedition into Bulgaria; but nothing
came of it.[3]

In 921, after writing to Nicholas that his terms involved
the deposition of Romanus,[4] Symeon marched again on
Constantinople; but at Catasyrtae, the scene of his victory four years before, Imperial troops under a certain
Michael, son of Moroleon, took him by surprise. The
Bulgarians probably suffered no great losses, but they decided to retire back on Heraclea and Selymbria.[5] In response to a further letter from Symeon, Nicholas offered
to go out and interview him there[6]; but Symeon did not
encourage him. He made it abundantly clear that he did
not want gold, or costly gifts, or even territory[7]; he insisted on Romanus's deposition. It was something quite
easy to do, he maintained, not like raising his Bulgar soldiers from the dead.[8] But Romanus was unlikely to consent to depose himself; and the Patriarch realised that he

---

[1] Nicholas Mysticus, *Ep*. xvi., p. 112.

[2] Constantine Porphyrogennetus, loc. cit. He says Paul had reigned
three years, but, in view of the sequence of events of these years, it would
be more correct to say that Paul was in the third year of his reign.

[3] Nicholas Mysticus, *Ep*. xvii., pp. 113 ff.

[4] Ibid., *Ep*. xviii., pp. 121 ff.   [5] Theophanes Continuatus, p. 400.

[6] Nicholas Mysticus, *Ep*. xix., pp. 125 ff.

[7] Ibid., *Ep*. xviii., pp. 121 ff.   [8] Ibid., loc. cit.

was being mocked.[1]   After spending the summer in
Thrace, Symeon went back to winter in his own country.

In 922 Symeon again appeared in the neighbourhood
of the city.   Romanus was anxious to save from his
devastation his palace at Pegae on the Bosphorus; he
sent out an army to guard it; but as it lay in the narrow
valley there, the Bulgarians swooped down and massacred
it or drove it into the sea.   After their victory Symeon
lingered throughout the summer in Thrace; but, later in
the year the Greeks made a successful sortie and destroyed
his camp.[2]   Again he had to retire, leaving nothing
permanent behind him.   During the winter his letters
grew slightly more pacific in tone; he even asked Nicholas
to send him an accredited ambassador.[3]

These gestures, however, were probably only the
reflection of Symeon's more despondent moments.   Even
while he made them he was arming himself.[4]   In the
spring of 923 he was ready to fight again, and laid siege
to Adrianople.   The great fortress was valiantly defended
by its governor, Moroleon, but no relief force came from
Constantinople; famine forced the garrison to surrender.
Symeon, thereupon, gave vent to his disappointed anger
against the Empire; Moroleon was brutally tortured to
death.[5]   But Symeon was unable to advance further.
Trouble broke out again in Serbia.   It was always easy
for Greek diplomats to point out how unnatural was an

[1] Nicholas Mysticus, *Ep.* xix., pp. 125 ff.

[2] Theophanes Continuatus, pp. 401–3.   No date is given for the sortie
but it almost certainly happened now.   The Empress Theodora's death,
(Feb. 922), Sophia's coronation (that month), and the visit of the Curo-
palates (τηνικαῦτα) are inserted in the chronicles between the account
of the battle of Pegae and it, but probably the three social events were
taken together to make a paragraph, irrespective of their accurate dating.

[3] Nicholas Mysticus, *Ep.* xxii., pp. 148–9.

[4] Ibid, *Ep.* xxi., pp. 137 ff.

[5] Theophanes Continuatus, p. 404.   Undated, but almost certainly early
in 923.   It was probably during this year that Symeon captured the city of
Bizya (Veza) in Thrace, as is mentioned in the *Vita S. Mariae Junioris.*

alliance between Serbia and Bulgaria; and Prince Paul saw the truth of it. But his attempt to escape from Bulgarian tutelage failed; Symeon's armies deposed him and set up Prince Zacharias in his stead.[1]

The distraction made Symeon more amenable to negotiation, while at Constantinople men felt correspondingly more cheerful. Romanus had gradually come round to a new policy, well illustrated in his failure to try to relieve Adrianople. He would let Symeon invade Thrace as often as he pleased, confident himself behind the walls of Constantinople, and hopeful that in the end Bulgaria would exhaust herself by her efforts. Meanwhile, his main armies were sent to fight more profitably in the east; he would employ foreign troops against Symeon. The Serbs, it was true, were always being defeated, but he was negotiating, with every prospect of success, with the Russians (now firmly established almost as far south as the mouth of the Dnieper), the Petchenegs, and the Magyars. Under the circumstances he was less anxious for peace than the Patriarch. And even Nicholas, writing to tell of these negotiations and of the defeat of the Saracen pirate, Leo of Tripoli, adopted a new, patronizing air.[2] But, with Serbia crushed, Symeon reverted as usual to his old insolence. He asked for an ambassador, but he made clear that he clung to impossible terms.[3]

---

[1] Constantine Porphyrogennetus, loc. cit., p. 157, dated three years after Zacharias's revolt. Henceforward my dating is radically different from Zlatarski's (op. cit.. pp. 427 ff.), as he dates the interview between Symeon and Romanus in 923 instead of 924.

[2] Theophanes Continuatus, p. 405: Nicholas Mysticus, *Ep.* xxiii., pp. 149, 156. He says that it was seventeen or eighteen years since Leo's victory at Thessalonica. As he was calculating roughly, there is no reason to prefer either seventeen or eighteen to nineteen. He also says that it is only in deference to his wishes that the Emperors are not attacking Bulgaria themselves.

[3] Ibid., *Ep.* xxvii., p. 173. Symeon's previous letters, answered by Nicholas (*Ep.* xxiv.–xxv., pp. 157 ff.), were apparently more encouraging.

Nicholas then tried a new method. Since Zoe's fall
relations between Rome and Constantinople had been
strained, but in 923 the Pope was at last induced to send
two legates, Theophylact and Carus, to Constantinople,
and then to Bulgaria, to use their influence in favour of
peace. Nicholas, in his anxiety, forgot his patriarchal
pride so far as to welcome this intervention, and wrote to
Symeon begging him to respect the Papal representatives. [1]
But Symeon had his own scheme for dealing with the
Pope. He knew the fragility of the alliance between Old
and New Rome. So he greeted Theophylact and Carus
amicably enough, but his conversations, as the sequence
was to show, were very different from what Nicholas
hoped. And meanwhile he was planning one more great
attempt against Constantinople. [2]

The attack was timed for the summer of 924. [3] Symeon
was wiser now; he realized that the land walls of the city
were impregnable. But Bulgaria had no fleet; he was
obliged to look round for an ally. The Fatimid Calif of
Africa was at war with the Empire and possessed many
ships. Symeon sent an embassy to the Court of Mehdia,
to suggest an alliance whereby the necessary sea power
should be loaned to him. The affair was successfully
arranged without the knowledge of the Greeks, and the

[1] Nicholas Mysticus, *Ep.* xxviii., p. 176.

[2] According to Maçoudi (*Prairies d'Or*, ii., p. 14), the Black Bulgars in
923 invaded the Empire as far as 'Phenedia' on the 'Greek Sea,' where
they met Arab raiders from Tarsus. If, as is probable, Phenedia was some
Greek town on the Aegean, the Black Bulgars must have passed through
Balkan Bulgaria. But whether they came as raiders to Bulgaria also or as
allies to their distant cousins we cannot tell. The raid seems to have been of
very little importance: though it inspired Professor Vasiliev (*Vizantiya
i Araby*, ii., p. 222) to see Symeon in relations with the Arabs of Tarsus.

[3] For my reasons for this date see my *Emperor Romanus Lecapenus*, pp.
246 ff. In that discussion I omitted to mention Zlatarski's argument that
the date is proved by the A.M. date in Nestor's chronicle, which by his interpretation of Bulgar dating (with which I agree) comes to 923. But why
Nestor's A.M. should be right when no one else's is and even his indiction is
wrong, I do not know. I do not think it can stand against the external
evidence.

Bulgarian ambassadors were returning with the African representatives, when the ship in which they were travelling was captured off the South Italian coast by an Imperial squadron. The Emperor at once sent to the Calif and offered him a profitable peace; which was gladly accepted—for the Africans had no desire to fight unnecessarily in the distant north-east; and he kept the Bulgarians prisoners.[1] But, at the same time, seriously alarmed by Symeon's preparations, he sent also to Bagdad, to the other Calif, to arange a truce, so that his main armies could come back to Thrace.[2]

In September Symeon in his panoply arrived before the walls of Constantinople. Once more the sight of them daunted him. Probably only then did he learn that the African fleet was never coming, and that, instead, the Imperial army was marching from the east. Once more, as eleven years before, while the city awaited his onslaught, he merely sent to ask to see the Patriarch.

Hostages were exchanged and Nicholas hurried out to meet him. Symeon, enjoying this subservience, demanded now that the Emperor should come instead. And even the Emperor came, though Imperial Majesty would not hurry and elaborate preparations had to be made. A strong, fortified pier was built out into the Golden Horn at Cosmidium and a wall erected across the middle; over the wall the monarchs would converse. But the delay made Symeon impatient. To show how terrible he was, how little awed by the venerability of the Empire, he spent the time wasting the countryside, and even burning one of its holiest sanctuaries, the old Church of the Mother of God at Pegae.

The interview took place on Thursday, September 9. Symeon came on to the pier by land, surrounded by a

[1] Cedrenus, ii., p. 536, undated, but clearly just before the 924 campaign.
[2] Ibn-al-Asir (in Vasiliev, op. cit., *Prilozheniya*, p. 106).

glittering escort, some to guard his person and some to
test the works of the Greeks—for Symeon was mindful
of Krum's experience—and others as interpreters; for
Symeon would not pay lip-service to the Empire by using
the Imperial language.   When hostages had been
exchanged he advanced to the wall.   The Emperor
Romanus was waiting there.   His coming had been in
contrast; he arrived with the Patriarch by water, in his
yacht, with a humble mien, clad in the holy cloak of the
Virgin, and with few attendants—for he knew that he
was attended by all the glory and tradition of Imperial
Rome.

Over the wall the monarchs greeted each other.
Symeon began to talk flippantly, teasing the Patriarch
for being unable to keep his flock from quarrelling.[1] But
Romanus brought the conversation to a higher level,
addressing a little speech to the Bulgar.   It was a kindly
homily to a foolish inferior, telling of the duties of a
Christian and the punishments in store for the wrongdoer.
Symeon was growing old now[2]; 'to-morrow you are dust,'
warned the Emperor: 'how will you face the terrible just
Judge?'   Moral considerations insisted that Symeon
should cease from staining his hands with the blood of
fellow-Christians; but at the same time Romanus hinted
that peace would be made financially advantageous to
the Bulgarian Prince.[3]

Symeon was very much impressed.   Indeed, peace was
now the only practicable policy.   He had won many
victories; from the walls of Corinth and Dyrrhachium to
the walls of Constantinople he controlled the countryside.
But the city was strong and he had no ships.   He had

[1] Nicholas Mysticus, *Ep.* xxxi., p. 189.

[2] Symeon was over sixty, according to Nicholas (*Ep.* xxix., p. 151, written
in the winter of 923–4).

[3] I quote the speech in full in my *Emperor Romanus Lecapenus*, p. 92.

arrived at the furthest limit of success within his reach, and it was not enough. And, faced with the Emperor's person, he was for a while overcome by the majesty of the Empire and the eternity of New Rome. Hemiargus, half-Greek, as he was, he learnt in his youth the magnificence, in conception and in execution, of the Imperial idea, which had lasted through the centuries before ever the Bulgars were heard of; but he realized now that he could never be more than half-Greek or half-Imperial. The other half was ineradicably Bulgarian, newly risen from barbarous heathendom. Boris had been wiser and more fortunate; he never tried to be, nor could have been, more than a Bulgarian prince; his aims were utterly opposite to Symeon's, national, not international. In his dealings with the Empire he was like a child, but an un-selfconscious child who hopes to grow up soon, and meanwhile means to help himself as best he can, by himself or through his elders. Symeon was like a clever, naughty child, who knows what a nuisance he makes himself and how gladly the adults would like him to keep quiet, who sees through their devices and understands their weaknesses and thoroughly enjoys annoying them, but who all the while is conscious that he is a child and they are adult, with something about them far beyond his grasp; and so he feels foiled and cheated and resentful. Similarly, as a naughty child is awed by a dignified scolding, so Symeon was awed by Romanus's speech. But, after a little while, the effect wears off, and the conscious naughtiness begins once more.

Meanwhile, as the monarchs conversed, Providence sent a symbol. High over their heads two eagles met and then parted again, the one to fly over the towers of Constantinople, the other turning towards the mountains of Thrace. The message was both to Symeon and to Romanus, to tell them that there would be two Empires now in the Balkan peninsula—for a while, at least; but eagles die.[1]

Forced now to recognize each other's independent existence, Symeon and Romanus agreed on terms for a truce. Possibly they even discussed them in person at this conversation, but more probably the details were arranged by their diplomats. In return for a large amount of bullion and other valuable gifts and a yearly present of 100 *scaramangia*—robes richly embroidered, one of the most luxurious articles manufactured in Constantinople— Symeon agreed to evacuate Imperial territory, especially the fortified cities on the Black Sea that he had captured, Agathopolis and Sozopolis, and possibly even Develtus and Anchialus, so as to allow the Emperor a route by land to his city of Mesembria.[2] After these arrangements were made Symeon retired peacefully home.

To some extent the peace was permanent; Symeon never invaded Thrace again. But he showed himself to be in no hurry to hand over his conquests on the Black Sea. Romanus wrote more than once to demand their restitution, and even refused to hand over the large consignment of gifts till it was effected; he was, however, willing to pay the yearly *scaramangia* if Symeon withheld from invasions. Symeon was quite agreeable to this. His

---

[1] Theophanes Continuatus, pp. 405–7: Georgius Monachus, pp. 898–9: Georgius Harmartolus, pp. 824 ff., etc.: Nicholas Mysticus, *Ep.* xxx., xxxi., pp. 185 ff.

[2] Romanus Lecapenus, *Ep.* i., ii. (ed. Sakkelion, pp. 40–5): Zlatarski, *Pismata na Romana Lakapena*, pp. 8 ff., 10 ff. The names of the Black Sea fortresses are never given. The simplest solution is to say that they were Agathopolis and Sozopolis, which may well have been captured by Symeon in 924 or at some previous date since 917. But I am inclined to think that Develtus and Anchialus were restored to the Empire in 927 (see below, p. 180), and they may well have been mentioned now. That would give a more cogent reason for Symeon's preferring to forfeit valuable gifts rather than give them up. Agathopolis and Sozopolis had no importance for him; but from Develtus an enterprising enemy could easily strike at Preslav.

retention of the Black Sea fortresses was hardly more than a gesture; the moral effect of the interview was wearing off, and he wished to show himself unawed by the Empire. Actually his policy was being completely altered. He could only be a Balkan monarch, but at least he would be Emperor of the Balkans. Hitherto, as one who hoped to sit on the Imperial throne, he had been punctilious in his use of titles, and willing also to recognize the spiritual suzerainty of the Patriarch; his future Government would thus escape complications. But now he had no such restraint. He decided to be Imperial even though he could not reign at Constantinople. Some time in 925 he proclaimed himself Emperor of the Romans and the Bulgars,[1] a title conceived to glorify himself and insult his enemies. The Emperor Romanus was extremely angry and wrote to protest; but Symeon did not answer.[2] Instead, he sent to Rome for confirmation of the dignity; and Rome, recently victorious over Greek interests in Illyricum, complied—the Popes had never quite lost hope of securing Bulgaria. In 926 a Papal legate, Madalbert, arrived at Preslav, bearing the Pope's recognition of Symeon as Emperor.[3] This was the fruit borne by that visit of Theophylact and Carus, of which Nicholas had had such sanguine hopes. But Nicholas had been already disillusioned. The interview had shattered his belief in Symeon's heart, and he understood that Symeon had no more use for him now. He wrote twice to Symeon after the interview, but both were the letters of an angry, bitter, ill old man. Then in May 925 a merciful Providence gathered him to his fathers, before he could learn of the

---

[1] 'Βασιλεὺς καὶ αὐτοκράτωρ τῶν Ῥωμαίων καὶ Βουλγάρων.'

[2] Romanus Lecapenus, *Ep.*, loc. cit.

[3] Innocentius III Papa, *Ep.* cxv., pp. 1112–3, referring to the fact that Symeon, Peter, and Samuel asked for and received Imperial crowns from Rome: Farlati, *Illyricum Sacrum*, iii., p. 103, telling of Madalbert's embassy. Madalbert held a synod at Spalato in 927 on his way home. See below, p. 176.

further enormities that his once beloved son would commit. [1]

The Emperor of the Romans and the Bulgars, whose cumbrous title was shortened by his people to the Slavonic word 'Tsar,'[2] determined to have his own Patriarch also.   His negotiations with Rome delayed the appointment—for the Pope could scarcely be expected to approve —consequently it was probably not till after Madalbert's departure, late in 926, that Symeon raised the Archbishop of Bulgaria, Leontius of Preslav, to the rank of a Patriarch.   This presumption passed unnoticed at Constantinople.   The Patriarch Nicholas was dead; his successor, Stephen, was the tool of the Emperor Romanus, who did not much care.[3]

Symeon's new policy not unnaturally terrified the Serbs. It was obviously to the west that Symeon would now seek to expand.   This was indicated by his failure to evacuate Northern Greece, where Bulgarian marauders remained till his death, raiding to the Adriatic coast and even invading and occupying parts of the Peloponnese.[4]   Under

[1] Nicholas Mysticus, *Ep.* xxx. and xxxi., pp. 185 ff.: Theophanes Continuatus, p. 410.

[2] Tsar is derived from Caesar, but probably came into use among the Slavs from the West when Caesar or Kaiser was the same as Emperor. At Constantinople it was a lower title.

[3] The foundation of the Patriarchate provides a difficult problem: the *Sinodik na Tsar Borisa* clearly shows that Leontius was the first Patriarch and had his seat at Preslav; but, according to the *List of Bulgarian Archbishops*, Damian of Dristra was the first.   As I explain below (p. 182), Damian was the first Patriarch recognized by Constantinople, in 927.   Leontius must therefore have been appointed by Symeon previously.   But, in spite of Zlatarski's conjectures, it seems quite impossible that a Pope as well informed and aggressive as John X should have sent a legate to Bulgaria and humoured Symeon's desire for a crown, had Symeon already appointed an autonomous Patriarch. The appointment must therefore have been made after Madalbert's departure, probably late in 926, but before Symeon's death (May 927).   Leontius thus only held his new post for a few months.

[4] See Bees, op. cit. passim, quoting a biography of St. Peter of Argos. He is also undoubtedly right in placing here the episode of the raid on the village of Galaxidi (on the Gulf of Lepanto), which took place in the time of the 'Emperor Constantine Romanus'—i.e., the Emperors Constantine VII and Romanus I.   Sathas, *Chronique de Galaxidi,* places the raid in about the year 996 (see below, p. 230), but in view of the Emperors' names, his arguments are unconvincing.

the circumstances very little Greek diplomacy was needed to induce Zacharias of Serbia to take the offensive, in 925. Symeon sent his generals, Marmaëm and Sigritze, the previous conquerors of the country, against him; but Zacharias was luckier than his forerunners. The Bulgars were routed, and the generals' heads sent as a pleasant gift to Constantinople. Symeon was unaccustomed to such an experience, and he would not let it go uncorrected. There was still another Serbian Prince living as hostage in Bulgaria, Tzeesthlav (Cheslav), whose mother was a Bulgar. In 926 a second expedition set out against Zacharias, accompanied by Tseesthlav. This time it was too much for the Serbian prince; he fled for refuge beyond the mountains to Croatia. The Serbian lords and *zhupans* were then summoned by the Bulgars to come and recognize Tseesthlav as their Prince. Under the promise of safe-conduct they came, only to be taken, prince and all, into captivity in Bulgaria. The Bulgar armies then set about unopposed the conquest and devastation of Serbia. The work was done thoroughly; the country became a wilderness and a desert. The inhabitants escaped if they could over the frontiers; those that remained were butchered. Symeon added a new but lifeless province to his Empire.[1]

It would have been well to stop now, but Symeon never knew when to stop. The annexation of Serbia brought him into direct contact with the Kingdom of Croatia. Croatia was a well-ordered State, with a great army at its beck; its king, Tomislav, was a figure of international importance. He had no quarrel with Symeon; his relations with Constantinople were cold, while he was closely in touch with Symeon's new friend, the Pope. There

[1] Constantine Porphyrogennetus, op. cit., pp. 157–8. The generals in command of the second expedition were called Cnenus, Hemnecus, and Etzboclia. No dates are given, but 925–6 seems correct.

might be a few Serbian refugees in Croatia, but they were not dangerous; the mountains made a satisfactory boundary-line. But Symeon, it seems, was jealous; he hated a neighbour to be powerful. His imagination had always been too grandiose, and now it verged on wanton megalomania. Determined to crush this rival, he ordered his general, Alogobatur, in the autumn of 926 to lead the Bulgarian armies into Croatia. Alogobatur crossed the mountains, but his war-worn troops were no match for the great Croatian levies. Their defeat was overwhelming; the general was slain with most of the army. A few fugitives survived to flee back and tell their fate to Symeon.[1]

The disaster came as a dreadful shock to Symeon. His health was failing, and his nerve began to go. With unaccustomed prudence he sought to make peace. The legate Madalbert was passing through Croatia on his return from Preslav, and he lent his services and goodwill. A peace was arranged, apparently on the lines of a *status quo*.[2] But Symeon never properly recovered.

Men believed at the time that everyone had an inanimate double[3]: that there was some object, a piece of statuary or a column, that was mysteriously bound up

[1] Constantine Porphyrogennetus, op. cit., p. 158: Georgius Monachus, p. 904. Theophanes Continuatus, written later, connects the war with Symeon's death (see below, p. 177). The Croatian war apparently happened close after the conquest of Serbia, probably in the same year, as Madalbert was able to make peace certainly before the second Synod of Spalato (927), and apparently before Symeon's death (May 927). It is pointless to explain the war as the result of a Greco-Croatian alliance as Drinov (*Yuzhnie Slavyane i Vizantiya*, p. 53), and Zlatarski (*Istoriya*, i. 2, p. 500) and others do. Constantinople had no relations with Croatia during these years; otherwise Constantine Porphyrogennetus would certainly have mentioned Tomislav. (I disregard the modern Croatian historians that say that Constantine knew all about him, but were mistaken about his name, as in that case Constantine must also have known the future a year or so ahead. (See my *Emperor Romanus Lecapenus*, pp. 208 ff.)) Symeon's megalomania provides a quite satisfactory reason. It is a well-known phenomenon for autocrats, particularly among races newly raised from barbarism, to be intoxicated by their power and so to reach a stage of semi-madness. For the name Alogobatur, see below p. 285.

[2] Šišić. *Priručnik*, p. 222. Farlati, loc. cit.

[3] The Greek word employed for this double was 'στοιχεῖον.'

with each human life, so that any harm that befell it was reproduced in its living correspondent. In May 927 an astrologer told the Emperor Romanus that Symeon's double was a certain column in the Forum. On May 27 Romanus, with his patriotic, experimental mind, had the column decapitated. At that very hour the old Tsar's heart gave out and he died.[1]

It was as though the light had gone out, and Bulgaria was left fumbling in the dark. Symeon had foreseen that chaos might follow, and had tried to make arrangements that would last. He left four sons, the issue of two marriages. His eldest son, the first wife's child, Michael, he considered unsuitable to succeed him; possibly Michael's mother had been of inferior birth, or possibly Michael himself resembled his uncle Vladimir. At any rate, he was compelled to retire into a monastery. Symeon's successor was to be Peter, the eldest of the second family, a child still; his maternal uncle, George Sursubul, was to act as regent for him and as guardian of his younger brothers, John and Benjamin. Symeon's testamentary wishes passed unchallenged; Peter mounted the throne, and George Sursubul took over the government.[2]

The Regent's position was by no means enviable. So long as he lived, Symeon's personality and prestige awed all his enemies abroad and silenced all opposition at home. But now everyone knew that the terrible Tsar could harm them no more; he was dead, and his Empire a corpse for

---

[1] Theophanes Continuatus, p. 412, which says that Symeon led his army to its defeat in Croatia in person, and just escaped with his life, and died soon after his return. Unfortunately none of the older chroniclers, e.g. Georgius Monachus, p. 904, nor the Logothete (Slavonic version), p. 136, mention the story of the ' στοιχεῖον,' which must therefore be dismissed as a later invention.

[2] Theophanes Continuatus, loc. cit. All the chroniclers tell us that John and Benjamin 'already wore the Bulgar robe.' The meaning of the phrase is very obscure. Possibly 'Bulgar' is used in contrast to the 'Roman' or Imperial robe worn by the Tsar, and the two princes wore it as a gesture against Peter's policy.

NE

vultures to feed upon. The neighbouring nations—Croats, Magyars, and Petchenegs—gathered on the frontiers and threatened invasion; even the Emperor Romanus was said to be preparing an expedition. George collected troops and sent them to make a demonstration in Thrace; but after fourteen years of unbroken warfare, marching to and fro over the wild Balkan mountains, and after the disaster in Croatia so few months before, the Bulgarian army, though it committed several atrocities,[1] was no longer really imposing. The Emperor Romanus continued his preparations. George saw that he must sue for peace.

There was apparently still a war-party in Bulgaria. Probably the remnant of the old Bulgar nobility was chiefly occupied in holding military posts, and feared for its existence in times of peace. At any rate, the Regent moved cautiously, and sent his first envoy, an Armenian monk, in the utmost secrecy to Constantinople, to suggest a treaty and a marriage-alliance. The Emperor agreed, and a peace conference was summoned to sit at Mesembria. The Imperial embassy sailed there by sea, and met the representatives that George, acting openly now, had sent. A truce was declared and terms roughly arranged; then the conference decided to adjourn to Constantinople, where the treaty should be ratified by the Emperor and the Regent in person. The Imperial ambassadors returned by land, through Bulgaria, accompanied by Stephen the Bulgar, a relative of the Tsar; George Sursubul, accompanied by the late Tsar's brother-in-law, Symeon, the Calutarkan and Sampses, and many of his nobility, followed shortly afterwards. At Constantinople George was permitted to see Maria Lecapena, Romanus's eldest granddaughter, the daughter of the co-Emperor

---

[1] *Vita S. Mariae Novae*, p. 300, which mentions the raid as being particularly barbarous.

Christopher. Well satisfied with her appearance, George summoned the young Tsar. Peter set out at once, and on approaching the city was met with honour by the Patrician Nicetas, Maria's maternal grandfather. He was allowed in to the Blachernae quarter, where Romanus interviewed him and greeted him with a kiss.

The royal marriage took place on October 8, 927, in the Church of the Mother of God at Pegae—the new church that replaced the victim of Symeon's wanton barbarism three years before. The Patriarch Stephen conducted the service; the witness on the bridegroom's side was his uncle the Regent, on the bride's the Protovestiarius Theophanes, chief Minister of the Empire. At the same time Maria was rechristened Irene, as a symbol of the peace. After the ceremony the bride returned with Theophanes to Constantinople; the Tsar, on the other hand, was not allowed to come within the walls. But three days later there was a reunion; Romanus held a sumptuous wedding feast at Pegae, at which Maria rejoined her husband. When the feast was over, she said good-bye to her relatives; her parents and Theophanes accompanied her as far as Hebdomum, and there they left her to her husband's sole care. The parting was very sorrowful; her parents grieved to see her go, and she wept to leave them for a strange country. But she dried her tears, remembering that her husband was an emperor and she the Tsaritsa of the Bulgarians. With her she took huge consignments of goods, luxuries and furniture, that she might not miss the comforts of her home.[1]

The marriage was a triumph to Bulgarian prestige. It was the first time for half a millennium that an Emperor's daughter had married out of the Empire; Bulgaria was shown to be no longer now a barbarous State with whose

---

[1] Theophanes Continuatus, pp. 412–5: Georgius Monachus, pp. 904–6: Logothete (Slavonic version), pp. 136–7.

people it was unseemly to be connected. Old-fashioned politicians in Constantinople regretted it as a degradation of the blood Imperial; but now that the Emperor had consented there was no more to be said.[1] The peace treaty, signed contemporaneously with the marriage, also increased Bulgarian self-importance and pride. Its final provisions, the work in the main of the Protovestiarius Theophanes,[2] fell under three headings—territorial, financial and titular.

The territorial settlement seems to have involved little change. Possibly the Bulgarians acquired a few towns in Macedonia, but the Empire recovered Sozopolis and Agathopolis and, apparently, the whole coastline to a river called the Ditzina, beyond Mesembria: though perhaps Develtus, right at the head of the Gulf of Burgas, remained in the Tsar's possession.[3]

About the financial settlement it is even harder to discover the truth. The Emperor apparently undertook to send some sort of yearly income to the Bulgarian Court —possibly the gift of 100 scaramangia promised to Symeon. This was apparently paid till the days of the Emperor Nicephorus Phocas, whose arbitrary refusal to do so gave rise to a war. But during that war the Bulgarians were

---

[1] Constantine Porphyrogennetus (*De Administrando Imperio*, pp. 87–8) deplores the marriage, and says that it was due to Romanus's lack of education that he permitted it; it must not be repeated. Actually, however, it created a precedent; Constantine's two granddaughters were married similarly—one to Otto II of the West, the other to Vladimir of Russia.

[2] Theophanes Continuatus, p. 413.

[3] Constantine Porphyrogennetus (op. cit., p. 79): talking of the Russians sailing along the Black Sea coast to Constantinople, says that from the Danube they 'καταλαμβάνουσιν εἰς τὸν Κωνοπάν, καὶ ἀπὸ τοῦ Κωνοπᾶ εἰς Κωνσταντίαν (Costanza), εἰς τὸν ποταμὸν Βάρνας (Varna), καὶ ἀπὸ Βάρνας ἔρχονται εἰς τὸν ποταμόν τὴν Διτζίναν, ἅπερ πάντα εἰσὶ γῆς τῆς Βουλγαρίας. Ἀπὸ δὲ τῆς Διτζίνας εἰς τὰ τῆς Μεσημβρίας μέρη καταλαμβάνουσιν ...' Clearly this implies that the whole coastline from the Ditzina, north of Mesembria, was Imperial except possibly for Develtus, which would lie out of the Russians' route. Zlatarski (op. cit., p. 525) says that the frontier remained the same as in 896 and 904, save that the Empire gave up Agathopolis, Sozopolis, and Develtus. He gives no references, nor can I find any reason for such a statement.

not the aggressors; the Emperor attacked Bulgaria by means of his Russian allies.[1] Another account of that time, mentioning no specific war, says that Peter, after his wife's death, sent humbly to renew the peace with Constantinople.[2] It is, therefore, probable that the gifts or tribute was only to be paid during the lifetime of the Tsaritsa—that it was a yearly income paid to the Imperial princess to help her to keep herself in the dignity that befitted her birth; and Peter was to put himself in the wrong by demanding the payment to be continued after her death. In connection with the financial settlement the Emperor received back a large number of prisoners. Whether they were ransomed at a price we do not know; Constantine Porphyrogennetus implies that they were released by the Tsar as a gift to Romanus in return for his granddaughter's hand.[3]

The arrangement of the question of titles was settled very satisfactorily for the Bulgars. The Imperial Court agreed to recognize Peter as an Emperor, and the head of the Bulgarian Church as an autonomous Patriarch. But it insisted on certain modifications. The patriarchal see must not be situated at Preslav, but at some other ecclesiastical metropolis. The Bulgarian patriarchate thus was to be dissociated from the Bulgarian Imperial Court, and so, it was hoped at Constantinople, would lose some of its national character and would, anyhow, escape a little from the lay control of the Tsar. It would even be possible to say that there were two patriarchal sees in the Balkan peninsula, not because Bulgaria insisted on spiritual independence, but because the increased number of civilized Christians necessitated such an arrangement. Thus Leontius of Preslav was degraded from

---

[1] Leo Diaconus, pp. 61, 80.
[2] Cedrenus, ii., p. 346. I return to this question below, p. 199.
[3] Constantine Porphyrogennetus, op. cit., p. 88.

his home-made patriarchate, and Damian of Dristra instead was elevated as a Patriarch, whose dignity and autonomy were recognized throughout the Eastern Christian world.[1]

A somewhat similar excuse could be given at Constantinople for Peter's Imperial title. The Emperor Romanus Lecapenus was generous in his bestowal of the Imperial dignity. His son-in-law was an Emperor before him, but he elevated no fewer than three of his own sons, and contemplated elevating a grandson. There was no reason, therefore, why he should not elevate his grandson-in-law: and the fact that the grandson-in-law already was an important independent monarch could be treated as irrelevant. Romanus also considered himself justified in withholding the title should Peter misbehave; indeed, it is possible that later for a time he did so.[2] The Bulgarians, however, did not see it in that light. They only knew that he was the first and only foreign potentate to be recognized as Emperor at New Rome; and, even if he had confirmed the title by marrying an Emperor's daughter, there was nothing derogatory in that.

A third concession was that Bulgarian ambassadors at Constantinople should have precedence over all other ambassadors for ever more. This was a natural corollary of the Imperial title; it much gratified the Bulgarians

---

[1] This, as Zlatarski (*Bolgarski Arkhiepiskopi-Patriarsi, passim*) suggests, is the only explanation of the *List of Archbishops of Bulgaria*, in which Damian of Dristra is named as first autonomous Patriarch, so recognized by Romanus Lecapenus, and as living till the time of John Tzimisces's conquest, and the *Sinodik na Tsar Borisa*, in which Leontius, Demetrius, Sergius and Gregory, as Patriarchs of Preslav. It is unlikely that Damian could hold the office for forty-five years. Probably on his death, at some earlier date, the Tsar restored the patriarchate to Preslav, but Constantinople never recognized the Patriarchs of Preslav.

[2] That Romanus recognized the title now is proved by the words, almost identical in all the chroniclers, that Maria rejoiced on reflecting that she was going to marry a 'Βασιλεύς.' I deal with the more complicated question raised by the *De Ceremoniis*, as to whether the title was taken away, in Appendix XI.

and it cost the Empire nothing: though later it was to offend touchy envoys from the Franks.[1]

Such were the fruits of Symeon's long war. Bulgaria had gained little land and little material wealth, but she owed now spiritual allegiance to no foreign pontiff, and her ruler was an Emperor, the acknowledged equal of the anointed autocrats of Rome, ranking far above all other princes, even the Frankish monarchs, the *soi-disant* Emperors in the West. And that was all the fruit; was it worth while ? An Imperial mantle is a cumbrous thing to wear for shoulders that are wasted.

For it had been won at a heavy cost. For fourteen years the war had lasted; for fourteen years Bulgarian soldiers had tramped from battlefield to battlefield, and at last to their death-trap in Croatia. What was left of Symeon's armies was now almost ridiculous.[2] The war must also have stupefied Bulgarian commerce; for many seasons the merchants trading in the Black Sea ports or conveying their caravans from the Danube to Thessalonica must have been delayed and thwarted and driven out of business. The Empire, with its widely flung interests, could afford such losses; but Bulgaria needed all its trade.[3] And, now that peace had come, the whole land was weary and discontented. Symeon by the force of his personality had stamped his will on his subjects; for all his wantonness, not one of them had lifted a finger against him. But he was dead, his heir a child, the Regent only a regent, not even of royal blood; and it was apparent to everyone how profitless the war had been. Tsar Peter had a hard task before him. His father had bought him his honour at a very heavy price.

[1] Liudprand, *Legatio*, p. 186.

[2] George Sursubul's demonstration in Thrace in 927 had been quite ineffective, and the Bulgars made no attempt to oppose the Serbian revolt in 931.

[3] e.g. Symeon's care for the trade early in his reign—going to war in its interests.

Chapter II

MEN OF GOD AND MEN OF BLOOD

FOR the rare length of forty years there was peace in the Balkan peninsula. But it was not a peace teeming with happy, tranquil prosperity; it was the peace of exhaustion. Bulgaria did not fight because she could not; while the Government at Constantinople was engaged in grandiose schemes far in the east. And so the years were punctuated by raids and risings that no one attempted to oppose. The foreign history of Bulgaria in Peter's reign is a melancholy story.

But it might have been worse. Save on the side of the Empire, the frontiers were strong, mountains guarding the country from the Slav nations farther west and the Danube guarding it from the Magyars and the Petchenegs. The cardinal principle of Peter's foreign policy was to keep on good terms with both the Empire and the Petchenegs. Everyone knew that the Petchenegs' allies were inviolable, for everyone was in terror of the Petchenegs; even the Magyars quailed before them. But a breach with the Empire might too easily mean a breach with the Petchenegs. When it came to bribery the Empire could always outbid Bulgaria, and Bulgaria lay temptingly close to the Petchenegs' homes. Even in Symeon's day it had only been the incompetence and the venality of the Imperial officials that had saved Bulgaria; now the danger was far greater. Thus it was a deliberate policy as well as the influence of a Greek Tsaritsa that made the Bulgarians submit uncomplaining to their high-handed treatment by the Emperor.[1]

[1] Constantine Porphyrogennetus, *De Administrando Imperio*, p. 71, tells how determined the Bulgarians were to keep on good terms with the Petchenegs.

Romanus indeed behaved often in a very unfriendly manner to his granddaughter's husband, whom at times he even, so it seems, refused to call by his Imperial title. In the year 933 Prince Tzeesthlav of Serbia escaped from his Bulgarian prison and returned to Serbia. His coming encouraged all the Serbian exiles to emerge from their refuges and to rally round him in re-establishing their kingdom. The country had lain desolate for seven years, ever since the Bulgar conquest, and Tzeesthlav had a hard task in restoring it to life. But any chance that Peter might have had in crushing the revolt was spoiled by the Emperor's actions. Romanus not only encouraged Tzeesthlav by gifts of garments and other articles of use or value, but he also accepted the suzerainty of the new State. Peter had to reconcile himself to the loss of Serbia.[1]

For the rest, the story of foreign affairs is a story of raids into Bulgaria by raiders on the way to Constantinople. In April 934 the Magyars made a great incursion into the Balkans. Their goal was Constantinople, but they utilized their passage through Bulgaria. The details of the raid are hard to decipher, but it seems that they reached Develtus, and the number of their captives, who must have been chiefly Bulgarian, was so great that a woman could be bought for a silk dress.[2] In April 943 they came again through Bulgaria, journeying to Thrace. How much this time the Bulgarians suffered we cannot tell; the Empire at once concluded a truce with them.[3] In 944 Bulgaria underwent a raid by the Petchenegs, set in

---

[1] Constantine Porphyrogennetus, op. cit., pp. 158–9, dated seven years after the Bulgar conquest.

[2] I deal in my *Emperor Romanus Lecapenus*, pp. 107 ff., with the problem of this raid, mentioned vaguely by the Hungarians (de Thwrocz, p. 147: Petrus Ranzanus, Index IV., p. 581), specifically by Theophanes Continuatus, p. 422, and other Greek chroniclers (dated April 934), and with details that cannot be ignored, though some are impossible (dated 932), by Maçoudi (tr. Barbier de Meynard, ii., p. 58).

[3] Theophanes Continuatus, p. 430.

motion by the vindictive restlessness of the Russians. The
whole incident showed the pathetic part now played by
Bulgaria. The Russians, from their southern centre at
Kiev, were now steadily growing in power; they were a
numerous nation, and they commanded the great trade
route from the Baltic to the Black Sea. In 941 they had
burst through the Petchenegs to make an attack by sea on
Constantinople, but, though the Emperor passed sleepless
nights in his anxiety, they had been heavily defeated.
Their Prince, Igor, burned for vengeance. In 944 he
induced the Petchenegs to accompany him in an enormous
raid by land. News of it reached Bulgaria; the Bulgars
were terrified, and sent the news on to Constantinople.
The Emperor Romanus, with customary prudence, at
once dispatched an embassy laden with gifts to the
Danube, and successfully persuaded the Russians to
negotiate. But the Petchenegs refused to be cheated of a
raid; so they crossed the river and paid a fierce and profitable visit to Bulgaria. Everyone was satisfied, except
the Bulgarians, who did not count.[1] After that humiliating experience there was a respite for several years; but
in 958 the Magyars returned, and again in 962,[2] till finally,
in 965, Peter, remembering the ways of his forefathers,
sought an alliance with Otto, the great King of Germany,
as a means for keeping them in check.[3]

How heavily these raids fell upon Bulgaria, we cannot say.
We only know of them because they penetrated into the
Empire and the ken of the Greek chroniclers. There may
have been others directed solely against the Bulgarians.

[1] *La Chronique dite de Nestor*, p. 35.
[2] Theophanes Continuatus, pp. 462–3, 480—undated, but their position
in the chronicle suggests these dates, while the first is rendered almost
certain, as in 943 a truce was made for five years, after which Magyar
Princes came to Constantinople to make a further truce, which would
naturally be for ten years. Both raids were checked by Imperial forces in
Thrace.
[3] Ibrahim-ibn-Yakub, quoted in Zlatarski, *Izviestieto na Ibrahim-ibn-
Yakub za Bulgaritie*, pp. 67–75.

This pitiable defencelessness was helped by the internal state of the country. Symeon, disastrous though his policy had been, was great enough and personified fully enough the aspirations of his people to carry them all with him and to suffer no insubordination. Under Peter the component parts of Bulgaria fell asunder. Peter's character was pacific and pious, his health was poor, [1] and he assumed the government very young—for it seems that, once the peace had been carried through, George Sursubul retired from the regency;—he had not the personality to awe and command a nation disillusioned and divided by failure. In the old days the Khan had maintained his position by playing off the Slav peasantry against the Bulgar nobility. Peter did not even succeed in that. Under his rule the Court party became a separate faction, distrusted by the rest of the country. Besides the Government at Preslav, it probably included the merchants, all naturally in favour of peace, and the official hierarchy, and no doubt took its tone from the Tsaritsa Maria-Irene, who, if she inherited at all the traits of her family, must have easily dominated her gentle husband. We know that she kept in close touch with Constantinople, at first often journeying there: though, after her father Christopher's death, in August 931, she only went there once again, with three of her children. [2]

The Bulgar nobility, so often crushed by the Khans, was not yet extinct; though probably it had by now lost its racial distinction, and was Slavonic-speaking and reinforced by the more powerful of the Slavs. Politically it appeared now as the war party. Its dissatisfaction with the Court was shown early in Peter's reign, in 929, when he discovered a conspiracy engineered against him to put

[1] According to Leo Diaconus, he died of an epileptic fit (Leo Diaconus, p. 78).
[2] Theophanes Continuatus, p. 422. A proof of the Tsaritsa's influence is that it was after her death that Peter fell under the sway of the war party.

his brother John on the throne. The conspiracy was put down, and the nobles involved were severely punished. John himself was imprisoned and made to take monastic vows. Peter then sent to Constantinople to announce his happy escape. But the Emperor Romanus determined to profit by the incident; his ambassador came to Preslav and somehow, no doubt at a heavy price, secured the person of the rebel Prince. John was given a palace at Constantinople, and very soon the Emperor had him released from his vows and married him to an Armeniac bride. The Imperial diplomats liked to have foreign pretenders in their power; Romanus could hold John as a threat over Peter's head.[1] After this failure the war party kept quiet, till, at the close of the reign, it took control of the Government.

The humbler classes were restless too. Occasionally they showed their sentiments in open lawlessness, as was shown by the career of another of the Princes. Michael, Symeon's eldest son, chafed under the monastic restraint that his father had put upon him; and about the year 930 he escaped and made off to the mountains in the west of Bulgaria, where he was joined by large numbers of Slav malcontents. He lived there successfully as a brigand king; and after his death his band still held together, displaying power and prowess enough to make sudden descents into the Empire and sack the city of Nicopolis.[2] And similar brigand companies probably existed all over the western provinces.[3] But the discontent of the main body of the populace took a very different and far more significant form.

[1] Theophanes Continuatus, p. 419. The incident is placed after the great frost of 928–9.

[2] Ibid., p. 420.

[3] In 926, before peace was signed, the Italian ambassador, travelling to Constantinople, fell in with Slav brigands on the frontier by Thessalonica (Liudprand, *Antapodosis*, p. 83). The peace probably hardly affected conditions there.

Those that are disappointed and weary and fearful for the future often take refuge in religion; and so it was with the Bulgarians. After Symeon's wars, a wave of religious activity swept over the whole country. Amongst its pioneers was the Tsar himself, well-known for his piety and for the zeal with which he sought out saints. Many of his subjects followed his lead. Crowds flocked to enter the monasteries; others sought even greater holiness by becoming hermits and settling down to lives of bitter hardness. Foremost among these was a certain herdsman called John, who, as Saint John of Rila (Ivan Rilski), has attained the eminence of patron saint of Bulgaria. John of Rila for many years lived in sanctity in a hollow oak; but at last the oak blew down, and he had to retire to the comfort of a cave high in the mountains of Rila. There he acquired considerable fame; and the Tsar, when hunting in the neighbourhood, took the trouble to find out his retreat and to pay him a visit. Peter had been annoyed by a homily that the saint had addressed to his huntsmen; but, meeting him face to face, he was deeply impressed by his holiness and eagerly gave him his patronage. When John died in 946 his body was buried in pomp at Sardica (Sofia); but later it was moved back to the mountains, to the great monastery that now bears his name.[1]

But this religiosity had another side. In its most perverted form it appeared in the case of the Tsar's own brother, Benjamin, the only one to abstain from political intrigue. Benjamin's life was given over to a study of the Black Arts; and he became so clever a magician that at will he could turn himself into a wolf or any other animal you pleased.[2] Many of his fellow Bulgars took too great

[1] *Zhivot Jovana Rilskog* (ed. Novakovitch), *passim*, esp. pp. 277 ff. (the account of Peter's interview): Ivanov, *Sv. Ivan Rilski*, pp. 1–20, *passim*.

[2] Liudprand, *Antapodosis*, p. 88.

an interest in fortune-telling and in demon powers,[1] but few could hope to acquire a proficiency such as his; and so, though in himself he might be actively unpleasant, he never attracted a large following. Far more influential and deplorable, politically as well as doctrinally, was a humble pope or village priest called Bogomil.

Pope Bogomil, the greatest heresiarch of all the Middle Ages, is a figure lost in obscurity. We cannot tell where or when he lived nor who he was. All that we know is that 'in the reign of the Orthodox Tsar Peter there was a priest called Bogomil, who was the first to sow heresy in the Bulgar tongue,'[2] that, following the custom of his sect of taking a second name, he was also called Jeremiah, that he was credited with the authorship of several parables and doctrinal pronouncements, and that his heresy was flourishing before the year 956.[3] Even the doctrines that he himself taught are somewhat hard to decipher. Of the writings of the Bogomils themselves—as Pope Bogomil's followers were called in Eastern Europe—nothing survives except a few legendary tales of Bible characters or saints and liturgies so simple as hardly to smack of heresy at all.[4] For the details of their belief and practices we have to resort to the evidence of their enemies; but even most of these are of a later date—and heresies, like orthodox religions, may change and elaborate their tenets considerably in a century or two. There are, however, two exceptions, two documents written against Bogomil himself either in his lifetime or soon after his death.

---

[1] Kozma inveighs against the prevalent taste for fortune-telling, etc.

[2] *Slovo Kozmy*, p. 4. The *Sinodik na Tsar Borisa*, p. 32, contains one short similar sentence.

[3] i.e. before the death of the Patriarch Theophylact of Constantinople. See Ivanov, *Bogomilski Knigi*, pp. 22 ff.

[4] See Ivanov, op. cit., where the theologically important writings are given; also Léger, *L'Hérésie des Bogomiles, passim*, and *La Littérature Slave en Bulgarie au Moyen Age: Les Bogomiles*, where some of their more popular legends are given.

The Patriarch Theophylact Lecapenus of Constantinople, the Tsaritsa's uncle, a prelate more often to be seen in his stables than in his cathedral, was sufficiently shocked by the growth of the Bogomil heresy to write about it to Tsar Peter—probably about the year 950; in 954 Theophylact had a severe riding accident, which incapacitated him during his remaining two years of life. [1] Theophylact was anxious that all the prevalent heresies should be anathematized, and so he did not distinguish between the Paulician teachings and those of Bogomil; but some of his remarks were clearly intended for the latter alone. More important is a work of considerable length, written probably about 975, by a Bulgarian priest called Kozma (Cosmas) purely against the heretics. [2]

From Theophylact and Kozma, as from all the later evidence, one fundamental doctrine appears. The Bogomil heresy was what was called at the time Manichaean[3]; though it only shared with Mani's faith the basis of Dualism. The Bogomils were frankly Dualist, contrasting God with Satan, good with evil, light with darkness, spirit with matter, and considering both Forces equal, though, it seems, in the end God would triumph. [4] Dualism has always been a natural and attractive religion; but Pope Bogomil was inspired by the Paulicians who were settled in the borders of Bulgaria. The Paulicians were an Armenian sect who had strained the dualism inherent in the New Testament to its utmost extent,

[1] This letter, the manuscript of which is in the Ambrosian Library in Milan, is printed in the *Izviestiya ot. Russ. Yazyka i Slov.*, vol. xviii., *knig.* 3, pp. 356 ff. Of its authenticity there can be no doubt.

[2] *Slovo Sv. Kozmy Presbitera na Eretiki* (ed. Popruzhenko). Kozma refers to Peter's reign as though it were over, but he was acquainted with the clergy of Symeon's time.

[3] Throughout the Middle Ages, in the West as in the East, Manichaean is used simply as synonymous with Dualist.

[4] Theophylact's letter, p. 364: God's ultimate triumph is foretold in Secret Book (Taïna Kniga), Carcassonne MSS, printed in Benoest, *Histoire des Albigeois*, p. 295, and in Ivanov, op. cit., p. 86.

putting great faith in the words of St. John's Gospel
(xii. 31 and xiv. 30) which attributed to the Devil the rule
of this world.   They rejected the ordinances of the
Orthodox Church or even the Armenian Monophysite
Church, and instead had their own rites and their own
ecclesiastical organization.[1] They had long been a source
of annoyance to the Empire, at times even forming
politically independent communities[2]; and one of the
methods employed to deal with them had been to trans-
plant them to Europe, especially to Thrace.   But their
migration never damped their ardour; already in the days
of Boris their missionaries were working in Bulgaria.[3]

But the Paulicians were a sect of some education,
versed in theology.   Bogomil's genius lay in his adaptation
of this intricate Armenian religion to suit the needs of the
European peasantry.   Probably he taught Paulicianism
as he understood it[4]; but his teaching was nevertheless
something new, and something so suited to its purpose
that before two centuries were over it had spread to the
mountains of Spain.   Besides the Dualist basis of their
creed, it seems that the Bogomils believed that the Mother
of God was not Mary, the daughter of Joachim and
Anna, but the Upper Jerusalem, and that Christ's life and
death were but fantasy—for God could never take on anything so evil as a material body; they rejected the Old
Testament, both the Mosaic law and the prophets, and they
restricted their prayers to the Paternoster; nor would they
cross themselves—for that would be a tactless reminder of

---

[1] The Paulician tenets may be found in Conybeare, *The Key of Truth*;
also in Petrus Siculus's diatribe.

[2] e.g. their republic at Tephrice, which Basil I had difficulty in capturing
in 871.   Basil's own family had been transported from Armenia to Adrianople, and possibly was itself originally Paulician.

[3] Nicolaus Papa, *Responsa*, p. 1015.

[4] 'Μανιχαισμὸς γάρ ἐστι Παυλιανισμῷ συμμιγής': Theophylact's letter,
p. 363.   The taking of a second name, e.g. Bogomil's assumption of the
name Jeremiah, was copied from a Paulician habit.

the wood on which God seemingly suffered. With regard
to Satan, called Satanail or Samail, there were two
schools of thought: had he always been evil or was he a
fallen angel? The former was the Paulician theory,
deriving from Zoroastrianism, and from the Paulician
settlements it seems to have enjoyed a considerable vogue
in the Balkans, especially in the Greek districts; the latter
was what Bogomil himself taught.[1] There were some
theories that Satan was either the elder or the younger son
of God and brother of Jesus. There was equal divergence
in their views of the origin of Adam and Eve, whose date
incidentally was 5500 B.C.: were they fallen angels trans-
formed into human beings, or created by God or by
Satan? It was also said that Eve was unfaithful; Abel
was her son by Adam, but she bore Cain and a daughter,
Calomela, to Satan.[2] Out of these stories arose a cycle of
popular legends. Pope Bogomil himself is said to have
pronounced on such subjects as 'how many particles
became Adam' and 'how Jesus Christ became a pope' or
'how he laboured with the flesh'; and he may too have
been the author of the story that tells how Saint Sisinni
met the twelve daughters of Tsar Herod on the shores of
the Red Sea, and they told him that they were come to
bring disease into the world.[3]

Thus far the Bogomil heresy, distressing though it was
theologically, need not have troubled the lay authorities.
But a faith that teaches that all matter is evil is bound to

[1] The Constantinopolitan Bogomils appear to have been followers of
the more Paulician school, which was probably the so-called Dragovitsan
Church after the village of Dragovitsa, near Philippopolis, in a Paulician
district. The same divergence appears to have separated the Cathari and
the Paterenes in the west.

[2] Theophylact's letter, pp. 364 ff.: *Slovo Kozmii, passim: Sinodik na Tsar
Borisa*, pp. 34 ff.: Euthymius Zigabenus, *Contra Bogomilos, passim*: Euthymius
of Acmonia in Ficker, *Die Phundagiagiten, passim*: The Secret Book (in
Ivanov, op. cit.). Summaries can be found in Ivanov, op. cit., pp. 24 ff.,
and Léger, *La Littérature Slave*.

[3] Quoted in Léger, op. cit.

OE

have serious social consequences. Many of the Bogomils'
habits were admirable; in contrast to the Orthodox
Bulgarians, who danced and drank and sang to their
gouslas all day and all night long, they were modest,
discreet, silent, and pale with fasting; they never laughed
out loud nor talked of vanities; food and drink came from
Satan, they said, so they took both in extreme moderation,
touching neither meat nor wine. But when they shut
themselves up in their houses for four days and nights on
end to pray,[1] employers of labour might well look
askance. Moreover, convinced as they were of the evil
of their bodies, they firmly discouraged marriage or other
less lawful methods of propagating the race. Indeed,
their abstention from women was so marked that among
their later disciples in France, often called the Bougres,
from the Bulgar origin of their doctrine, it aroused the
prurient suspicions of the Orthodox; and their name in its
English translation still preserves the meaning of an alternative form of vice. Pope Bogomil was not hopeful
enough to expect the whole of his followers to commit
racial suicide; so, following the practice of the Paulicians,
he set aside certain persons known as the Elect, whose
abstinence from sexual intercourse was complete, and
from bodily nourishment and comforts as nearly complete
as possible; they were the aristocracy among the Bogomils,
and their spiritually feebler brethren ministered to them.[2]
Their democratic instincts made them averse to authority.
In their early days they even had no clergy—Bogomil
and his chief disciples, Michael and Theodore, Dobr,
Stephen, Basil, and Peter, had no official position—but
later they seem to have recognized the orders of deacon,
priest, and bishop[3]; and by the thirteenth century there

---

[1] *Slovo Kozmy*, pp. 36 ff.
[2] Ivanov and Léger, loc. cit.: Ivanov, p. 123 *n*.
[3] Ivanov, op. cit., pp. 29–30. The names of the heresiarchs are given
in the *Sinodik na Tsar Borisa*, loc. cit.

existed in Bulgaria a spiritual potentate known throughout Christendom as the Black Pope himself.[1] But what made the Bogomils an inevitable menace to the State and necessitated their persecution was their view, based on their dislike of things that were temporal, that it displeased God if a servant worked for his master or a subject worked for his prince.[2]

The method and extent of the persecution employed by the Government to combat so dangerous a heresy are unknown to us, as are most of the details of Bulgarian history during these years. The Patriarch Theophylact had recommended the employment of secular authority in crushing them, and his advice was no doubt followed. But Bogomilstvo was a faith for which its adherents would gladly suffer martyrdom; and it increased in strength. Its success was greatly helped by the political and social atmosphere of the country. It was the expression of discontent by the poorer classes, the Slavs, members of a race that has always had a democratic bias. The people had long been opposed to the aristocracy, which still was for the most part alien by birth, if no longer in speech; they had lost touch with their old ally the Khan, who now as Caesar was bravely imitating the autocracy and luxury of New Rome. The orthodox Bulgarian clergy were proving unsatisfactory; they were probably under the control of the Court, whose interests they pursued, and, unlike the Greeks, whose culture and learning had at first dazzled the Bulgarians, the average priests were lazy and debauched and little better educated than their congregations—the Bogomils called them blind Pharisees—while the higher clergy were out of touch with the

[1] He is mentioned in a letter of the Legate Conrad written in 1223, (Gervasii Praemonstratensis, *ep.* 120, p. 116). But his actual existence is uncertain—it was generally misunderstood in the West that every Eastern village priest was called a pope.

[2] *Slovo Kozmy*, pp. 40–1.

people. The Bogomil Elect provided a remarkable and impressive contrast, just as the ordinary Bogomils—so Kozma had to admit—compared very favourably in their manners with the orthodox laity. It was scarcely surprising that the best of the crushed and disillusioned peasantry should feel the world to be an evil place and all its matter the work of Satanail, and should follow Pope Bogomil, who was of their number and understood their souls. Nor could so well suited a faith long remain confined by the frontiers of Bulgaria; it spread southward to Constantinople itself and the provinces of the Empire, it spread eastward to Serbia and to Bosnia and Croatia, and across to Lombardy and the Alps, finding its second great home in the land of Languedoc, between the Cevennes and the Pyrenees: till at last that poor land was cleansed and purified by the blood-baths of de Montfort and the fires of Saint Dominic. [1]

But the history of the Bogomils in France and Italy in centuries to come, or of their baneful influence on the Balkan lands that was to last till the Ottoman conquest, is outside of our limits here. In Peter's time and in the years that followed close after, they had not yet reached their full notoriety; but, though they worked invisibly and humbly, their work was that of a worm gnawing at the heart of Bulgaria. The decline and fall of her first Empire came very largely from the unceasing labours and increasing strength of the followers of Pope Bogomil.

For the rest, life in Bulgaria under Peter seems to have passed without much incident. Trade probably returned

[1] The descent of the Albigeois heretics from the Bogomils is sometimes denied; e.g. H. Lea, in his *History of the Inquisition in the Middle Ages* (i., p. 90), dismisses the Bogomils in a footnote as a side-track. However, mediaeval writers (e.g. Reinerius Sacchoni and Moneta) trace the Albigeois from them, and certainly the Languedoc heretics looked to Bulgaria as the source of their faith. Some historians like to consider any traditional opinion as being therefore wrong; but any doubt on this question must vanish before a comparison of the Slavonic Bogomil literature with the Latin-Languedoc literature of the Cathars and Paterenes, as is given in Ivanov, op. cit.

with peace and flourished, and the mines were no doubt
worked.   That churches and palaces and monasteries
were built throughout the country is certain: though we
can assign no extant building confidently to these years.
Of the arts in detail we know nothing; nothing has survived.   Literature was extremely fashionable; the priest
Kozma complained bitterly that everyone wrote books
instead of reading them.   These books were mostly translations of Greek religious works or romances; but Kozma's
own writing shows the advance in Slavonic literature that
had been made in the last half-century.   Not only was it
the first original work of any length written in the Bulgarian vernacular, but it has a maturity of form and flexi-
bility of language far in advance of the writing of Symeon's
day, of Khrabr or John the Exarch.[1]   Moreover, the
Bogomils introduced a popular literature, telling legends
that sooner or later were written down.   These too were
mostly translations or adaptations from the Greek, some
even showing traces of Indian mythology, but others were
original compositions.   But, in spite of this activity, the
general standard of culture and comfort was low.   Even
at the Court it did not probably extend far beyond the
furniture and trappings that the Greek Tsaritsa would
bring with her on her journeys from her home.   When,
after her death, her daughters visited Constantinople,
they travelled not in the litters that would convey any
lady of quality in the Empire, but in chariots whose wheels
were armed with sharp scythes.   The Bulgarian ambassador at Constantinople in 968 was even less civilized; he
shaved his head like a Hungarian and wore a brass belt,
apparently to keep his trousers up, and was quite unwashed.   Bishop Liudprand of Cremona, ambassador of
Otto I, was furious at such a creature having precedence

[1] Kozma probably wrote after Peter's death (see above, p. 191), but I treat
of him here, as he considered himself a disciple of the Preslav school of
Symeon's day.

over him—and yet the North Italians themselves were
none too clean in the tenth century.[1] But probably this
ambassador was a member of the war-party—a *boyar* who
would despise the decadent cleanlier habits of the Court.

Thus for close on four decades Bulgaria lay in this weary
parody of peace. At last, in 965, the Tsaritsa Maria-Irene,
eponymous leader of the peace party, died. Years had
brought Peter no greater strength of character, and almost at once, deprived of his wife's pacific influence, he
fell under the control of warlike *boyars*, who counselled
him to show a brave, aggressive front against Constantinople. Things had changed in Constantinople. The
Emperor Romanus Lecapenus, Symeon's adversary, had
fallen long since, and had died a repentant monk; Constantine, the Porphyrogennetus, restored to his rightful
place, was dead now too; even his son, the second Romanus, grandson of old Lecapenus, had died. The Imperial crown was now worn officially by two little boys,
the sons of Romanus II—the younger an indolent child
called Constantine, the elder called Basil, who would
later bear a surname dreadful to Bulgarian ears. Their
mother, the lovely Empress Theophano, warned by the
fate of Zoe Carbopsina, had maintained herself in power
by a second marriage; her husband had been the Imperial
Commander-in-Chief, Nicephorus Phocas, grandson of
the first Nicephorus Phocas and nephew of the victim of
the Achelous. Nicephorus, from his prowess and from
this marriage, was now firmly seated with his stepsons on
the Imperial throne, co-Emperor and Regent of the Empire.
    It would have been wise not to provoke the warrior-
Emperor who had conquered Crete from the Infidel and

---

[1] Liudprand, *Legatio*, pp. 185–6. Ibrahim ibn Yakub describes the
Bulgarian ambassador at Otto I's Court in 965 as wearing a similar
costume. See above, p. 186.

was conquering in the east. But the Bulgarians hoped that Nicephorus would be too fully occupied in his schemes against the Saracens not to yield to the demands of Bulgaria, should she show a warlike spirit. And so, when Nicephorus revisited Constantinople for the winter of 965-6, fresh from his capture of Tarsus, he was accosted by an embassy from the Tsar, sent to receive the 'customary tribute.' [1]

This tribute was the old income that the Empire had agreed to pay, by the peace of 927, during the lifetime of the Tsaritsa. Peter's demand for it after her death was an act of unwarrantable aggression; and to call what was practically a dowry paid in instalments tribute was an intolerable insult. The ambassadors' reception was short and painful. Nicephorus was furious; rhetorically he asked his father, the Caesar Bardas, what could they mean by demanding tribute from the Roman Emperor. He then turned on the ambassadors and poured abuse on them, calling their race one of filthy beggars, and their Tsar, not an emperor, but a prince clad in skins. [2] His refusal was categorical; the unhappy Bulgarians, amid blows from the humbler courtiers, were dismissed from the Presence.

It was an audience almost unparalleled in the history of Imperial etiquette, similar only to Alexander's reception of Symeon's envoys in 913. But Peter was not Symeon; nor was Nicephorus Alexander. His rage was real, not the product of drunken bravado, and he did not confine himself to words. At once he moved with a large army to the frontier, and even captured a few of the Bulgarian forts that still guarded the Great Fence; but he had no wish to go campaigning in Bulgaria, that difficult country

[1] I give my reasons for my disentanglement of Nicephorus's wars with Bulgaria in Appendix XII.

[2] Leo Diaconus, p. 62.

where so many Imperial lords and soldiers had been slain
—he still had work to do in the east. He thought of an
easier way to deal with Bulgaria, a method dictated by
the traditions of Byzantine diplomacy. The Russians
were a vigorous race and lay beyond Bulgaria. They
could do his work for him. But for the moment there
was no work to be done. Peter was terrified by the result
of his bellicose gesture. Hastily he sent to make peace,
withdrawing, we may presume, his demand for 'tribute,'
and handing over his two sons, Boris and Romanus,
as hostages to the Emperor—an act that was not as
humiliating as it might seem; the young men were simply
going, as Symeon had gone, to finish their schooling at
Constantinople, the one place where they would receive
an education worthy of civilized princes. That they were
there in the Emperor's power could be regarded as a side-
issue.

The episode gave Nicephorus food for reflection. For
close on forty years the Empire had ignored Bulgaria; but
Bulgaria had not lost her warlike temper. It was only
weariness that kept her tranquil; if she were allowed time
to recover, the age of Symeon might come back again.
Nicephorus proceeded with his negotiations with the
Russians.[1]

The Imperial ambassador sent to the Russian Court
was the Patrician Calocyras, son of the chief magistrate
of Cherson, the Imperial colony in the Crimea, the starting
point of most of the missions into the Steppes. Calocyras,
who had lived most of his life in his native district, was
admirably fitted to deal with the savage neighbouring
tribes, knowing their languages and their habits well.
Moreover, he took with him a sum of money enormous

---

[1] Zlatarski's suggestion that Nicephorus called the Russians into Bulgaria
to keep them from attacking Cherson is, I think, unnecessary. Cherson
could be defended easily still by calling in the Petchenegs.

even in those days of the wholesale bribery of nations—
1,500 lb. of gold. The Russian monarch, the heathen
Varangian Prince Svyatoslav, fell an easy prey to the
ambassador's bribes and blandishments. He was a
young man, only recently released from the tutelage
of his stern Christian mother, the Grand Princess Olga;
already he had waged wars successfully against his neighbours on the Steppes, and he was ambitious and eager to
show his prowess further afield. By the summer of 967
the Russians were ready to descend upon Bulgaria.

In June 967 the Emperor Nicephorus marched to the
frontier to inspect its defences—a useful precaution when
war was to be let loose beyond it. At the same time, he
wished to salve his conscience for calling in heathen barbarians against a Christian country with which he was
at peace. So from the frontier he wrote to the Tsar ac-
cusing him of having so often allowed the Magyars to
cross the Danube and penetrate to the Empire. Peter
had no answer. He would gladly have prevented the
Magyars from raiding in his country, but he had not been
strong enough; but naturally, when they did invade, he
encouraged them to pass on as quickly as possible into
the provinces of some other ruler. His reply was inevitably unsatisfactory; and so Nicephorus could consider
himself justified.[1] Confident that the Russians would do
his work thoroughly, he turned his attention again to the
east.

In August Svyatoslav crossed the Danube with Calocyras to guide him and sixteen thousand men. The Bulgarians had been warned, and sent twice that number to
oppose his landing on the southern bank; but they were
badly defeated and fled to the fortress of Dristra. Svyatoslav

---

[1] Zonaras, iii., p. 512–13, says that Nicephorus was actuated by a Magyar
invasion. Cedrenus (Scylitzes), however (ii., p. 372), on whom Zonaras
based his chronicle, implies that it was a general pretext. The invasion in
Zonaras is clearly due to his misinterpretation of the passage in Scylitzes.

overran the north of the country, capturing twenty-four towns, and established himself for the winter in that very district of Onglus where Asperuch the Bulgar had lived, holding his Court in Preslav-on-the-Danube, Little Preslav, the fortress that commanded the river delta. Thither the Emperor sent him additional subsidies[1] ; and next spring he invaded southward again, devastating the land even more fiercely than before.

The Bulgarians were in despair. The Tsar Peter's health was affected by the disasters; he had an apoplectic fit from which he never properly recovered. His Government, however, kept its head sufficiently to apply the only possible remedy; it called in the Petchenegs. The Petchenegs were only too glad to intervene; the Russian power was rivalling their own, and already their prestige was diminishing compared to the better ordered hordes of the Varangians. Moreover, Svyatoslav had violated their territory in marching to the Danube; for they still roamed over the Wallachian plain and the Steppes on the Black Sea coast. They banded themselves together in the summer of 968 and marched in full force against Kiev. The Grand Princess Olga defended the city as best she could, but her forces were outnumbered and famine intervened. The news at last reached Svyatoslav, and reluctantly he saw that he must return. He arrived back in time to save his capital: while his people reproached him for adventuring in foreign lands and neglecting his own. But, though Bulgaria thus won a respite, his heart was set on going there again.

The ailing Tsar took a second precaution. That same summer he swallowed his pride and humbly sent an ambassador to Constantinople—the unwashed Patrician whose precedence so vexed Liudprand of Cremona.

---

[1] This is clearly what is meant by 'Nestor's' assertion that the 'Greeks paid him tribute there.'

Nicephorus received him non-committally; he was as yet undecided in his policy. But as the year wore on alarming news came from Russia. The Patrician Calocyras had succeeded only too well in winning Svyatoslav's confidence; he now was planning to use it against his Emperor. Continually he urged the Russians to invade the Balkans again, hoping either to be carried on Russian arms to the Imperial throne itself, or more probably so to divert the Emperor that he could return to his native Cherson and establish himself there independently. Svyatoslav fell eagerly in with his plans. The south tempted him; he wished to hold his Court for ever at Preslav-on-the-Danube; for there, he said, was the centre of his lands; there all the riches came, from Greece, silver, stuffs and fruits, and varied wines, from Bohemia and from Hungary, silver and horses, from Russia, skins and wax and honey and human slaves.[1] It was indeed a fine site for a capital, so near the mouth of the great river and commanding the gate to the rich Balkan world. It was all that his mother Olga could do to restrain him, to keep him with her at Kiev till she died; for already she was very ill.[2]

Nicephorus learnt from his spies that the situation was really serious; he himself thought that war with Russia was unavoidable. He hastily sent to fortify the Imperial possessions in the Crimea,[3] and at the same time instructed the Patrician Nicephorus Eroticus, and Philotheus, Bishop of Euchaïta, to proceed to the Bulgarian Court and propose an alliance. The Bulgarians received them delightedly; the need for Imperial help, they said, was very urgent indeed. Everything was arranged for a common defence of the peninsula. At Nicephorus's suggestion the

---

[1] *Chronique dite de Nestor*, pp. 53–4. [2] Ibid., loc. cit.

[3] It is this fact that makes me believe that Cherson was at first Calocyras's objective.

204 THE FIRST BULGARIAN EMPIRE

alliance was to be further cemented by a marriage between two little Bulgar Princesses[1] and the two young purple-born Emperors. This clause was enthusiastically accepted; and the two princesses set out in scythe-wheeled chariots to Constantinople, to be trained in their future high duties. But these marriages never took place; and we only hear of them once again. Early on the December night on which the Empress Theophano had her husband Nicephorus murdered, she came to talk to him about the upbringing of these foreign girls, and left him to make some arrangement for them.[2]   After that nothing is known of them. They soon lost their political importance; probably they were given as brides each to some respectable gentleman of Constantinople.[3]

In the midst of these arrangements the Tsar Peter died, on January 30, 969.[4] He had reigned nearly forty-two years, a good man, but a bad king. His task had been almost impossible; he had inherited a weary kingdom, and he had not been strong enough to hold it together. If he kept the peace he aroused the irritation of his *boyars*; but his show of warlike temper at the end was even more disastrous. And all the while he had to face the passive but increasing hostility of the peasant heretics. His had not been a happy life; even in his youth he was a disillusioned man, murmuring to Saint John of Rila that, however great your longing for riches and for glory may be, they will not

---

[1] It is uncertain who these Princesses were. They can hardly have been the children of Peter and Maria, as is generally said, for they were married forty-one years previously, whereas the Princesses were clearly quite young. They were probably the children either of Boris II (though one gathers that Boris was hardly old enough), or of some elder but now dead son of Peter's.

[2] Leo Diaconus, p. 86.

[3] Such was the fate of the Princesses of Samuel's family (see below, p. 257).

[4] The date (Jan. 30) is supplied by the Office of Tsar Peter (see Ivanov, *Bulgarski Starini*, p. 83). For the year, see Zlatarski, *Istoriya*, i., 2, p. 589. As he shows, 969 must be correct, though I disagree with some of his other dates.

bring you peace.[1]   And Peter had not even lived glori-
ously.   Death alone was kind to him, for it spared him the
woes that were coming to his country.

On Peter's death the Emperor sent his sons back to
their homes from Constantinople; and the elder, Boris,
ascended the throne.   Boris was probably in his middle
twenties.   In character and ability he was alike mediocre;
the only thing about him that was really remarkable was
his thick red beard.[2]   His accession brought with it no
new policy.   Indeed, under the circumstances, there was
nothing to be done, save to put the country into some
state of defence, and then await the inevitable onrush of
the Russians.

The storm broke in the early autumn of that year (969).[3]
The great Princess Olga died during the summer, and
Svyatoslav now had nothing to retain him at Kiev.   He
set off at once with an army of Russians and Petchenegs
and Magyar subjects or mercenaries for his new capital of
Preslav-on-the-Danube, and from there marched into the
heart of Bulgaria.   Whatever defences Boris may have
organized, they fell utterly to pieces before the Russian
hordes.[4]   They swept down through the northern provinces, on to Great Preslav itself; after a sharp battle the
capital fell into their hands, and in it they took prisoner
the Tsar, his brother Romanus, and all his family.[5]   From
Preslav they moved to Philippopolis, the greatest town of
the south.   Philippopolis, it seems, made a brave but

---

[1] Zhivot Jovana Rilskog, p. 279.   [2] Leo Diaconus, p. 136.

[3] For the dating see Appendix X.

[4] 'Nestor' says that the Russian army was only 10,000 strong (p. 56);
the later Greeks, however, considered it thirty times as large (300,000;
Zonaras, iii., p. 524: 308,000; Cedrenus, ii., p. 384).   'Nestor's' number
probably represents the pure Russians; but there were the additional Petcheneg, Magyar, and, later, Bulgarian auxiliaries.   Probably Leo Diaconus's
estimate (p. 109) of 30,000 is fairly correct.

[5] Cedrenus, ii., p. 383: *Chronique dite de Nestor*, p. 55.   Here I think Pereia-
slavets is Great Preslav, not, as before, Preslav-on-the-Danube.

feckless show of resistance; Svyatoslav in revenge impaled twenty thousand of its inhabitants.[1] By the fall of winter the Russians had overrun and held firmly the whole of Eastern Bulgaria, as far as the Thracian frontier of the Empire. There they paused to winter, Calocyras still with them and urging them on. His ambitions were boundless now; the Russians should carry him in triumph to Constantinople, and there, as Emperor, he would reward them with his province of Bulgaria.[2]

There was great alarm in Constantinople; and it was not allayed by a grand tragedy in the Palace. On December 10, 969, the Emperor Nicephorus was murdered by the order of his wife Theophano and her lover, his best general, John Tzimisces. In the retribution that followed the Empress was deserted and dispatched into exile; and John, doubly traitorous, became Emperor.[3] John was an excellent soldier and an able statesman, younger and less scrupulous than his predecessor. The Empire had no reason to regret his elevation. But for Bulgaria it was less felicitous.

John at first attempted to negotiate with Svyatoslav. He sent to him offering to complete the subsidies promised by Nicephorus—their payment had presumably been stopped when Nicephorus allied himself with Bulgaria; and he requested him to evacuate what was, he said, a rightful possession of the Empire. Those words must have fallen strangely on the ears of the Bulgarian captives at the Great Prince's Court. But Svyatoslav's reply was to order John to cross into Asia; he would only consider a peace that gave him all the European lands of the Emperor, and if he were not given them he would come and take them. Despite this ferocity, John sent a second message, sterner but still conciliatory, probably to gain more

---

[1] Leo Diaconus, p. 105.   [2] Cedrenus, loc. cit.

[3] Leo Diaconus, pp. 84 ff.

time.   Again Svyatoslav issued an insulting message to the Imperial ambassadors.   So both sides settled down to war.[1]

It was a war that was miserable for Bulgaria.   The Bulgarians, weary and disunited, had at last met the fate for which diplomats at Constantinople so long had plotted; they had succumbed to barbarians from the Steppes.   And now they had to watch the barbarians and the Imperial armies fighting over their lands, knowing that, whichever might be victorious, neither would give them back their independence.   They were a melancholy sight—the Tsar a captive in his palace, his soldiers taken off to swell the ranks of the Russians, while the merchants and the farmers watched the ruined tracks of war and the heretic peasants sulked in passive indolence.   Only in the west, where the Russians never penetrated, was there still some active national life and feeling: which would bear fruit later.

In the summer of 970 the Russians advanced into Thrace.   The Emperor sent his brother-in-law, Bardas Sclerus, out to meet them.   After preliminary skirmishes there was a great battle at Arcadiopolis, the Lule-Burgas of to-day.   It was a long-drawn-out contest, full of heroic hand-to-hand combats; but in the end the Russians were beaten, and swept back, with their numbers sadly reduced, to Bulgaria.   But the Imperial army did not follow up its advantage.   Probably the year was too well advanced; and John Tzimisces wished to make fuller preparations before adventuring an army into the Balkan mountains.[2]

---

[1] Leo Diaconus, pp. 105 ff., after giving a rough and inaccurate history of the early Bulgars: *Chronique dite de Nestor*, pp. 55 ff., giving it all in a light flattering to Russian pride: Cedrenus ii., pp. 383 ff.

[2] Ibid., pp. 108 ff.: Cedrenus, ii., pp. 384 ff.   The attempts of Russian historians (e.g. Drinov, *Yuzhnye Slavyane i Vizantiya*, p. 101) to prove that this was really a Russian victory are a scandalous piece of misguided patriotism, as Schlumberger (*L'Epopée Byzantine*, i., pp. 57–9) has shown: though, of course, the figures given by Greek chroniclers of the casualties have been exaggerated owing to similar patriotism.

But the delay was made longer than the Emperor had hoped.   Throughout the autumn of 970 and the winter he assembled troops and prepared his fleet; but in the early spring of 971 news came to Constantinople of the serious revolt at Amassa of Bardas Phocas, the late Emperor's nephew.   John's armies had to march to Asia instead of to the north.   Thus the season was lost, and the Russians remained, keeping their heavy yoke upon Bulgaria.   As the year moved on they recovered some of their confidence, and in the autumn conducted some raids round Adrianople.   Their task was made the easier by the gross incompetence of the local Imperial governor, the Emperor's cousin, John Curcuas, a man abnormally fond of eating and drinking.[1]

By the new year of 972 the rebel Bardas Phocas was defeated, and the ships and the soldiers were almost ready for the Bulgarian campaign.   When spring came the Emperor set out from Constantinople, blessed by the holiest of the city's relics, at the head of a huge, well-trained, and richly furnished army.   Meanwhile his fleet of fire-shooting galleys sailed to the Danube, to cut off the Russians' retreat.   Russian spies in the guise of ambassadors waited on the Emperor at Rhaedestus, but he let them go free.   He marched on through Adrianople, and in the last days of Lent crossed the frontier and began to wind his way through the Pass of Veregava and the other defiles of the Balkan mountains on the road to Preslav. By a strange good fortune the Russians had left these passes unguarded.   Whether, as John himself suggested, they had not expected the Emperor to go campaigning in Holy Week, or whether, as is more likely, the Bulgarian population was restive and the Russians had not enough

---

[1] Leo Diaconus, p. 126.   This John was probably the grandson of Romanus I's general, John Curcuas, John Tzimisces's great-uncle : his father was called Romanus.

troops to spare, they certainly neglected the one satisfactory opportunity of checking John's advance.

On Wednesday, April 3, the Emperor arrived before Great Preslav. The city was defended by Svyatoslav's third-in-command, Svengel, a Varangian of immense stature and bravery,[1] and by the traitor Calocyras. Svyatoslav himself was at Dristra, on the Danube, probably trying to keep open communications with Russia in the teeth of the Imperial fleet. The Russians at once gave battle, but after a terrible and long-undecided conflict they were severely defeated and fell back behind the city walls. Next morning, on Holy Thursday, reinforcements reached the Emperor, including his latest machines for shooting fire. Thereupon he gave the order for assault of the city to begin.

During the night Calocyras, who had noticed the Imperial insignia among the attacking force, and who knew what his fate would be were he captured and recognized, slipped out of the city and fled to Svyatoslav's camp at Dristra. Svengel, however, defended the walls as best he could; but the Russians, weakened by the previous day's battle, could not man the huge enceinte properly against the outnumbering assailants, and they were no match for the Greek Fire. After a few hours' desperate fighting they retired, as many as could, into the inner city, the fortress-palace of the Tsars.

The Emperor's troops burst into the outer city and overran it, slaying what Russians they met. Many, too, of the Bulgarian inhabitants perished, guilty or suspected of having helped the heathen barbarians. In the midst of the butchery they came upon Tsar Boris and his wife and two children, for over two years the prisoners of the Russians.

---

[1] 'Σφέγκελος.' Drinov (op. cit., p. 104) identifies him with 'Nestor's' Svienald, a Varangian chief who had served under Igor and who was mentioned in the peace of 972, but, according to Leo Diaconus, he was killed before Dristra.

PE

This miserable family was brought before the Emperor. John deigned to receive them graciously, saluting Boris as Prince[1] of the Bulgars, and saying he was come to avenge the injuries inflicted on Bulgaria by the Russians. But, though he released Bulgarian prisoners, his actions put a curious interpretation on his words.

Meanwhile, his soldiers besieged the Palace, a vast, well-fortified group of buildings forming, like the Great Palace at Constantinople, a town within the city. The Russians resisted with some success till the Emperor brought fire to his aid. Flames swept over the palace buildings, burning the Russian warriors or forcing them out to the open, to their deaths. Svengel, with a small bodyguard, fled through the Imperial army to Dristra. Thus by the evening all Preslav was in the Emperor's hands.

Good Friday morning broke on a mass of smouldering ruins and streets choked with corpses. It was the end of Great Preslav, the city that so few years before had been the largest and wealthiest of all the cities of Eastern Europe, save only Constantinople. The Emperor John spent the Easter week-end there, restoring order and refreshing his army, and sending a curt embassy to Svyatoslav at Dristra, to bid him either lay down his arms and beg for pardon, or meet the Imperial armies and be slain. A few days later he set out in full force for Dristra. Before he left, he rebuilt the fortifications of Preslav and rechristened it after his own name, Ioannupolis. Henceforward it should be a minor provincial city of the Empire, distinguished only for the vastness of its ruins.

Svyatoslav at Dristra heard of his troops' disaster in a wild fury. There were large numbers of Bulgarian hostages or unwilling auxiliaries at his camp, and on them he

---

[1] 'Κοίρανον,' not 'βασιλέα' in Leo Diaconus (p. 136). However, Leo speaks of him as 'βασιλεύς,' and Cedrenus says that John called him 'βασιλέα' (ii., p. 396).

gave rein to his rage. Suspecting treachery from their
compatriots, knowing that even Imperial rule was better
in their eyes than his, and, determining to terrorize them
into alliance, he threw the Bulgarians in his power into
chains, and beheaded all the magnates and the *boyars*, to
the number of three hundred.[1] Later, as the Emperor
approached, he released the humbler Bulgarians and en-
rolled them in his armies; but he ordered his Petcheneg
allies to mow them down without mercy should they
attempt treachery or flight.

From Preslav John marched to Pliska, the ancient
capital, and thence, by way of a town called Dinea, to
Dristra. He arrived before the city on Saint George's
Day; and at once the two armies met in battle on the
plain outside the walls. It was another hard, heroic contest, but by nightfall the Russians were driven back with
heavy losses behind their fortifications. John could not,
however, proceed at once with the siege; his fleet had not
yet arrived to cut the Russians off on the river side. He
spent April 24 in fortifying his camp on a hillock close
by, but on the 25th impatiently ordered an assault. This
attack failed, as also a rival sortie of the Russians; but in
the evening the Emperor saw his great fleet come sailing
up the Danube. On the 26th, after a third great battle,
the siege of Dristra began. John had hoped to take the
city by storm, but almost at once he realized its impossi-
bility. Restraining his army's ardour, he waited, closely
guarding every access to the city.

The weeks passed by, full of stirring episodes. The
Russians made many murderous sorties, but they never
could break right through the besiegers' circles; nor could
their arrows keep the Greek Fire from burning their ships.

[1] The number is supplied by Scylitzes (Cedrenus, ii., p. 400), who,
however, has an unfailing habit of exaggerating numbers. He also says that
the Bulgarian prisoners in Dristra numbered 20,000.

The Bulgarians recognized that it was only a question of time now. Many of their northern cities, including Constantia (Kostanza) sent deputations to the Emperor's camp, handing over their keys to him and offering him help. Nevertheless, while John sat before Dristra, fortune almost upset his whole career; the restless and vindictive family of the Phocae once more rose in rebellion, in Constantinople itself; and only the energy of the eunuch Basil the Paracoemomenus, son of Romanus Lecapenus and a Bulgarian woman, saved John his throne.

As July wore on, the Russians grew desperate. They had lost many of their finest heroes, including Svengel, the defender of Preslav, and their food was running short. Finally, on July 21, Svyatoslav held a council with his generals, at which, after long discussions, they decided, at the Great Prince's exhortation, to make one last attempt to fight their way to freedom. On the 24th[1] they burst out of the city with all the force and courage of despair. So furious was their attack that the Imperial forces almost gave way before them; and for a moment their fate hung in the balance.

In Constantinople everyone waited eagerly for news from the Danube. On the night of the 23rd a pious nun had a dream; she saw the Mother of God herself, protectress of the city, summon Saint Theodore Stratilates, the soldier, and bid him go to the aid of their beloved servant John. At Dristra during the battle men noticed a noble warrior on a white horse dealing destruction amongst the pagan hordes. When, afterwards, the Emperor sought him out to thank him, he could not be found. Saint Theodore may have saved the Empire. The battle

[1] Leo Diaconus (p. 152) dates it *Friday*, July 24; but in 972 July 24 was a Wednesday. In Cedrenus (ii., p. 405) the day before Svyatoslav's council of war is dated July 20; the attack would therefore fall on July 22. I follow Leo's monatal dating, as he is usually the more reliable, but, considering that he is self-contradictory, the whole thing remains unsatisfactory.

certainly was full of strange incidents; John even offered to
settle it in single combat with Svyatoslav. But the Imperial victory was in the main due to John's adoption of
the old Parthian tactics of a feigned retreat. By nightfall the Russians were routed, this time beyond all hope
of a recovery.

On the morning of the 23rd, Svyatoslav bowed to fate
and sent envoys to the Emperor. He only asked now to
be allowed to cross the river without an attack from the
terrible fire-shooting ships, and to be given a little food
for the starving remnant of his men.[1] In return he promised to hand over all the prisoners that he had made, to
evacuate Dristra and all Bulgaria for ever, and never to
invade Cherson. He also begged that the previous commercial treaties and arrangements about the Russians in
Constantinople should be renewed. John Tzimisces,
almost equally weary of fighting, accepted his terms; and
so the war was ended. Bulgaria had no voice in the
treaty.

Before the Varangian prince retired to his northern
country, he asked for an interview with the Emperor.
The monarchs met on the edge of the great river. John
rode down clad in his golden armour, with a splendid
retinue; Svyatoslav came in a little boat, rowing with the
other rowers, distinguished from them only in that his
plain white robe was slightly cleaner than theirs; and he
wore one golden earring, set with two pearls and a car-
buncle, and from his shaven head fell two long locks,
signifying his rank. For the rest, he was of medium
height, very well built, with fair hair, blue eyes, an
aquiline nose, and long moustaches—a true Norseman.
Their conversation was very short, but the two mortal
enemies were enabled to see one another—the Swede that

[1] Leo Diaconus (p. 156) says that 22,000 Russians remained, 38,000
having perished in the war. These numbers might well be true.

ruled over Russia meeting the Armenian Emperor of the Romans, after this long contest for the land of the Bulgarians.[1]

And so Svyatoslav returned sadly towards Kiev, sailing in his little ships down the Danube and along the coast to the mouth of the Dnieper. Then he began his laborious journey up the river through the territory of the Petchenegs. Winter overtook him there, and cold and hunger added to his humiliations. Meanwhile the Petchenegs, forgetting the troops that they had sent to help him, and rejoicing in his downfall, waited hungrily by; they could not believe that he was bringing back no treasure from the war. The old Imperial ambassador, Philotheus of Euchaïta, was at the Court of Kouria, chief prince of the Petchenegs, making a separate peace in which they promised never to cross the Danube. But when he asked them in the Emperor's name to be merciful and let the Russians through, they angrily refused. In the early spring Svyatoslav moved on up the Dnieper. At the great Cataracts the Petchenegs lay in ambush, and as he came they fell on him and slew him. Of his skull they made a drinking-cup, even as Krum had done with the skull of an Emperor.[2]

John's return home was very different. He rested in Dristra, rechristening it Theodorupolis, after the saint that fought by his side; then he journeyed southward in glory, the royal family of Bulgaria following in his train. All

---

[1] The main source for the campaign is Leo Diaconus (pp. 105–159), whose account is very full and who himself was alive at the time. Scylitzes's account (Cedrenus, ii., pp. 392–413) is less detailed, but provides one or two additional facts. Zonaras merely recapitulates him (iii., pp. 523–32). *La Chronique dite de Nestor* (pp. 53–59) is crude and over-patriotic, but brings out facts such as Olga's restraining influence. There is an excellent modern critical account of the war in Schlumberger's *Epopée Byzantine*, vol. i. chapters i.–iii.

[2] *La Chronique dite de Nestor*, pp. 59–60, saying that the Greeks provoked the attack. Cedrenus ii., p. 412, shows that the opposite was the case. Philotheus of Euchaïta is called here Theophilus of Euchaïta.

Eastern Bulgaria lay in his power, from Preslav-on-the Danube and the new Theodorupolis, to Philippopolis and the Great Fence frontier to the sea. Soon, he hoped, he might confirm his rightful power over the turbulent poorer provinces of the west. In the meantime he celebrated his triumph in Constantinople. A long and splendid procession wound from the Golden Gate down the Triumphal Way to Saint Sophia. After rows of warriors and captives, there came a golden chariot in which was borne the most precious of all the spoils, the icon of the Virgin of Bulgaria. Whence this icon came we do not know, but the Emperor revered it exceedingly and draped it in the Imperial mantle of the Tsars. Behind it rode the Emperor John on his white horse; and after him, on foot, there came the Tsar of the Bulgarians. At the cathedral John laid the icon and the crown-jewels of Bulgaria on the altar of God's Wisdom; the crown itself was a thing of marvellous richness and beauty. The Court then moved to the palace, and there, before all the dignitaries of the Empire, Boris of Bulgaria abdicated his throne. [1]

Vengeance had fallen on the seed of Krum and of Symeon. The Empire in the end had conquered. The Emperor treated the fallen monarch kindly; he was given the title of Magister, and took his place amongst the Imperial nobility. His brother Romanus was made a eunuch. [2] The abdication of the Tsar had released the Empire from its legal obligations; the Emperor could declare Bulgaria to be forfeited to himself. At the same time he abolished the independence of the Bulgarian Church. A quiet end was given to the patriarchate of Preslav, whither the see had been moved after the death of

---

[1] Leo Diaconus, pp. 158–9: Cedrenus, ii., pp. 412–13.

[2] Ibid., loc. cit. When Romanus was captured and when he was castrated are alike unknown. He appears as a eunuch a few years later (Cedrenus, ii., p. 435), having been castrated by the Paracoemomenus Joseph. Boris's two children were probably daughters, as we hear no more of them.

Damian of Dristra.[1] Bulgaria, like any other province of the Empire, should depend on the Oecumenical Patriarch of Constantinople.

In Eastern Bulgaria, by the old capitals of the Balkan invaders, men were too war-worn to protest. But Bulgarians still lived on the slopes of Vitosh and of Rila, and in the valleys and lakesides of Albania and Upper Macedonia. There the Russians had never come spreading desolation, nor the Emperor in all his might to combat them, and to reap the harvest that they had sown with blood. There the Bulgarians were proud and unconquered, scorning the decrees that were issued on the Bosphorus. The house of Krum had faded in ignominy; but, even as the afternoon was passing into night and the shadows had gathered, the sky was lit up in the west with golden and with red.

[1] See above, p. 182, and references given there.

CHAPTER III

THE END OF AN EMPIRE

IN the west of Bulgaria, at the time of the Russian invasions, there lived a count or provincial governor called Nicholas. By his wife Rhipsimé he had four sons, whom he named David, Moses, Aaron, and Samuel; to the world they were collectively known as the Comitopuli, the Count's children.[1] Of what province Nicholas was governor we do not know, nor when he died. By the time of the abdication of Tsar Boris, his sons had succeeded to his influence; and to them the Western Bulgarians looked to preserve their independence.

Of the history of this revolution we know nothing. The Emperor John Tzimisces was apparently unconcerned by troubles in Bulgaria after his victory at Dristra. His attention was mainly turned to his eastern frontier. We only hear that, following the old Imperial policy, he established large numbers of Armenians, Paulician heretics, round Philippopolis and on the borders of Thrace.[2] This would dilute and weaken the Slavs; but it weakened them chiefly in the one way which as a pious Emperor he might regret—it increased the vigour of the Dualist heresy. To the provinces further to the west he paid no attention. It

---

[1] In Drinov (op. cit., p. 88) and Jireček (*Geschichte*, pp. 173, 186, 189), and other works, we hear of a certain Shishman who was the father of the Comitopuli. His existence is deduced solely from a list of the Tsars of Bulgaria interpolated probably as late as the eighteenth century, in the Register of Zographus (see Zlatarski, op. cit., pp. 638–9). The Charter of Pincius (see Farlati's *Illyricum Sacrum*, iii., pp. 111–12), calling the Tsar 'Stephen' in 974, is equally suspicious (Zlatarski, loc. cit.). The names Nicholas and Rhipsimé are given in a deed of Samuel's (op. cit., p. 637), and in Bishop Michael of Devol's MS. of Scylitzes (Prokič, *Die Zusätze in der Handschrift des Iohan. Scylitzes*, p. 28.)

[2] Cedrenus, ii., p. 382.

was only after his death, in January 976, that statesmen at Constantinople fully realized the fact that, not only were there large numbers of Bulgarians quite unconquered, but they were restively and aggressively airing their independence. [1]

Already they had looked around for foreign support. At Easter time in 973 the old Western Emperor, Otto I, was at Quedlinburg, receiving embassies from many varied nations; and among them were envoys from the Bulgarians. But Otto was dying, and his son had other cares. Nothing came of this mission. [2]

Meanwhile, at home, Samuel, the youngest of the Comitopuli, was establishing himself in sole supremacy. How the brothers organized the independent kingdom is uncertain; possibly they each took over a quarter of the country and ruled it as some form of a confederacy, with David, the eldest, as their head. [3] Fortune, however, favoured Samuel. David was soon killed by Vlach brigands at a spot called the Fair Oak Wood, between Castoria and Prespa, in the extreme south of the kingdom. Moses set out to besiege the Imperial town of Serrae (Seres), probably in 976, on the news of the death of the terrible Emperor John; there a stray stone cast by the defenders ended his life. [4]   Aaron had a gentler temperament

---

[1] Cedrenus, ii., p. 434, says that the Comitopuli revolted on John Tzimisces's death; but we know that they were independent in 973 (see below). Probably the West Bulgarian question lay dormant, till on John's death the Bulgarians became actively aggressive. Drinov's theory (loc. cit.) of an independent Western Bulgaria that seceded in 963 depends on the existence of the mythical Shishman and on a paragraph in Cedrenus, ii., p. 347, which has clearly been interpolated out of place. Drinov has, however, been copied by Jireček and Schlumberger and the *Cambridge Mediaeval History.*

[2] *Annales Hildesheimenses*, p. 62.   An embassy from Constantinople arrived at the same time.

[3] Zlatarski (op. cit., p. 640) definitely divides up the country between them. I think that rather too confident.

[4] Cedrenus, ii., p. 435. He mentions Aaron's death at the same time as David's and Moses's, though actually it occurred later. The legend of

than his brothers, it seems, for it was his pacifism that was to prove his ruin in the end. At the moment he was content to play second fiddle to Samuel, who probably by the year 980, if not before, was enjoying the title of Tsar.[1]

From the Peace of Dristra till his death in 976 the Emperor John had ignored the west, though probably he intended to deal with it later, when an occasion should arise. On his death the young Basil II, already for thirteen years a nominal Emperor, succeeded to the full authority. But for four years Basil's hands were tied by the great rebellion of Bardas Sclerus in Asia. Even till 985 his position was insecure; he himself was gay and careless, while all his ministers and generals plotted against him.

These years gave Samuel his opportunity. Already in 976 the Comitopuli had been aggressive enough to attack Seres; and, though that attack failed, under cover of such action they were able to establish themselves over all of Peter's former Empire west of a line drawn south from the Danube considerably to the eastward of Sofia; though Philippopolis lay to the east of it. At the same time Samuel sought to add prestige and spiritual force to his dominion by refusing to acquiesce in the extinction of the independent patriarchate. The old seats, Dristra and Preslav, were no longer available; but, it seems, a Patriarch, called Gabriel or Germanus, was established first in Sofia, and later moved to Vodena, and thence to Moglena and to Prespa; on his death his successor, Philip, had his

---

David's retirement, as the sainted Tsar David, into a monastery, given in Païssius (*Istoriya Slaveno-bolgarskaya*, pp. 33, 63, 66, 70), and in Zhepharo-vitch's *Stemmatigraphion* (eighteenth-century works, though compiled from older sources), is obviously of no historical value. See Zlatarski (op. cit., pp. 646–7).

[1] For Aaron's career see below, pp. 230-1. With regard to Samuel, I think that he already called himself Tsar by the time of Boris's and Romanus's escape (see below, pp. 220-1); but Constantinople never recognized the title.

seat at Ochrida.[1]   These peregrinations probably coin-
cided with the movements of Samuel's Court, which, after
visiting Sofia and Vodena, settled for about the last fifteen
years of the century at Prespa, and soon after 1000 moved
to Ochrida, the holy city of Clement and of Nahum, the
real centre of Western Bulgarian civilization.[2]   The
presence of a patriarchate under his close control must
have greatly strengthened Samuel's hands, especially as
Samuel, unlike Peter, could not be suspected of leanings
towards the Greeks.   But Samuel also seems to have dealt
tactfully with the Bogomils.   We have no direct evidence;
but throughout his career he seems never to have come
into collision with the people.   Probably the aristocracy
of his realm was more Slav than Bulgar, and therefore
there was less cause for friction than there had been in
Peter's reign, round the old Bulgar capitals.   Possibly,
too, the Bogomil heresy never penetrated far into Macedonia, where Clement had established the orthodox faith
on more popular foundations.

Samuel's consolidation was very nearly wrecked by an
embarrassing escapade on the part of the sons of Peter.   Soon
after the Emperor John's death the ex-Tsar Boris and his
brother Romanus escaped from Constantinople and set
out for Samuel's court at Vodena.   It would have been
difficult for Samuel to know how to receive his former
sovereign; and Boris probably did not realize that he was
seeking refuge with a rebel.   However, fate intervened.

[1] In Ducange's List of Bulgarian Archbishops (op. cit., p. 175), Gabriel-
Germanus, the first after 972, resided at Vodena, then Prespa.   In Basil II's
ordinances about the Bulgarian Church, quoted in Gelzer (in *Byzantinische
Zeitschrift*, ii., pp. 44–5), Sofia (Sardica, Triaditza, or Sreditza), Vodena,
Moglena, and Prespa appear as having been seats of the patriarchate.
Gabriel's successor, Philip, is placed in Ducange's list (loc. cit.) at Ochrida.

[2] Zlatarski (op. cit., p. 640) makes Sofia Aaron's capital; but I do not think
that the land was divided up so definitely.   I think that the capital
moved with the patriarchate.   By 986 (the capture of Larissa), Samuel's
capital was Prespa (see below, p. 222; also Presbyter Diocleae, p. 294).
By 1002 it was Ochrida (see Zlatarski, *Istoriya*, i., 2, pp. 702-3).

As the brothers reached a wood on the frontier, a Bulgarian outpost took them to be Imperial spies; and Boris was shot dead by a Bulgarian arrow. Romanus managed to save his life, hastily explaining who he was. At first the soldiers received him with enthusiasm as their Tsar. But their zeal died down when they learnt that he was a eunuch, and they took him to Samuel. It has always been a cardinal principle that no eunuch can sit upon a throne, so Romanus by himself presented no difficulty. Samuel took him into his service and gave him various honourable positions.[1]

Secure in his own dominions, Samuel soon indulged in further aggressions abroad. All along the frontier, in Thrace and Macedonia and on the Adriatic coast, there were ceaseless and destructive Bulgarian raids. But from the year 980 onwards he concentrated particularly on the Greek peninsula, directing his main attention against the city of Larissa in Thessaly. Every spring, before the harvest was reaped, he led his army down into the fertile plain and sat before the city. But Larissa was defended by a wily soldier. In 980 a certain Cecaumenus, of Armenian origin, was appointed Strategus of Hellas—the theme in which Larissa was included. Each year, as Samuel approached, Cecaumenus hastily made his submission to him: until such time as the season's harvest was gathered and the city amply provisioned; then Larissa

---

[1] Cedrenus, ii., p. 435, who tells of the brothers' escape and of Boris's death, and announces that he will tell more of Romanus later, which he does on p. 455. Yachya of Antioch (translated in Rosen, *Imperator Vasilii Bolgaroboïtsa*, pp. 20–1) amplifies the story by saying that Romanus was proclaimed Tsar, and proceeds as though it was Romanus who conducted the war against Basil. But Yachya apparently did not realize that Romanus was a eunuch, which would prevent him occupying the throne. Zlatarski (op. cit., pp. 650–60) assumes from Yachya that Romanus was Tsar with 'Comitopulus' working for him; but it was unheard of that a eunuch should reign; moreover, Yachya, writing at a distance, clearly mistook Romanus for Samuel most of the time, especially with regard to his death (p. 58), which is an utter muddle. I think that Uspenski is right, in his review of Rosen's book, not to take Yachya too seriously.

reannounced its allegiance to the Emperor, who highly approved of this manœuvre. Samuel, who could not, or did not wish to, attempt to storm the city, thus found it, on its revolt from him, in a fit state to stand a protracted siege. And so for three years he was foiled in his ambitions against it. But in 983 Cecaumenus was recalled, and the new strategus was unwise and honest in his loyalty. When next Samuel invaded Thessaly he found the country openly hostile; so he destroyed all the crops. After three seasons of such treatment, in 986 Thessaly was more or less in a state of famine; and when that summer he began a close blockade on Larissa, the city was soon face to face with starvation. To such straits were the inhabitants reduced that a woman was found eating the thigh of her late husband: whereupon the authorities decided to surrender. Samuel treated the population with severity, selling them all as slaves, with the exception of the family of Niculitzes, one of the local gentry. For some reason Niculitzes, who was a connection of Cecaumenus, was spared, and showed his gratitude by taking service under Samuel.[1] Amongst the captives was a little girl called Irene, whose beauty was later to raise her to a fatal eminence. Along with the population, Samuel transferred the city's holiest relics, the bones of its bishop, Saint Achilleus, to decorate and sanctify his new capital at Prespa.[2]

The capture of Larissa scandalized Constantinople. Already there had been growing anxiety there about the Bulgarian menace. In 985, when a great comet trailed across the sky, the poet John Geometrus wrote an ode

---

[1] *Cecaumeni, Strategicon*, ed. Vassilievsky and Jernstedt, pp. 65–6, written by the Strategus's grandson. The date is fixed by evidence provided by an anonymous writer in the same MS., whose grandfather, Niculitzes, probably the father of the turncoat of Larissa (ibid. p. 96), was Strategus of Hellas in 980. See preface (ibid., pp. 4, 7) and the excellent account in Schlumberger, op. cit., pp. 622 ff.

[2] Cedrenus, ii., p. 436.

entitled with grim punning ' To The Comitopulus,' in which he presaged woe and called for his great hero, the Emperor Nicephorus Phocas, to rise from the dead and save his Empire.¹ But, though Nicephorus was gone for ever, the Emperor Basil was ready to act as his step-father's substitute. In 985 he had disgraced the great Paracoemomenus Basil, on the suspicion of some vast plot, the secret of which has never been unravelled.² The strain of the experience utterly changed the young Emperor's character. He was now aged twenty-seven. Hitherto Basil had been gay and dissipated and idle; henceforward he threw all that aside, and schooled himself into a state of relentless asceticism, unrivalled in Byzantium save among the holiest saints. He hardened his body to welcome discomfort and his mind to distrust culture. Henceforward his energy was unflagging; he thought nothing of campaigning at seasons when armies usually reposed in winter quarters; he was unmoved by horrors or by pity. He became a terrible figure, chaste and severe, eating and sleeping sparsely, clad in un-relieved dark garments, never even wearing the purple cloak nor the diadem on his head. He concentrated on one thing only, the establishment and consolidation of his own personal power, as Emperor, for the harmony of the Empire.³ Tsar Samuel, a Bulgarian rebel in the Emperor's eyes,⁴ might well fear such an adversary, for all his own boldness and ruthlessness. But as yet the

¹ Joannes Geometrus, *Carmina*, p. 920.

² This episode is admirably told in Schlumberger, op. cit., pp. 573 ff.

³ Psellus, *Chronographia*, pp. 16–19—a portrait and character sketch of Basil II.

⁴ Cecaumenus, in his correspondence with the central Government, talks of the 'Rebel Samuel' (*Strategicon*, p. 65). According to Matthew of Edessa (p. 34), Basil ordered the Bulgarian rebels to submit in 986. Asoghic (pp. 124–5) traces the war to a story of the Bulgarian king asking for an Imperial wife and having a substitute foisted off on to him. This must be a complete legend.

change brought no result. The Emperor was young and untried.

Moreover, his first trial of strength against Bulgaria was disastrous. In the summer of 986, as soon as possible after the news from Larissa had reached him, he set out with a large army into the heart of the Balkans, along the old Roman road past Philippopolis. His objective was Sofia, the capture of which would prevent the Bulgarians from expanding into their old eastern provinces. The Emperor's approach brought Samuel hurrying back from Thessaly, and, with Aaron and the eunuch-prince Romanus, he marched up to defend the city. The Imperial troops successfully passed up the River Maritsa, and through the Gate of Trajan (the Pass of Kapulu Derbend) into the plain in which Sofia lies; there they encamped at a village called Stoponium, just beyond the pass, some forty miles from Sofia, to wait for the rear-guard to come up. Meanwhile Samuel had time to occupy the mountains near the city. At last, at the end of July, Basil moved on again and reached the walls of Sofia. But his attempted siege was marked with ill success. Owing to mismanagement or lethargy—it was the height of summer—or mere treachery, his soldiers conducted themselves half-heartedly: while a surprise Bulgarian attack on his foraging parties made the whole army short of provisions. After only twenty days Basil gave the order to retreat. Already discouraged and depressed, he had heard disquieting rumours. He had left the Magister Leo Melissenus to guard the passes through which he came. The Domestic Contostephanus now spread a report that Melissenus, of whom he was desperately jealous, was engaged in deserting his post and betraying the Emperor. Melissenus had played a somewhat equivocal part in Syria shortly before ; and so the Emperor's suspicions were easily roused against him. Basil would not risk his throne by remaining in the depths of Bulgaria.

The first day of the retreat passed quietly enough; but the Imperial army, encamping that night in a wood, was reduced almost to panic by a rumour that the Bulgarians were in possession of the passes and by the passage of a brilliant meteor across the sky. Next day, Tuesday, August 17, as it entered the defiles, Samuel suddenly swooped down from the mountains. The carnage was tremendous, and all the Imperial baggage was captured. The author, Leo Diaconus, was only saved by the agility of his horse. It was with a pathetically small remnant of his army that the Emperor Basil reached Philippopolis. On his way he discovered that Melissenus had remained at the passes with perfect loyalty, and that the perfidious conspirator was Contostephanus. Humiliated and angry, Basil reached Constantinople, vowing that some day he would be avenged. Giving voice to the disappointment of the Empire, John Geometrus wrote another ode, entitled ' To the Woe of the Romans in the Bulgarian Defile.' [1]

Of the next years we know little. Samuel apparently followed up his victory by overrunning Eastern Bulgaria, capturing the old capitals, Preslav and Pliska, and establishing his power as far as the Black Sea coast. [2] Soon afterwards he turned his attention to the west, against the great Imperial city of Dyrrhachium. How, or exactly

---

[1] Joannes Geometrus, *Carmina*, p. 934. Leo Diaconus took part himself in the campaign, of which he gives a vivid account (pp. 171-3), though he does not mention the treachery of Contostephanus. That is told by Scylitzes (Cedrenus, ii., pp. 436-8). Leo's failure to mention it does not, I think, render the story suspect. Basil would certainly try to keep it at the time from his soldiers. Moreover, Leo mentions that there was a rumour that the passes were in Bulgarian hands. Asoghic mentions the campaign, but with fictitious details.

[2] Basil had to recapture them in his 1001 campaign (see below, p. 235). They were probably occupied now; indeed, Basil's attack on Sofia seems to imply that Samuel was known to be contemplating an eastern campaign.

Q E

when, it fell into his hands we do not know; probably it was before the year 989. The government of the city was given to the Tsar's father-in-law, John Chryselius.[1] The capture of Dyrrhachium gave Bulgaria an outlet on the Adriatic, and put the country in direct touch with the West. Samuel had, it seems, already received a confirmation of his Imperial title from the Pope—probably from some creature of Saxon Emperors such as Benedict VII, at the time of the Emperor Otto II's wars against the Eastern Empire in 981 or 982; certainly the Pope did not, or could not, insist that his recognition should be accompanied by a declaration of his spiritual suzerainty.[2] At present, however, Samuel could hope for little aid from the West. The ruler of the West was a Greek, the Empress-Mother Theophano, sister to the Eastern Emperor Basil.

Basil had been unable to prevent Samuel's expansion. From 986 to 989 he was distracted again by great rebellions in Asia, those of Bardas Phocas and Bardas Sclerus. The year 989 was the gloomiest of all at Constantinople. On April 7 the Aurora Borealis lit up the sky with terrible pillars of fire, presaging woe; and soon news came that the Russians had captured Cherson and the Bulgarians had captured Berrhoea.[3] The Russians soon gave up their conquest, tamed by conversion to Christianity and appeased by the gift of an Imperial bride to their Great Prince—Basil's own sister Anna was sacrificed in marriage to Vladimir, son of the savage Svyatoslav. But Basil could not so easily dispose of the Bulgarians.

Berrhoea, situated among the foothills of Macedonia,

[1] Yachya (p. 27) and Joannes Geometrus, *Carmina*, p. 955, both make allusions to Samuel's aggressions in the west about 988–9. Probably these refer especially to the capture of Dyrrhachium, which remained in Samuel's hands till 1005. (See below, p. 239.)

[2] Innocent III (*Ep.*, p. 1112) refers to Samuel as having been papally recognized as Emperor.

[3] Leo Diaconus, p. 175.

was one of the strongest fortresses that guarded the approach to Thessalonica; and it was soon clear that the great seaport was the object of Samuel's present ambitions. After Berrhoea, the Bulgarians, under Samuel's lieutenant, Demetrius Polemarchius, managed by a ruse to capture the fortress of Serbia (Selfidje) [1] ; and Bulgarian marauders began to occupy the countryside right down to the Aegean coast. Things became so serious that Basil was forced into fresh action. Already in 988 he had attempted to guard against Bulgarian encroachments by establishing colonies of Armenians on the Macedonian frontier; but they had proved ineffectual. By the end of 990, however, his troubles in Asia and with the Russians were settled, and he could plan more drastic steps.

Early next spring the Emperor set out for Thessalonica. At the end of February he passed through the Thracian village of Didymotichum, where the old rebel Bardas Sclerus was living now in retirement. Basil went to interview him, and invited him to come to the war; but Bardas refused, on the plea of old age and infirmity—with justification, for he died a few days later, on March 7. [2] Meanwhile Basil reached Thessalonica, where he paid his vows at the altar of Saint Demetrius, patron of the city and one of the most helpful of all the saints that watched over the Empire. He also won the support of a living local saint, called Photius, who prayed for him nightly throughout his campaigns. [3]

But of these campaigns we know nothing, save that for four years the Emperor remained in Macedonia, capturing many cities, razing some and garrisoning others, and

[1] Cecaumenus, *Strategicon*, pp. 28–9—undated, but this seems to be the most probable occasion. Demetrius caught the Imperial commanders bathing outside the walls.

[2] Yachya, p. 27.

[3] Encomium of Saint Photius of Thessalonica, quoted in Vasilievski, *Odin iz Grecheskikh Sbornikov*, p. 100–1.

eventually returned to Constantinople with a large amount
of prisoners and booty. Among the recaptured cities was
Berrhoea.[1] It is to be doubted that Basil spent all four
years in the field; probably he made frequent journeys to
his capital to superintend the government. We are told
of various Armenian warriors who took over the command
in the Emperor's absence. All seem to have fought bravely,
but in the end were worsted by the Bulgar. Foremost
amongst them were princes of the dispossessed house of
Taron, which for some time past had intermarried with
the aristocracy of the Empire. Samuel's movements during these years are very obscure. Probably he kept to
the mountains, following the old Bulgar practice of avoiding a pitched battle save when the enemy should be caught
in a difficult position, in some valley or defile. But Basil,
wilier now, never gave him the opportunity. This caution, however, kept Basil from completing his work. He
never risked advancing into the wild country that Samuel
made his headquarters[2]; and so, for all his booty and
captured fortresses, the Bulgarian menace was only very
slightly lessened when in 995 the Emperor was summoned
again on urgent business to the east.

Basil left behind him, as commander on the Thessalonican front, Gregory, Prince of Taron.[3] On the news
of the Emperor's departure, Samuel came down from the
mountains and advanced to Thessalonica. Deceived by
the meagre force with which Samuel demonstrated before the walls, Gregory sent his young son Ashot, with
too few troops, out to meet him. They were ambushed

---

[1] Yachya, pp. 27–8. Scylitzes (Cedrenus, ii., p. 447) merely says that
Basil visited Thessalonica, to see to its defences and pray to Saint Demetrius. Asoghic (ii., p. 145) refers to the recapture of Berrhoea and tells of
the Armenian soldiers.

[2] Ibn-al-Asir (Rosen, op. cit., p. 246) says that Basil reached the centre
of Bulgaria. This probably refers to his previous campaign against Sofia,
then known as Sredetz (the centre).

[3] Cedrenus, loc. cit.

by the main Bulgarian army and for the most part slain;
Ashot himself was taken alive. Gregory, hearing of it,
lost his head and rashly hurried out to rescue his son.
But he too fell into a Bulgarian trap, and was butchered
with almost all his army, fighting bravely.[1]

This disaster to the garrison was very serious, but Samuel
did not venture to attack Thessalonica itself. Instead,
after ravaging the countryside and recapturing Berrhoea,
he took his prisoners back to his capital. Basil was too
busy to come back to Europe himself; but he sent one of
his ablest generals to command against the Bulgarians,
Nicephorus Uranus, who arrived with reinforcements at
Thessalonica in the course of the year 996.[2]

Samuel was spending the season of 996 in the Greek
peninsula. He had held its gateway Larissa for ten years
now, and he was able to advance unopposed up the Vale
of Tempe and through Thermopylae and Boeotia and
Attica to the Isthmus of Corinth. There was a panic in
the Peloponnese; even the Strategus Apocaucus was
affected by it, and fell ill from worry and uncertainty as
to how he could organize a defence. It needed all the
tact and spiritual gifts of Saint Nicon Metanoitë to soothe
his shattered nerves. But, as everyone waited anxiously
for the attack, the news came that the Bulgarian army
was in full retreat for the north.[3]

Nicephorus Uranus had followed Samuel into the peninsula, and succeeded in recapturing the fortress of Larissa.
Leaving his heavier accoutrements there, he passed on
through Pharsalia and over the hills of Othrys to the
valley of the Spercheus. On the far bank of the river the

[1] Cedrenus, ii., p. 449.
[2] Ibid., loc. cit.: Berrhoea, retaken by Basil in 991, had to be again
retaken in 1003. Samuel must therefore have recaptured it now.
[3] Ibid., loc. cit.: *Nicon Metanoitë*, ed. Lampros, pp. 74–5. This incident
must occur now (not, as Schlumberger says, in 986)—the only occasion
when we know that Samuel advanced on the Isthmus of Corinth.

Bulgarians were encamped, laden with the spoils of Greece. The river was flooded from the summer thunder-showers; and Samuel thought himself secure. But by night the Imperial troops forced their way through the turgid torrent and fell upon his camp. The Bulgarians were slaughtered as they slept. Samuel and his son Gabriel-Radomir were wounded, and only just managed to escape with a few followers. Their losses were terrible; all their booty was recovered, and all their prisoners released. Uranus returned in triumph to Thessalonica, and later to celebrate in Constantinople the glory of having driven out the invaders from Greece. [1]

Yet, despite this victory, Basil could not venture on a final crushing campaign; he was still too heavily committed in Asia. And so the next few years remained probably the most splendid in Samuel's career. After the first shock of his defeat he had written to the Emperor offering to submit on terms; but soon he withdrew his offer, realizing that he was not at the moment to be attacked. According to a rumour current in Antioch, he was negotiating when he heard that the rightful Tsar (Romanus, son of Peter) had died in captivity at Constantinople. He at once broke off the negotiations and proclaimed himself Tsar. But Romanus, so far from being a Tsar imprisoned in Constantinople, was a eunuch in Samuel's own service, and lived on for many more years. Probably it is now that we must place the story told earlier by Scylitzes of Samuel's last surviving brother, Aaron. Aaron, more peaceful than Samuel, urged for terms to be made with the Empire, and probably succeeded in winning the support of a large proportion of the Bulgarians. His influence and his policy were alike distasteful to

---

[1] Cedrenus, loc. cit. Sathas, *Chronique de Galaxidi*, and Schlumberger (op. cit., ii., pp. 139 ff.) place here the story of the Bulgarian attack on the village of Galaxidi on the Gulf of Lepanto. See above, p. 174.

Samuel; and so he was taken and summarily put to death
with all his children, save one son only, John Vladislav,
who was saved by his cousin Gabriel-Radomir.   Thus
Samuel was left sole and undisputed Tsar; but the news
reached the eastern frontier of the Empire in a rather
vague form, which the local historians amended in their
own imaginative way.[1]   Samuel's ruthlessness cowed the
peace party; and so when he decided to break off relations again with the Emperor there was no opposition left.

The internal history of Samuel's reign is a blank to us.
We only know of his system of taxation, namely that every
man to possess a yoke of oxen was obliged to pay yearly
a measure of corn, a measure of millet, and a flagon of
wine.[2]   This was no doubt a very old Bulgarian system.
It seems that the people, Bogomils as well as orthodox,
made no complaint against his rule, either from indiffer-
ence or from terror.   His lieutenants, on the other hand,
used all too frequently to betray him.   This was probably
due to the greater prospects of material comfort and luxury
that the Empire could offer; for Samuel's Court in the
Macedonian mountains was lacking somewhat in refinement.   The Comitopuli do not seem to have extended
the same patronage over letters and culture as did the
monarchs of the house of Krum.   On the other hand,
Samuel was a great builder.   Not only did he throw great
fortifications round his strongholds; but from these years
date several churches, still standing in part to this day.
Near Prespa the Church of Saint Germanus, and the
church built on the island to hold the relics of Saint
Achilleus from Larissa, and in Ochrida—which became

[1] Yachya (in Rosen), p. 34: Cedrenus, ii., p. 435. I do not think that
Yachya deserves much credence with regard to Bulgarian affairs. Scylitzes's account is much more likely to be true. We know that Aaron was
living in 986 (from Michael's MS. of Scylitzes, Prokič, p. 29). This seems
to be the most likely occasion for his pro-Greek policy to have been a
menace, and also his death may well provide the origin of Yachya's story.

[2] Cedrenus, ii., p. 530. Basil continued this system.

his capital soon after the turn of the century—the Churches
of Saints Constantine and Helena and Saint Sophia show
his architectural zeal.   The devastations and improvements of subsequent generations make it hard now to
pronounce upon their style.   They appear to belong in
temper to the provincial Byzantine school, as opposed to
the Imperial school of Constantinople—a school in close
touch with Armenian architecture.   Possibly Samuel's
architects were Armenian captives from the colonies in
Macedonia; but more probably these churches represent
the first ambitious artistic efforts of the native Bulgarian-
Slavs.

Comforts might be crude, but there was romance too in
the Bulgarian Court.   The Tsar, by his wife Agatha Chry-
selia, had several children whose wild passions brought
love into Bulgarian history.   Samuel had brought Ashot,
the captive Prince of Taron, to his capital and kept him
there imprisoned.   But Miroslava, the Tsar's eldest daughter, caught sight of him and lost her heart.   Vowing to
kill herself unless she became his bride, she secured his
release.   After their marriage, Ashot was sent by his
father-in-law to help in the government of Dyrrhachium.
They betrayed the Tsar later.[1]

About the same time—probably in 998—Samuel,
checked for the moment in the south and the east, determined to expand to the north-west, along the Adriatic
coast; the possession of Dyrrhachium showed him the
value of being an Adriatic Power.   He was too cautious to
attempt, like his predecessors, to conquer the valleys of
inland Serbia; instead he kept to the coast, where an
excellent opportunity was given to him.   The principality
of Dioclea, modern Montenegro, was suffering from the
weak rule of a child, Vladimir.   Samuel invaded his
country, capturing the town of Dulcigno and the person

[1] Cedrenus, ii., p. 451: Prokič, p. 29.

of the young Prince without any effective opposition. Vladimir was sent into captivity at Prespa, and Samuel moved northward and made himself suzerain of Terbunia, the principality that lay next along the coast. In consequence of this Bulgarian aggrandizement, the Emperor Basil, who could not afford to maintain squadrons so far away, formally handed over the policing of the Adriatic to his loyal vassal-state of Venice.[1]

Again one of Samuel's daughters intervened. Like her sister, the Princess Kosara was stirred by the thought of a handsome young captive; and before long she fell in love with the Dioclean prince. Samuel listened to Kosara's prayers; Vladimir was released and restored to his throne, with Kosara as his consort. At the same time Vladimir's uncle, Dragomir, was established in Terbunia. Both the princes acknowledged the overlordship of the Bulgarians, and Vladimir at least abode loyally by his fealty.[2]

The fame of Samuel's prowess reached even to the Magyars; and their king, Saint Stephen of Hungary, sent to make an alliance with Bulgaria. Its terms were somewhat vague, but they were sealed by a marriage-alliance; Stephen sent his daughter to wed Samuel's son and heir, Gabriel-Radomir. But the Hungarian girl was not as lucky in love as were her sisters-in-law. There was at the court of Ochrida a slave called Irene, who had been captured as a child at the fall of Larissa, a creature of marvellous beauty. The Princess, probably all too well endowed with the looks of her father's race, the race that gave its name to ogres, could never hope to rival the radiant Greek captive. Gabriel-Radomir forgot his wife's high lineage, that her father was a king and her

---

[1] Presbyter Diocleae, pp. 294–5. Undated, but it probably was the cause of Basil's formal cession of the Adriatic to Venice (Dandolo, p. 227).

[2] Ibid., loc. cit.

mother a princess of the Imperial blood of the West, and
left her for the low-born Irene. Samuel, always sympa-
thetic to his children's passions, condoned the desertion
and recognized the marriage with Irene—the Hungarian
alliance was of very little value. Of the further fate of the
Princess, nothing is known. Deserted and divorced, in
this wild Court far from her home, she probably sought
refuge in a convent. One son was born of her marriage,
Peter Delean, who probably died young; many years
later, after the fall of his dynasty, he was impersonated by
an ambitious but unsuccessful rebel against the Emperor.[1]
But while these love-dramas were still incomplete, probably even before the Hungarian marriage, the Emperor
Basil returned to the field. In about 998 Samuel's cause
had seemed so flourishing that several of the European
nobility of the Empire contemplated deserting to his
allegiance. Basil was informed, and arrested two of them
at Thessalonica, the Magister Paul Bobus and the Protospatharius Malacenus, and deported them—the latter to
Asia, the former to Constantinople; whereupon some of
the intending traitors at Adrianople, Vatatzes and Basil
Glabas, fled at once to Samuel. Basil imprisoned Glabas's
son for three years, but could take no other action.[2] It is
probable that Nicephorus Uranus continued to lead yearly
expeditions against the Bulgarians, but we know nothing
of them. In the spring of 1001, however, Basil made
peace on his eastern frontier and was able to turn his full
attention to the west. For four years he campaigned
regularly in Samuel's dominions.[3]

The first of these campaigns, in 1001, was directed

---

[1] Cedrenus, ii., p. 529: Prokič, pp. 31, 36.

[2] Cedrenus, ii., pp. 451–2.

[3] In Cedrenus (ii., p. 452) the first campaign is dated 999; but we know
from Yachya (in Rosen, p. 42), who is very reliable about eastern affairs,
that Basil did not leave the east till 1001. Cedrenus must therefore be two
years out throughout these four years.

against Sofia. Making Philippopolis his starting-point—
he left it strongly garrisoned under the Patrician Theodorocanus—he marched through the Gates of Trajan, and
captured many castles round Sofia, though he did not
attack the city itself, before retiring to winter at Mosynopolis, the modern Gumuldjina, in south-western Thrace.
The reason of this campaign was to cut Samuel off from
his eastern provinces; and so next year Basil sent a large
army under Theodorocanus and the Protospatharius
Nicephorus Xiphias to conquer the districts between the
Lower Danube and the Black Sea, the old centre of
Bulgaria. He himself probably waited near to Sofia, to
intercept any help that Samuel might send. The
manœuvre was successful; the former capitals, Little Preslav, Pliska, and Great Preslav fell once more into the
Emperor's hands. [1]

In 1003 Basil struck in Macedonia. As his great arma-
ment approached Berrhoea, Dobromir, the Bulgarian
governor, took fright and surrendered without a struggle.
Basil always attempted to attach former Bulgarian
commanders to the Empire by giving them titles, and
sometimes posts in provinces far enough away for them
to be able to do no harm. Dobromir was honoured with
the dignity of Anthypatus and sent to Constantinople.
From Berrhoea the Emperor attacked Serbia. The town
was defended by Niculitzes, the traitor that Samuel had
spared at Larissa. Niculitzes made a valiant resistance,
but in the end the town was taken. Basil treated the
defenders leniently; despite Niculitzes's past history, he
was made a Patrician, and accompanied the Emperor
back to Constantinople, some time in the summer of
1003, when Basil thought it advisable, after his recent
successes, to pay a short visit to his capital.

But the fierce traitor could not be won by a title. After

[1] Cedrenus, loc. cit.

a few days he escaped and made his way back to Samuel. Samuel, in the orthodox Bulgarian fashion, had remained in the mountains during the Emperor's invasion, resolutely avoiding any pitched battle. On Basil's departure he came down with his army, and with Niculitzes, attempted to recover Serbia. But Basil was well informed, and moved swiftly. Forced marches brought him back to the borders of Thessaly; and Samuel and Niculitzes fled. The latter was soon captured in an ambush and sent to imprisonment in Constantinople. A few years later he escaped once more. The Emperor spent the next month or two in Thessaly, rebuilding the castles that the Bulgarians had destroyed and recapturing those that they still held. The Bulgarian garrisons were sent to colonize the district of Volerus, where the Maritsa flows into the Aegean Sea. From Thessaly Basil turned northward, to the great fortress of Vodena, placed on the edge of the high Macedonian plateau, by where the river of Ostrovo falls in grand cascades into the valley below. A Bulgarian called Draxan made a valiant defence, but in the end was forced to surrender, probably in the late autumn. The garrison was sent to fill up the colony at Volerus, but Draxan obtained permission to reside at Thessalonica. There he married the daughter of one of the chief clergy that attended to the shrine of Saint Demetrius. His subsequent history was strange. After two children had been born to his wife, he suddenly fled to the Bulgarian Court. He was soon recaptured and pardoned, on his father-in-law's intercession. But shortly afterwards he repeated his flight, with the same result. He then waited in Thessalonica until two more children were born: whereupon he fled once more. This time the Emperor's patience was exhausted. When he was recaptured, he was summarily impaled.

In 1004 Basil determined to complete the conquest of

Danubian Bulgaria, and very early in the year¹ set out to besiege Vidin, on the Danube, the easternmost fortress left to Samuel. Against these well-organized and carefully led expeditions Samuel could do nothing, but now he attempted a diversion that almost succeeded in forcing the Emperor to raise the siege. On August 15, when the citizens of Adrianople were on holiday, celebrating the Feast of the Assumption of the Virgin, the Bulgarians suddenly fell upon the city. Adrianople was utterly taken by surprise; no one had ever expected Samuel to advance so far from his centre. He massacred and destroyed without hindrance, and then retired as suddenly as he had come, with a long train of prisoners and booty. But this brilliant foray was too late; Vidin, after an eight months' siege, was on the point of falling. Basil waited until he could storm the city, probably early in September; then, garrisoning it strongly, he hastened southward to catch the Bulgarians on their return. His march, up the Timok and the Morava, through hostile, unconquered country, was as bold an achievement as Samuel's to Adrianople.

The Emperor caught up the Tsar and his army near Skopie (Uskub), on the banks of the Vardar. The river was in flood; and Samuel had not learnt his lesson sufficiently at the Spercheus. The two armies encamped on either bank, the Imperial troops with due precaution, the Bulgarians with an insolent carelessness, confident that the river could not be crossed. But a Greek soldier found a ford that was passable; and the Emperor crept over secretly at the head of his troops. The Bulgarians were too suddenly surprised to attempt to fight; they all hastily fled in confusion, Samuel amidst them. The Tsar's own

¹ Probably in January, as Vidin fell after an eight months' siege soon after the raid on Adrianople. Basil, as Psellus tells us, thought nothing of campaigning in the depths of winter.

tent was captured, and the camp, with all the booty from Adrianople, fell into the Emperor's hands.

After the battle, the Bulgarian governor of Skopie came down to hand over the keys of his city to the Emperor. It was Romanus, the eunuch son of Peter, last scion of the house of Krum.[1] Basil received him gently and created him a Patrician. He finished his strange career as governor of Abydos.

From Skopie Basil marched eastwards to attack the castle of Pernik, which commanded the upper valley of the Struma. But Pernik was impregnably placed and magnificently defended by the ablest of Samuel's generals, Krakra. Basil, after losing many of his men, and finding Krakra to be incorruptible, abandoned the siege and moved back, late in the winter of 1004, to his head-quarters at Philippopolis. Thence he soon returned to Constantinople.[2]

Thus in four years Samuel had lost half his Empire. From the Iron Gate of the Danube to Thessalonica all the east of the Balkan peninsula was in the Emperor's hands, except only for Sofia and Strumitsa and a few castles around Pernik and Melnik in the western slopes of Rhodope; and Imperial garrisons were stationed on the borders of Thessaly and along the River Vardar. The campaign had been among the most glorious in the history of Byzantine arms; it had shown that the Imperial troops, when they were ably led, were still the finest machine for warfare that the world at that day knew; it had shown that the Bulgarians, for all their courage and ardour, their ruses and their traps, were no match for them now. Samuel, like every great Bulgar general, had avoided pitched battles, trusting to his speed and to

[1] We hear now that he was also called Symeon, after his grandfather; but there is no reason to suspect him of being any other son of Peter than the eunuch Romanus.

[2] Cedrenus, ii., pp. 452–6, for the whole campaign.

ambushes and sudden descents; but now he had to face an
adversary that could make forced marches across the
wildest enemy country and yet never now be caught
unguarded in a valley or a mountain-pass—an adversary,
too that had rid himself of distractions, that had determined not to cease from fighting till Bulgaria should be
no more.

Even Samuel's own followers were beginning to see the
true state of things. In 998 Imperial magistrates had
broken their allegiance to pay homage to him, as the
rising sun; but now, with treacherous foresight, his own
officials were beginning to transfer their services to the
Emperor. Every desertion was a heavy blow to him; it
was on his governors and generals and the soldiers that
they commanded that his whole strength lay. The common people, it seems, were too poor or too indifferent or,
as Bogomils, too conscientiously passive, to help or to
hinder his cause.[1] Samuel, though as yet no foreign army
had reached the high lakes where he held his Court, might
well feel apprehensive of the future.

In 1005 the canker of treachery entered into the heart
of his family. His daughter Miroslava and her husband,
Ashot the Taronite, fled from Dyrrhachium, where he
held a command, to Constantinople. Ashot had long
yearned to return to his former home, and had persuaded
the Princess that a wife's duty ranked before a daughter's.
But Miroslava was not the only traitor in the family.
Ashot brought with him to the Emperor a letter from the
Tsar's own father-in-law, John Chryselius, who was left
in charge of the fortress. John offered to hand Dyrrhachium over to Imperial troops in return for money for
himself and the title of Patrician for both his sons. The

[1] The whole internal history of Samuel's reign is so unknown that even
such generalizations must be qualified. It seems, however, that Samuel
never became nor has become a popular national hero, as Symeon did:
though Symeon did infinitely more harm to his country.

offer was accepted; and the Patrician Eustathius Daph-
nomelas took a fleet to the Adriatic and received back the
city.   Ashot was made a Magister, and Miroslava a
Girdled Patrician, becoming thus one of the greatest ladies
at the Imperial Court.[1]

The loss of Dyrrhachium hit Samuel hard, both in his
affections and his power.   He had no outlet now to the
western sea, save through Dioclea, the territory of his
faithful son-in-law, Vladimir.

The story of the next nine years is lost in obscurity.
From 1006 onwards it seems that the Emperor Basil
yearly invaded Bulgaria[2]; and in 1009 there was a battle
at a village called Creta, probably somewhere near Thessalonica, where he heavily defeated Samuel.[3]   All through
these years the Imperial troops were pressing nearer and
nearer to the centre of the Tsar's dominions.   Only the
mountains of Upper Macedonia and Albania remained in
Samuel's hands, and the valley of the Upper Struma, where
Krakra held out.   It was probably from Krakra that
Samuel learnt that the Emperor journeyed each year on
his way to the war through the narrow pass of Cimbalongus, or Clidion, that led from Seres into the upper
valley of the Struma.   Samuel conceived the plan of occupying this pass, and thus either checking the Emperor on
his way or forcing him to make a détour that would leave

[1] Cedrenus, ii., p. 451. He tells of it out of its place, after talking of
Ashot's capture and marriage. The date, however, is supplied by Lupus
Protospatharius, writing at Bari, just across the sea (ad. ann. 1005, p. 41).
The Theodore whom he mentions as having carried out the transaction was
no doubt a son of the aged John Chryselius. It is uncertain who really
commanded Dyrrhachium. It seems unlikely that John was placed under
his foreign grandson-in-law, though Cedrenus implies so, merely calling
Chryselius one of the chief magistrates, though in Bishop Michael's MS. of
Scylitzes he is 'πρωτεύων.' Probably he was retired, as he must have been
old.

[2] Cedrenus, ii., p. 457, says Basil invaded the country yearly. Matthew of
Edessa (p. 37) talks of Basil inaugurating a long war against the Bulgars in
1006.

[3] Reported in the life of Saint Nicon Metanoeite (Vasilievski, op. cit.,
loc. cit.). See Zlatarski (op. cit., pp. 849–50).

the enemy strongly entrenched in his rear. In 1014 Samuel carried out his scheme, and took possession of the pass, fortifying its entrance with wooden palisades. Meanwhile he sent other troops, under Nestoritsa, to create a diversion near Thessalonica. But Nestoritsa was routed by the Imperial strategus, Theophylact Boteniates, who then was able to join the Emperor's army as it approached Cimbalongus.

At the sight of the strong Bulgarian palisades, Basil hesitated, and, after a few futile attacks, was in despair. But his lieutenant, the strategus of Philippopolis, the general Nicephorus Xiphias, suggested taking a detachment over the forest-covered mountainside and attacking Samuel in the rear; he thought that it was just feasible. Basil agreed, and Xiphias set out through the forest of Balathistes (the Sultanina Planina of to-day), and at last managed to arrive behind the Bulgarian army. On July 29 Basil made a grand onslaught on the palisades. At the same moment Xiphias fell unexpectedly on Samuel's rear. The Bulgarians were taken by surprise and caught. Many were slain, and many more were captured. Samuel himself was only saved by the endurance and the bravery of his son, and fled away to his fortress of Prilep. The captives numbered fourteen or fifteen thousand. Basil, whose clemency had come to an end, determined to teach the Tsar a bitter lesson. All the captives were deprived of their sight, save for one in every hundred, who had one eye left to him. Then, with these one-eyed men to guide them, they were set free to grope their way back to their master.[1]

Meanwhile Basil turned to the north, to clean up the districts of Western Rhodope, where Krakra valiantly

---

[1] Cedrenus, ii., pp. 457, 459. He numbers the prisoners at 15,000; Cecaumenus (*Strategicon*, p. 18) numbering the prisoners at 14,000. Michael Attaliates (p. 229) also refers to the battle.

RE

held out.   He advanced to Strumitsa, and captured the neighbouring castle of Matrucium.   Thence he sent Boteniates with some troops to burn the palisades that the Bulgarians had thrown across the road to Thessalonica.   Boteniates performed his task successfully, but on his return fell into a Bulgarian ambush, where he perished with all his men.   This victory heartened the Bulgarians, but it was of little avail.   The Emperor continued in the district—one of the many called Zagoria, 'across the mountains'—and even its strongest fortress, the impregnable castle of Melnik, surrendered itself to him.   After its capture he retired for a while to Mosynopolis; and there, on the 24th of October, joyful news reached the Imperial camp. [1]

The blind victims of Cimbalongus at last found their way back to the Tsar.   Samuel was at Prespa, ill with anxiety and fear.   The ghastly procession of his former grand army was too much for him.   He fell to the ground in an apoplectic fit.   A glass of cold water brought him to his senses for a moment, but he passed again into unconsciousness, and two days later, on October 6, 1014, he died. [2]

It was the end now.   The last red streak of sunset had shone on Bulgaria in the defiles of Cimbalongus.   Now it was twilight, and dim figures hurried to and fro to ward off the inevitable darkness.   Nine days after Samuel's death, his son Gabriel-Radomir, whom the Greeks called Gabriel-Romanus, was proclaimed Tsar; he had probably been away with the army at the time of his father's death, and it took him some time to reach the Court.   Gabriel-Radomir, for all his valour and his magnificent physique, had none of his father's greatness.   He could command

[1] Cedrenus, ii., p. 460.
[2] Ibid., ii., p. 458.   The date of the death is given in Bishop Michael's MS. (Prokič, p. 30).   Lupus Protospatharius refers to it (p. 41, ad ann. 1015).

none of the same awe and respect; and almost at once his throne began to totter.[1]

On the news of the great Tsar's death, Basil at once recommenced his campaign. Leaving Mosynopolis, he marched to the valley of the Cherna, as far as the great town of Bitolia (Monastir) where Gabriel-Radomir had a palace. The destruction of this palace was the only act of violence that the Emperor now committed. From Bitolia Basil turned back—to advance on higher in the depths of winter would be unwise—and he descended the Cherna, while his troops captured Prilep and Shchip (Ishtip, Stypeum). Thence he returned by way of Vodena to Thessalonica, where he arrived on January 9, 1015.

At the beginning of spring he set out again. Through treachery the Bulgarians had recovered Vodena; so Basil at once flung his whole army at it and terrorized it into submission. Again its garrison was transported to the colony at Volerus, while, to keep it securely in his hands, he built two castles to over-awe it, one called Cardia, the other Saint Elias. He then went back to Thessalonica. As he sojourned there, a Greek soldier called Chirotmetus (as he had lost one hand) came to the Emperor with a letter from the Tsar promising his submission. But Basil feared a ruse, and dismissed Chirotmetus without an answer. Instead he sent his army under Nicephorus Xiphias and Constantine Diogenes to besiege the city of Moglena, one of the strongest cities left to the Bulgarians in Macedonia. Moglena was under the command of the local governor, Elitzes, and the Kavkan Dometian, one of the Tsar's most intimate counsellors. So firmly was

[1] Cedrenus, ii., p. 458–9. He says that Gabriel-Radomir was proclaimed on Sept. 15, Ind. xiii., i.e. Sept. 15, 1015; but that must be a mistake for Oct. 15, Ind. xiii., i.e. Oct. 15, 1014. This date fits with Oct. 6 as the date of Samuel's death, and Oct. 24 as the date when Basil heard the news. Cedrenus is wrong here about the slave girl of Larissa. As Michael's MS. shows (see above, p. 234), she was Gabriel-Radomir's wife, not Samuel's.

the fortress defended that Basil himself had to come and
conduct operations. It was only when he had diverted
the river that surrounded the city and undermined its
walls that the garrison was driven to surrender. The
Emperor deported them far away, to the borders of
Armenia; the city was destroyed and burnt, and the
same fate befell the neighbouring castle of Enotia.[1]

Five days after the fall of Moglena, in August 1016,
Chirotmetus again appeared at the Emperor's camp, this
time with a more sensational story. The Tsar Gabriel-
Radomir had been murdered while out hunting at the village of Petrisk on the Lake of Ostrovo, by his cousin,
Prince John-Vladislav, Aaron's son, whose life he once
had saved[2]; and John-Vladislav was master of the remnant
of Bulgaria. With Gabriel-Radomir had perished his
wife, the lovely Irene of Larissa.[3] Chirotmetus brought
with him various servants of the new Tsar and letters
offering submission. Basil was at first half convinced, but
about the same time another *kavkan*, the brother of the
Kavkan Dometian, joined the Emperor, by whom he was
well received; and probably he explained the duplicity of
the letters. Basil at once set out for the enemy country,
and moved up into the Macedonian highlands, past
Ostrovo and Sosk, blinding every Bulgarian that he
captured.[4]

[1] Cedrenus, ii., pp. 461–2.

[2] Ibid., ii., pp. 459, 462. Petriscus is not Petrich in the Struma valley;
there is a fifteenth-century MS. at Rila in praise of Saint Demetrius which
gives a full account of the death, and makes it occur at Sosk (Zlatarski, op.
cit., pp. 850–2). No doubt the Tsar was residing at Sosk, but hunting in the
neighbourhood of the village of Petrisk on Lake Ostrovo, where the murder
occurred. Yachya (in Rosen, pp. 58–9) has a confused account where he
gives the protagonists their fathers' names. The date must be c. Aug.
1015, as Gabriel-Radomir reigned for less than a year.

[3] Ibid., p. 469.

[4] Ibid., ii., p. 462. Presbyter Diocleae, p. 295, referring to the
murder, says that it was due to Basil's intriguing. The account in Scylitzes
seems definitely to contradict this; the priest probably had heard of the
subsequent negotiations, though there was certainly a good deal of treachery
at the Bulgarian Court.

Gabriel-Radomir's death threw the country into further disorder. John-Vladislav was a usurper, probably little more than a party leader; and in the chaos every Bulgarian general began to consider his own interests. But John-Vladislav had a considerable ruthless energy. He retired to the north-west before the Emperor, into the Albanian mountains, to rally his forces. There he summoned Vladimir of Dioclea as his vassal to consult with him; he probably wished to secure a safe retreat there, and was angry that Vladimir's gentle nature inclined towards peace with the Emperor. The good prince wished to go, but his wife, Kosara, Samuel's daughter, distrusted her brother's murderer, and, fearing for her husband's life, determined to go in his stead. John-Vladislav received Kosara with such cordiality that at last, on a safe-conduct guaranteed by David, [1] the Bulgarian Patriarch, Vladimir set out to the Tsar's Court. When he arrived he was summarily beheaded, on May 22, 1016, and his body was denied burial, till it performed so many miracles that even his murderer was impressed. Kosara received permission to bury it at Kraina, by Lake Scutari; and she herself, broken-hearted, took the veil in a convent close by. [2] The murder removed the danger of treachery in the rear, but otherwise it did little save to add to the general disorder. The Bulgarians soon lost their hold over Dioclea.

Meanwhile the Emperor had penetrated far into the heart of the Macedonian mountains, into that mysterious land of high lakes and valleys where Samuel had held his Court. In the early autumn of 1015 he reached Ochrida, the capital. But barely had he occupied the city when he

[1] The Patriarch David, who features several times in Cedrenus (see below, *passim*), is not mentioned in Ducange's list, but he is almost certainly the same as John, who succeeded Philip (see above, p. 219). In Michael of Devol's MS. he is called John, both here and when he subsequently appears (Prokič, op. cit., pp. 32, 33, also his *Jovan Skilitsa*, p. 146).

[2] Cedrenus, ii., p. 463: Presbyter Diocleae, pp. 295–6, giving date May 22. The year must be 1016.

heard that John-Vladislav was attacking Dyrrhachium. At once Basil left a garrison in Ochrida and marched down to save the great seaport. But there worse news arrived. On his march to Ochrida he had left the Strategus George Gonitziates, and the Protospatharius Orestes, with a considerable army, to remain in the foothills guarding the road to the mountains. But George had been led into an ambush by the Bulgarian general, Ivatsa, a soldier of notorious brilliance, and had been butchered at the head of all his army. Basil was forced to leave Dyrrhachium to its fate—a fate which, however, was averted—and hurried across the mountains in pursuit of Ivatsa, to reopen the road. But Ivatsa avoided his path and retired to the south; he managed, however, to recover Ochrida for the Tsar, and to re-establish the Court there. The Emperor returned to Thessalonica and thence to Mosynopolis. There he divided his forces into two portions; one he sent under David Arianites to attack Strumitsa, the other under Xiphias against Sofia. Arianites succeeded in capturing a fort near Strumitsa called Thermitsa, and Xiphias various castles near Sofia, including Boyana. The Emperor himself went to Constantinople, where he arrived in January 1016.

Later in the year Basil returned to the field, and himself led an expedition against the Bulgarian districts of the Upper Struma. The centre of resistance was Pernik, where the brave and loyal Krakra—he was loyal to each Tsar in succession—still held out. Once again Basil attempted to storm the stronghold; and once again his attempts cost him so many men that he gave up the siege. As autumn came on he turned south, to winter and to refresh his men at Mosynopolis.

In the first fine days of 1017 the old Emperor took the field again. He sent David Arianites and Constantine Diogenes to raid on the Upper Vardar; he himself took the castle of Longus.[1] The Imperial armies captured vast numbers of men and herds of cattle and sheep—the chief wealth of the country. The prisoners were divided into three portions; one was shared by Imperial troops, one went to the Russian auxiliaries—the beginnings of the famous Varangian Guard—and the third to the Emperor himself. From Longus, Basil moved southward to besiege Castoria. But as he lay before its strong walls he received a letter from the Strategus of Dristra, to announce that John-Vladislav and his viceroy in Rhodope, Krakra, were attempting to negotiate with the Petchenegs, who roamed in strength beyond the Danube. Basil took no risks. At once he lifted the siege and hastened northward to be at hand should anything occur. As he passed by, he stormed and burnt the castle of Bosograd or Vishegrad,[2] and ordered the ruined walls of Berrhoea to be rebuilt, and then, coming up to Ostrovo and Moliscus,[3] destroyed every Bulgarian castle that he found still standing. When he arrived there he heard that the Tsar's alliance with the Petchenegs had failed; the Petchenegs would not risk arousing the enmity of the terrible old Emperor.

Basil returned southward again, and captured the town of Setaena (the present village of Setina on the Brod, on the edge of the valley of the Cherna). Samuel had had a palace there; and Basil found great stores of provisions. The palace was burnt and the food distributed to the troops. The Tsar and his army came hurrying to the neighbourhood, to see what might be done: whereupon Basil sent out to find him Constantine Diogenes and the troops of the European themes. But Constantine fell into a trap laid by John-Vladislav, and was on the point of perishing, when Basil, who somehow had heard of it and

[1] Its position is unknown—probably not far to the north of Castoria.
[2] Probably not far to the north of Castoria.
[3] Presumably near Ostrovo.

was anxious, suddenly rode up with a picked band of soldiers and joined in the battle. The Bulgarians, well-nigh victorious, were aghast: 'Fly, fly ! The Emperor !' [1] they cried, and all followed that advice. In the rout, many were left dead on the field; two hundred fully armed horsemen were captured, with all the baggage of the Tsar and his nephew.

After this victory Basil moved to Vodena and strength-ened its garrison; then, in January 1018, he returned to his capital. [2]

Every season the Emperor was more firmly established in Bulgaria; but John-Vladislav, in his restless energy, did not despair. No sooner had Basil left the field, than he came down from the mountains to attack with all his remaining strength the city of Dyrrhachium. It was his last effort. As he fought before the walls a warrior attacked him, in whom he suddenly thought that he recognized Vladimir of Dioclea, the saint that he had murdered. In a mad frenzy he cried for help, but none could reach him. And so the unknown warrior, were he a spectre, or some casual Greek, or even a Bulgarian traitor, struck the Tsar dead. [3]

His death meant the end of Bulgaria. His sons were young and inexperienced, and even the most fervent Bulgarian leaders began to see that further resistance was hopeless. The Emperor, on the news, set out from Con-stantinople. As he journeyed across the peninsula, various of his old opponents came to make their peace. At Adria-nople he met the son and the brother of Krakra, who brought him news of the great general's submission and the surrender of his impregnable fortress Pernik. Basil

---

[1] 'Βεξεῖτε, ὁ Τσαῖσαρ,' i.e. Begaite, Tsesar—fly, the Tsar.

[2] Cedrenus, ii., pp. 462–8. Who the nephew of the Tsar was, we do not know.

[3] Ibid., pp. 466–7: Presbyter Diocleae, p. 266, giving the miraculous intervention of Vladimir.

received them kindly and gave them high Imperial dignities; Krakra was created a Patrician. At Mosynopolis,
legates came from Bitolia, Morovizd, and Liplyan,[1]
handing over the keys of their towns. At Seres, Krakra
himself joined the Emperor, with the commanders of the
thirty-five castles that he had held; he was shortly followed
by Dragomuzh, the governor of Strumitsa. Dragomuzh
brought with him John the Chaldee, who had been captured by Samuel twenty-two years before, when the
Taronites were routed. The Emperor made Dragomuzh
a Patrician, and moved towards Strumitsa. As he approached the city a new embassy came up to him, headed
by David, the Patriarch of Bulgaria.

On John-Vladislav's death, his widow Maria took over
the government, and at the Patriarch's advice decided to
surrender, on a few conditions as to her family's safety.
Her eldest son Prusian and two of his brothers objected
to this policy, and left Ochrida for the mountains; but the
bulk of her Court agreed with her. David was now
bearing her letters to the Emperor. At the same time
a high official called Bogdan arrived; he was commander
of the 'inner castles,' and had favoured the Imperial cause
to the extent of slaying his warlike son-in-law. As a
reward he became a Patrician.

From Strumitsa Basil crossed to Skopie, where he
stationed David Arianites with a strong garrison. He
himself, in a triumphant progress, moved back to Shchip,
and thence to Prosek on the Vardar, and passed on southward and then westward, and so up to Ochrida. At the
city gates the Tsaritsa herself met the Emperor, bringing
with her all the royal family that was at the Court—three
of her sons and her six daughters, a bastard son of Samuel,

---

[1] Bitolia is called here Pelagonia, after the district of which it was chief
town. The other towns, 'Morobisdus' and 'Lipenius,' were situated close by
Bitolia.

and the two daughters of Gabriel-Radomir and his five
sons, one of whom had been blinded. Basil received them
kindly and accepted their submission. He found there
too the treasury of the Tsars, which he had not had time
to open during his former brief occupation. It was filled
with golden pieces, and garments sown with gold and
golden diadems set with pearls. The money, to the extent
of a hundred centenaria, he divided amongst his troops.
Then, leaving the city well garrisoned under Eustathius
Daphnomelus, he set out southward. More Bulgarians
joined his camp—Nestoritsa and the younger Dobromir,
with all their men. Even Prusian and his brothers, the
Tsaritsa's elder sons, came down from the wild slopes of
Mount Tomor, whither Basil had sent to pursue them,
and threw themselves on his mercy. Basil received them
at Prespa. Prusian he created Magister, the others
Patricians. It was now the middle of August.

At Prespa Basil received another distinguished, but less
willing supplicant. The general Ivatsa had been living in
proud independence in his castle on the Devol, surrounded
with fair gardens. For nearly two months the Emperor
had been negotiating with him, seeking his bloodless
submission; but Ivatsa had grandiose ambitions to be
Tsar and was only playing for time. In August Ivatsa, as
he had always done, invited his friends and relatives to
celebrate with him the Feast of the Assumption of the
Virgin. As the negotiations were still being carried on,
Eustathius Daphnomelus asked to be allowed to come too.
Ivatsa was surprised, but delighted, that an enemy should
place himself in his hands, and welcomed Eustathius with
outward cordiality. After the feast was over, Eustathius
demanded a private interview with Ivatsa. It was held in
a distant orchard, for secrecy's sake. There, when they
were alone, the Greek suddenly overpowered the Bulgarian, and gagged him and put out his eyes. Two

servants of Ivatsa heard his first smothered cries and summoned the company. The Bulgarians rushed up, enraged at this abuse of hospitality against their friend. But Eustathius waited for them calmly, and as they approached harangued them for their folly in opposing the Empire. His words and his confidence impressed them, and they realized their ultimate impotence against the mighty Emperor. Prudently they bowed to fate and accompanied Eustathius and the blind Ivatsa back to the Emperor at Prespa. As a reward Eustathius was made Strategus of Dyrrhachium and given all Ivatsa's possessions.

At the same time Niculitzes, the traitor of Larissa, who had been hiding in the mountains and now found himself deserted by his followers, wearily gave himself up one night into the Emperor's hands. Basil, however, would not see him, but sent him to a prison in Thessalonica.

From Prespa Basil made a détour, to arrange things in Dyrrhachium, Colonea, and Dryinopolis in Epirus, and then came to Castoria. There he found two daughters of Tsar Samuel, who were brought to his camp. When they saw there the Tsaritsa Maria, their rage knew no bounds. It was with difficulty that they were kept from doing her serious bodily harm. To relieve himself from further distressing scenes of this type, Basil sent the captive royal family to Constantinople. The Tsaritsa was appointed, as the Princess Kosara had been, a Girdled Patrician. The Emperor himself journeyed southward, his work over, to visit his province of Hellas. As he passed through Thessaly he saw the bones of the Bulgarians bleaching on the banks of the Spercheus, where Uranus had slain them in their thousands, and he marvelled at the great fortifications built after that battle to guard the narrows of Thermopylae; and then he came through Boeotia to the glorious city of Athens.[1]

[1] Cedrenus, ii., pp. 470–6.

Meanwhile Xiphias received the homage of the remaining free Bulgarians. He strengthened the garrisons of Serbia and Sosk, and as he waited at Stagi in Thessaly, the last of the unconquered generals, Elemagus of Berat (Belograd) made his submission. Bulgarian independence was dead, save only in the distant north, where Sermon, governor of Sirmium, established himself for a few months longer as an independent prince, even striking his own coins. But in 1019 Constantine Diogenes extinguished this last flicker [1]; and even the princes of Serbia and Croatia hastened to announce their vassaldom. [2]

The Emperor Basil saw his life-work finished. All his reign, for more than forty years, he had striven to destroy the Empire of the Bulgarians. At last it was done, and he would be famous throughout the coming ages as Bulgaroctonus, the Bulgar-Slayer. Here in Athens, in the Church of the Mother of God, he rendered up his thanks to his Creator—in the church known, in an earlier Virgin's honour, as the Parthenon. [3]

[1] Cedrenus, ii., p. 477. For Sermon's coins see Schlumberger (op. cit., p. 417).

[2] Ibid., p. 476: Lucius, p. 297.　　　　　[3] Cedrenus, loc. cit.

EPILOGUE

EPILOGUE

THE Bulgarian Empire was ended. Worn out by its weakness within and by the everlasting, ever-reviving strength of Imperial Rome, it had finally succumbed; and for nearly 170 years Bulgaria would be numbered among the Imperial provinces. Of its history during those years we know little, nor does it concern us here. The Emperor Basil, with the wise moderation that characterized the great statesmen of Byzantium, who preferred when they could to respect local customs and institutions, made few changes that would affect the common Bulgarian people. The country was divided into two themes, Bulgaria and Paristrium. The former contained the bulk of Samuel's empire, the latter the Danubian province and the older capitals; probably the former frontier fortresses, such as Philippopolis, had already been included in existing Imperial themes. The governor of the Bulgarian theme enjoyed the title of Pronoëtes and was apparently one of the governors who found their salaries out of the local taxes. Basil, however, ordained that Samuel's system of taxation—payment in kind—should be maintained; and, though later governors were to provoke revolt by attempting to alter the system, it actually endured throughout the period of Imperial rule. With regard to the Church, Bulgaria was granted by Basil concessions unknown in any other of his provinces. The whole ecclesiastical organization was revised, and the patriarchate abolished. But the Archbishop of Bulgaria, installed at Ochrida in the Patriarch's place, only owed a faint allegiance to the Patriarch of Constantinople; and the thirty Bulgarian bishops and the 685 ecclesiastics obeyed him alone. We do not know how far these thirty bishoprics instituted by Basil corresponded with the old bishoprics of the Bulgarian Empire; but their seats had all been Bulgarian towns in Samuel's heyday. Basil so far relied on the loyalty of the Bulgarian Church to the new Government that in several dioceses he increased its jurisdiction at the expense of the dioceses of former Imperial provinces, no doubt in districts chiefly inhabited by Slavs, who would appreciate the Slavonic liturgy. How far he proposed controlling the Church himself, or through the Patriarch of Constantinople, we do not know. He kept on the Bulgarian Patriarch David as Archbishop of Bulgaria; but on David's death the Imperial Government adopted the custom of appointing Greeks to the Archbishopric—save once when they appointed a converted Jew—thus keeping the whole fabric in close connection with Constantinople. Among the Archbishops thus appointed was Theophylact of Euboea, who occupied his time in that wild country in writing the lives of its martyrs and of its great saint, Clement. [1]

Bulgaria, on the whole, acquiesced in its annexation. The aristocracy, worn out by its resistance, was glad to sink into the luxurious service of the Empire. The merchant classes, such as they were, welcomed peace. Those of the peasantry that held political views were almost all of the Bogomil heresy, equally but passively opposed to all Governments. Twice during the next sixty years the misgovernment of Imperial officials was to provoke the Bulgarians into serious revolt; but both rebellions were soon put down; and, so long as the Government remained competent, Bulgaria was content to rest in peace: till, at the close of the twelfth century, the whole Empire fell into

[1] The ecclesiastical settlement is given in Basil's ordinances, published by Gelzer, in vol i., pp. 245 ff., and vol. ii., pp. 2 ff. of the *Byzantinische Zeitschrift*. The best complete account of the reorganization of Bulgaria under Basil is given in Schlumberger's *Epopée Byzantine*, vol. ii., pp. 418–32, where the meagre information is fully summarized and discussed.

chaos under the rule of the feeble house of Angelus, with Western Europe stabbing it in the back.

As for the actors of the final scenes, the princes and princesses of Bulgaria and the great generals, they were merged into the functionaries of Byzantium. They walked before the Emperor on his triumphal entry into Constantinople; then the men were given Imperial posts and titles and the women husbands from among the aristocracy. Of the fate of Tsar Samuel's few surviving descendants nothing is told; but many of John-Vladislav's family enjoyed a certain eminence. Of his sons, Prusian, the eldest, created a Magister on his surrender, became the strategus of the important Bucellarian theme, till he quarrelled with his colleagues so badly that he had to be exiled. Aaron, as Catepan of Vaspurakan, later played a prominent part in the Armenian campaigns of the Empire. Of Trajan, Radomir, and the youngest son of all we have no information; but Alusian, the second son, after being made a Patrician (on his surrender to Basil) and, later, strategus of the theme of Theodosiopolis, involved himself disgracefully in the Bulgarian rebellion of 1048—the rebellion kindled by an impostor who claimed to be Peter Delean, son of Tsar Gabriel-Radomir and the Princess of Hungary. Alusian first betrayed the Emperor for him, and then betrayed him to the Emperor. Of John-Vladislav's six daughters, one married Romanus Curcuas, who was involved in Prusian's quarrels and was blinded; another, the Princess Catherine, sat for a while on the Imperial throne itself, as the wife of the nervous Emperor, Isaac Comnenus. Of the next generation, Alusian's son, the Vestarch Samuel-Alusian, fought with distinction in the desperate Manzikert campaign of Romanus Diogenes, while his daughter was the first wife of that unhappy Emperor. Aaron's son, Theodore, became strategus of the theme of Taron in Armenia; while Trajan's daughter,

SE

Maria, married Andronicus Ducas. One of their daughters, Irene Ducaena, became the wife of the Emperor Alexius Comnenus and the ancestress of that great dynasty. And so, after long journeying, through the Angeli and the Hohenstaufen and the houses of Castile, of Hapsburg and of Bourbon, the blood of the last Tsar of the first Bulgarian Empire flows in the veins of the first Tsar of modern Bulgaria and his present successor.[1]

The First Bulgarian Empire was ended. Its end was not inevitable nor foredoomed—unless it be that everything is foredoomed. But history is so full of accidents improvised by a whimsical providence that it is idle to explore the roads of what might have been. Nevertheless, the First Bulgarian Empire was planned by fate in its grandest, most sweeping scale. There is the small beginning, the nomads entering the Balkan peninsula, and gradually, by the ability of the Khans of the House of Dulo, establishing themselves there with increasing strength: so that even the chaos and disasters that followed the dynasty's extinction could not remove them thence. Then we come to Kardam and the swift revival, and the greatness of Krum and his successors, when Bulgaria was numbered among the great Powers of Europe, and wooed and feared by the East and the West, and so to Boris, the Christian Prince, the greatest of them all, who outwitted

---

[1] The fate of John-Vladislav's descendants can be found in various passages of Cedrenus—ii., pp. 469, 483, 487, 497 (for Prusian), 469, 470, 531 (Alusian), 469, 573-4 (Aaron), 469—and Prokič—pp. 34 (Trajan and Radomir), 678 (Samuel-Alusian), 483 (the wife of Romanus Curcuas), 628, 650 (the Empress Catherine). Psellus, p. 63-4, calls Alusian brother, not son, of John-Vladislav, but we know that John had no surviving brothers. Bryennius (p. 19) calls Catherine Samuel's daughter, but dates make it unlikely, and Cedrenus provides circumstantial evidence. See also Prokič, p. 36. Bryennius also (pp. 106-7) tells of Trajan's daughter Maria's marriage, calling Trajan Samuel's son. But Prokič, p. 34, shows this to be wrong. Bryennius probably had only heard of Samuel, and not of John-Vladislav. Aaron's son, Theodore, is identified by evidence given in Skabalonovitch, *Vizantinskoe Gosudarstvo*, p. 198. Attaliates (p. 123) mentions Samuel-Alusian.

the Pope and used the Patriarch to secure his country
the Church that he desired. After Boris was Symeon
and the summit. For Symeon was the hero of a Greek
tragedy, too prosperous, too triumphant, too defiant of
Nemesis, wearing out Bulgaria with too many victories
and dying in disappointment. The curve swerves down-
ward, in the long afternoon of Peter's reign: while Pope
Bogomil gave form to the discontent of a disillusioned
people. The first shadows of evening were terrible amid
the Russian storms; but the sunset was lit with splendour
before the night came at last. But the tragedy is not perfect. Bulgaria did not bear within herself all the seeds of
her decline and fall. Bulgarian history must always be
read with Constantinople in sight. It was Byzantium,
the Empire, that decided its destiny. The Bulgars had
come into the Balkans at a time when the Empire was
weak, when the Roman world was still shaken by the first
sudden blows of Islam; and they had established themselves there before the Empire had recovered. But since
the middle of the eighth century the Empire had gradually
been growing in power though the growth had been veiled
by the development of Bulgaria and by periodical set-
backs, usually more spectacular than really disastrous.
It was at the climax of Symeon's career and of the whole
Bulgarian Empire, at Symeon's interview with Romanus
Lecapenus, that the truth was revealed. The Emperor,
for all his armies' defeats, was the victor. After that, the
end was as inevitable as anything in this world can be;
and, though much blood was shed before Bulgaria was
extinguished, the length of the struggle was due rather
to Samuel's genius and Imperial dissensions than to uncertainty as to the ultimate result.

Nor need Bulgaria stand ashamed. It is a tribute rather
to the greatness of her rulers that they could, as no other
invaders had been able to do, build up a nation at the

very gates of the mightiest empire of Christendom. Not only was Byzantium supreme amongst her neighbours in material wealth and organization, but, as the heir of Rome, she held unbroken the conception and prestige of the Universal Empire; and her civilization was the highest of its hemisphere. Sooner or later she would surely absorb the close inhabitants of the Balkan peninsula, for all that a line of brilliant Khans had knit together Slav and Bulgar and all the remnants of races that lingered there into a nation. At times, indeed, great monarchs, lured by the siren call of Constantinople, would attempt to make the absorption of their doing, but in vain—and fortunately so; for that would be the wrong way round, as was proved by the greatest crime in history, the Crusaders' sack of the Christian city in the year 1204.

And, indeed, the absorption was no bad thing for Bulgaria; for it did not happen too soon. The Bulgarian monarchs had had time to instil into their country a consciousness that was strong enough to survive. In the meantime, peace and the penetration of the Imperial civilization came as a boon to the weary country and taught the Bulgarians more than they could have learnt in a long struggle for independence. But now they had their memories and, still more, their Slavonic Church to remind them who they were; and not all Pope Bogomil's teachings and his followers ever broke that down. And so, when the time came, and the Empire no longer was wise and beneficial, Bulgaria was ready to assemble again round an independent standard raised by the noble House of Asen at Tirnovo.

So it had been worth while—and worth while, too, to countries outside of Bulgaria. The Bulgars had brought order to the Slavs and had lifted them out of chaos, setting an example for the whole Slav world to follow. The Serbian tribes could profit by it; and, moreover, had not

Bulgaria lain between, they might never so have freed themselves from the influence of Constantinople, to form a proud nation, until it was too late: while, similarly, the same bulwark preserved the Empire from many harmful barbarous invasions. But the great gift of Bulgaria to Europe lay in her readiness to take over the legacy of Cyril and Methodius, so carelessly thrown away by the Moravians. This work had been initiated in Constantinople and greatly helped by the Patriarch Protius and the Emperor Basil, with that strange mixture of philanthropy and political cunning that characterized Byzantium. But it was Boris of Bulgaria that brought it to completion, and thus put all the Balkan peninsula and all the Russias into his debt. To his lead those countries owe their Churches, Churches well suited to them— Churches that kept their pride alive through all the dark days that they were to endure, at the hands of fierce and infidel barbarian invaders.

Though clouds pass at times over the face of Bulgaria, she may well be content with her history. The First Empire has left her memories rich in glory. It is a splendid procession that stretches backward into the far-off darkness, past Samuel and his passionate Court beside the high mountain-lakes of Macedonia; past Symeon on his golden throne, his silken raiment weighed down with studded pearls; past Boris, issuing from his aureoled palace with angels to escort him; past Krum, with bowing rows of concubines, crying 'Sdravitsa' to his boyars as he drank from an Emperor's skull; past Tervel, riding in to Constantinople by the side of a slit-nosed Emperor; past Asperuch and his brothers, and his father, King Kubrat, and past the princes of the Huns, back through dim ages to that wild marriage from which her race was born, the marriage of the wandering Scythian witches to the demons of the sands of Turkestan.

APPENDICES

ORIGINAL SOURCES FOR EARLY BULGARIAN HISTORY

THE original sources for a history of the First Bulgarian Empire do not, on the whole, present any great problems, except for their paucity, which obliges us to remember that we have only a one-sided account of almost every event, and that we must therefore use them cautiously, ready to discount prejudice and ignorance wherever our judgement raises our suspicions.

The main sources are provided by the writers, chroniclers, hagiographers, and letter-writers of Constantinople and the Empire, writing for the most part (and after the seventh century entirely) in Greek. Indeed, with the one important exception of the Bulgarian Princes' List, which I discuss in Appendix II, we are absolutely dependent on them until the ninth century. For the pre-Balkan history of the Bulgars we have occasional references in the rich crop of histories written during or shortly after the reign of Justinian I, such as those of Procopius, Agathias, Menander, Malalas, &c. As regards Bulgarian history these need no comment; the other problems that they raise are admirably summarized in Bury's Appendix I to the fourth volume of his edition of Gibbon's *Decline and Fall*. From the middle of the seventh century onward till the ninth, we are almost entirely reduced to two Greek histories, those written by the Patriarch Nicephorus and Saint Theophanes, who both wrote in the early ninth century. For this period both seem to have used the same source or sources, now lost to us. This is the more unfortunate, in that both had the same strong anti-iconoclastic views. Nicephorus's history ends in the year 769; it is a poor piece of work, clearly written with the aim of pleasing the populace; and it is valuable only because of the general dearth of contemporary histories. Theophanes is a much abler writer; though the later part of his Chronography, which extends to 813, is so coloured by his anti-iconoclastic opinions as to leave out events that reflected credit on his opponents. The extent of his high-minded dishonesty during these last years is equalled by that of a very valuable fragment known as *Scriptor Incertus de Leone Armenio*,[1] a work of additional importance to students of Bulgarian history in that it deals largely with Krum's later campaigns. Theophanes' dating also is unsatisfactory; he employs a system of mentioning the Annus Mundi, the Indiction year, and the regnal year of the Emperor and the Calif (earlier, that of the Persian King). As each year began on a different day, the results do not always coincide as well as they should.[2]

With the ninth century our information becomes fuller, as both Latin and native Bulgarian records begin to be of value. Setting them aside for the moment, we must notice the increased activity of the Greek chroniclers towards the end of the ninth and beginning of the tenth centuries, who treated of the ninth century. The oldest is George the Monk, who based his work on Theophanes, but continued it to 842; but his ecclesiastical interests make him tend to ignore foreign politics. But the main sources for the century are two groups of chronicles, both written in the middle of the tenth century. The one consists of the history of Genesius, which extends to 886—an important but prejudiced work, bearing the obvious marks of official patronage—and the work known as the Continuation of Theophanes, Books i. to v., also written at the behest of the Emperor Constantine Porphyrogennetus, who himself contributed a chapter on his grandfather, Basil I; the other consists of the synoptic chroniclers, based on the

---

[1] An example of the necessity for corroborative evidence to the *Scriptor Incertus* is given in Appendix VII.

[2] For two periods, during most of the seventh century and again for the middle of the eighth century, his datings do not coincide. See the references given above, p. 41, n. 2.

chronicle of the mysterious Logothete, who wrote a work reaching down to 948. This work is unpublished, but its Slavonic translation and the redactions of Leo Grammaticus and Theodosius of Melitene probably represent with fair accuracy its original form, and the Continuation of George the Monk is closely akin. Book vi. of the Continuation of Theophanes is, as far as the year 948, based on the Logothete, with a few current traditions added; from 948 to 961 it apparently depends on contemporary knowledge.[1]

After 961 the chroniclers again become fewer. For the reigns of Nicephorus Phocas, John Tzimisces, and the early years of Basil II we have the valuable testimony of a contemporary, Leo Diaconus. Otherwise, for Samuel's reign and Basil II's Bulgarian war, we are dependent solely on the chronicle written by John Scylitzes in the middle of the eleventh century, dealing with the period 811 to 1079. He derived his material from all the previous chronicles that covered the period, but claimed to have seen through their prejudices—that is to say, he introduced fresh prejudices. He also made use of one or more sources now lost to us. His work (as far as 1057) was copied out word for word (about the year 1100) by Cedrenus in an otherwise unimportant compilation, and is most easily accessible in that form. But there is also a MS. of Scylitzes copied by the Bulgarian bishop, Michael of Devol, who inserted various addenda, such as names and dates, all of great importance to Bulgarian historians, of which we would otherwise be ignorant.[2] The remaining Greek chroniclers that cover the period of the Bulgarian Empire, epitomes such as Zonaras, Manasses, Glycas, &c., are of no great importance to us here.

[1] During the 'synoptic' period I refer to Theophanes Continuatus rather than the others, as its account is the fullest. But there are occasions when its story is embroidered by legends that must be taken with caution—e.g. over the death of Symeon, where its details run counter to the Logothete's account. On such occasions I refer also to the older version.

[2] These very important additions are tabulated in Prokič's *Zusätze in der Handschrift des Johannes Skylitzes*, and further discussed in his *Jovan Skilitza*.

Besides the chronicles, there are throughout the period various Greek hagiographical biographies. By far the most important are the works of Theophylact, Greek Archbishop of Ochrida in the late eleventh century. Theophylact wrote a work on the early Bulgarian martyrs, and edited the life of Saint Clement, the famous apostle of Cyril and Methodius. For both of these he must have drawn on local Bulgarian traditions, and possibly written sources; and they, therefore, must rank as the first native examples of Bulgarian historical literature.   There are other purely Imperial works. which by casual references throw very valuable sidelights on Bulgarian history—lives of Patriarchs such as the *Vita Nicephori* by Ignatius, the *Vita Ignatii* by Nicetas, or the very important anonymous *Vita Euthymii*, or of local saints such as the *Vita S. Lucae Junioris*, the *Vita S. Niconis Metanoeite*, the *Vita S. Mariae Novae*, &c. The incidental nature of their evidence makes it all the more reliable: though all the local biographers are sparing in their use of dates.   Even more important, though few in number, are the collections of letters written by various Greek ecclesiastics and statesmen—the letters of the Patriarchs Photius and Nicholas Mysticus (the latter of immense importance for Symeon's career) and Theophylact, of the Emperor Romanus Lecapenus, and, most interesting of all, the correspondence of the Imperial ambassador Leo the Magister, which includes some of Symeon of Bulgaria's replies. With regard to these letters, it must all the while be remembered that their authors were engaged in politics and held strong views and desired definite results; their evidence is therefore highly partial. This is particularly true of the great Patriarchs. With these hagiographical writings must be included the List of Bulgarian Archbishops (quoted in Ducange) and the ordinances of Basil II about the Bulgarian Church after his conquest of the country. Finally, there are various Greek treatises, of which the best known and most important are the works of the Emperor Constantine Porphyrogennetus, especially

that strange compendium of history, ethnography, and
diplomatic advice known as the *De Administrando Imperio*.
Unfortunately and curiously, Constantine never deals
directly with Bulgaria, a subject on which he must have
had copious information.[1] Almost as important, in that
they deal with the obscure period of Samuel's reign, are
the two treatises joined together under the name of the
Strategicon of Cecaumenus, one by Cecaumenus and the
other by a relative of his, probably surnamed Niculitzes.
Of the authors we know little, except that their relatives
played considerable parts in Basil II's Bulgarian wars.
The treatises contain a number of general precepts, with
frequent citations of historical examples and precedents.
There are also references to the Bulgarians in the curious
Lexicon compiled in the tenth century by Suidas.[2]

The few Oriental sources must be taken in connection
with the Greek. The Arab geographers took little interest
in Balkan Bulgaria; and the Arab and Armenian chroniclers only repeat, very occasionally, items that trickled
through to them from the Empire: though the Armenians
took a flickering and unreliable interest in the adventures
of Armenian soldiers in Basil II's Bulgarian wars. Only
two of the Oriental chroniclers were really interested in
Balkan affairs. Eutychius, the Patriarch of Alexandria,
as a Christian, kept watch on events at the Imperial Court.[3]
His chronicle ends at the year 937, and he died in 940. His
continuator, Yachya of Antioch, who died in 1040, is more
important. When he wrote, Antioch was a Christian city
under the Empire; he therefore was in touch with all the
contemporary history of the Empire. He makes frequent and
important references to Basil II's Bulgarian wars; but their
importance has, I think, been exaggerated.[4] Our anxiety

[1] For Constantine Porphyrogennetus's works, see Bury's commentaries,
the treatise *De Administrando Imperio*, and *The Ceremonial Book*.

[2] There is also an unsatisfactory but clearly significant reference to the
Bulgarians in Cameniates's description of the sack of Thessalonica.

[3] e.g. his interest in Symeon's marriage scheme. See Appendix X.

[4] By Rosen, who practically discovered him, and by Zlatarski. Uspenski
and Schlumberger take a more temperate view.

for additional evidence for this dark period should not
blind us to the fact that Yachya is undeniably muddle-
headed about Bulgarian affairs, e.g. on the relations
between the Comitopuli and the sons of Peter, of which he
obviously had no clear idea himself; his information probably came from hearsay and underwent alterations before it
reached Antioch. Yachya's great value lies in his accuracy
on Basil's eastern campaigns, his clear dating of which en-
ables us to amend the dating of the Bulgarian campaigns.

Latin sources are non-existent till the ninth century:
except for those early Imperial historians—e.g. Ennodius or
the Goth Jordanes—who occasionally mention the pre-
Balkan Bulgars. In the ninth century the westward
expansion of Bulgaria resulted in connections with the
Western Empire. The Carolingian chroniclers begin to
make simple, but well-dated, references to Bulgarian wars
and embassies. After the coming of the Hungarians
at the end of the century these references practically
cease. However, the conversion of Bulgaria and Boris's
ecclesiastical policy brought the country into close
relations with Rome, and for a while Papal correspondence lights up Bulgarian history. Most important
among these is the long letter written by Nicholas I to
answer Boris's questions as to the desirability of various
Bulgarian habits and customs. At the same time, Bulgarian affairs are recorded in the official lives of the
Popes.[1] After Boris reverted to the Eastern Church these
Papal sources soon cease, but occasional mention is still
made of the Bulgarians in Italian chroniclers, e.g. Lupus
Protospatharius, who wrote at the Imperial city of Bari,
and in Venetian and Dalmatian writers, especially when,
in Samuel's reign, Bulgarian influences extended up the
Adriatic, and later, retrospectively, by the first Hungarian
historians. Besides these chroniclers and ecclesiastical
writers, there is one Latin author who, from his personal

[1] Information on the Bogomils is given fitfully in various of the later
Latin authors who wrote on the Albigenses; but they lie somewhat outside of
our scope.

experience of politics in the East, deserves special
mention, Liudprand, Bishop of Cremona, whose relatives and who himself went often on embassies to Constantinople.   Liudprand was a gossipy and unreliable
historian with a taste for sensational rumours; but he was
a contemporary, he liked vivid details, and, until his
second embassy, he was interested and unprejudiced. He
therefore ranks among the most important authorities.

The Slavonic sources are few, but most of them are of
great importance. I deal with the Princes' List below;
apart from it we have no Slavonic evidence on Bulgarian
history till the Conversion. The literature of the Conversion of Moravia, the lives of Cyril and of Methodius,
touch on Bulgarian affairs, and are the beginnings of a
stream of Slavonic hagiographical writings, all of considerable importance. For the First Empire I would cite
particularly the *Life of Saint Nahum*, and, to a less degree,
The Miracles of Saint George. The birth of Bulgarian literature naturally introduces a valuable new element, though
most of the works were merely translations from the
Greek.[1] But prefaces and epilogues supply, not only an
occasional date, but also a picture of the civilization at the
time; there are also original works of great significance,
such as Khrabr's and Kozma's. I have dealt with them
more fully above (p. 139). In addition to these sources
there is the important Russian chronicle known, certainly
wrongly, as *The Chronicle of Nestor*. It is derived partly
from a Bulgarian translation of George the Monk and his
continuator, partly from various Greek and Slavonic religious writings, partly from oral information and native
Russian records.[2] Where it touches on Bulgarian history
its value is obvious; but it also requires notice with regard
to its dating, which I discuss in connection with the
Princes' List. The native writings of the Bogomils,

---

[1] These Slavonic hagiographical works have been carefully edited by
various Slavonic savants, and any problems that they present are there
discussed.

[2] For 'Nestor's' sources, see the preface to Léger's *La Chronique dite de
Nestor*.

though for the most part they belong to a later date, are important for the light that they throw on the political situation of the sect.

Besides the literary sources, there are various archaeological sources. By these I mean the excavations that have been undertaken at various important old Bulgarian sites. Those at Preslav-on-the-Danube have produced little results, but at Pliska the work has thrown great light on the civilization of the ninth-century Khans. The work at Great Preslav has not yet produced results of the value that had been hoped. I also include in these sources the inscriptions written in crude Greek by which the ninth-century Khans recorded on columns or stones various events of importance. The significance of these sources is obvious.[1] It is always possible that new excavations and the discovery of more inscriptions may necessitate considerable emendations in our present knowledge of early Bulgarian history.

Appendix II

THE BULGARIAN PRINCES' LIST

THE Bulgarian Princes' List is a document of such importance to early Bulgarian history that it demands separate notice. It exists in two practically identical manuscripts, one at Leningrad, one at Moscow, written in old Slavonic, and contains a list of the Bulgarian rulers from Avitokhol to Umor, with dates; but its great interest lies in that the entry clearly indicating the date of each accession is in an unknown language, which must be old

---

[1] The Pliska excavations and most of these inscriptions have been fully recorded in the volume *Aboba-Pliska*, compiled by MM. Uspenski and Shkorpil.

Bulgar. Translated into English, the List runs as follows:
'Avitokhol lived 300 years, his race Dulo, and his years
dilom tvirem: Irnik lived 100 years and 5 years, his race
Dulo, and his years *dilom tvirem*: Gostun as regent 2 years,
his race Ermi, and his years *dokhs tvirem*: Kurt reigned 60
years, his race Dulo, and his years *shegor vechem*: Bezmer 3
years, his race Dulo, and his years *shegor vechem*. These 5
princes held their rule, with shorn heads, on the other side
of the Danube for 515 years; and after, there came Prince
Isperikh to this side of the Danube where they are now.
Isperikh, prince, 60 years and 1 year, his race Dulo, his
years *ber enialem*: Tervel 21 years, his race Dulo, and his
years *tekuchitem tvirem*: . . . 28 years, his race Dulo, and
his years *dvansh ekhtem*: Sevar 15 years,¹ his race Dulo, and
his years *tokh altom*: Kormisosh 17 years, his race Vokil,
and his years *shegor tvirem*: this prince changed the race of
Dulo, that is to say Vikhtum²: Vinekh 7 years, his race
Ukil, and his years *shegor alem*: Telets 3 years, his race
Ugain, and his years *somor altem*, he too of another race:
Umor 40 days, his race Ukil, and his [years] *dilom tutom*.'

There is one obvious emendation to be made; to make
the five first princes' reigns add up to 515 we must alter
the length of Irnik's into 150 years.³ But nothing else can
be done until we discover the significance of the Bulgar
words. As they stand, there is no means of finding out
their meaning: though the Bulgarian, Tudor Doksov,
writing early in the tenth century, apparently used the
same system. But, though a few scholars⁴ attempted to
bring Turkish and Mongol philology to bear on the question, they could evolve no definite equation between this
dating and any known dating. It was not till some thirty

¹ From the photographs of both the MSS. I read here '∊ι'' which must
be intended for 15; but Bury, Marquart, and Mikkola all take it to be 5.
² This rendering is a little doubtful; after 'Dulo' the text goes 'Vrek-
shevi Khtun.'
³ Jireček, *Geschichte*, pp. 127 ff.: Bury, however (op. cit. below), thinks the
change unnecessary.
⁴ e.g. Kuun (*Relationum Hungarorum*) and Radloff (*Die Alttürkischen
Inschriften*).

TE

years ago, when Russian excavators discovered the Chatalar inscription, that a point of contact was found; Omortag's foundation of Preslav was dated in the 15th Indiction (i.e. September 821–September 822), or the Bulgarian date σιγορελεμ, *shegor alem*.

It would take too long to give a detailed account of the results that savants have evolved from this additional evidence. I shall merely deal generally with the chief investigators and state which I follow. Bury was the first serious investigator. In 1910 he published a clue to the Bulgar words,[1] which, he declared, fitted all known facts, though he emended the text with regard to the later princes, to reconcile it better with the data of the Greek chroniclers. His theory demanded a cycle of 60 lunar years—a cycle not unfamilar among Oriental tribes—the first series of figures—e.g. *dilom*—represented the units, the second the decades. He claimed for this system that it was free from the dangerous trap of linguistic similarities. Unfortunately the dates that he thus evolved upset known history, as Marquart pointed out.[2] In particular, the Bulgars had to cross the Danube 20 years earlier.

Marquart's criticisms were damaging, but not constructive. However, in 1914, Professor Mikkola of Helsingfors fell back on to the help of philology, and evolved a key,[3] which provided a twelve-year cycle, in which each year was given the name of some animal—the first Bulgar word being therefore a name, not a number—a suggestion that had already been tentatively put forward by Petrovski. Analogies with Turkish and Cuman words (e.g. *dvansh* = Turkish *davšan*, a hare; *tokh* = Cuman *taok*, a hen) and the order of the years in their cycles enabled Mikkola to translate these Bulgar names and fix their order in the cycle. The second Bulgar words he took to be the ordinal numbers of the months, and, on analogous linguistic comparisons, he arrived at an order for them.

---

[1] In the *Byzantinische Zeitschrift*, vol. xix., pp. 127 ff.

[2] Marquart, *Die Altbulgarische Ausdrücke*, pp. 1 ff.

[3] Mikkola, *Tyurksko-Bolgarskoe Lietochislenie*, pp. 243 ff.

Mikkola's philological arguments are convincing and
have now generally been accepted. But his dates do not
fit with the dates known from our Greek sources, particularly with regard to the Khans living in the time of Copronymus. To produce better results, Mikkola made one or
two later emendations, but ineffectively.[1] The matter remained unsatisfactory till Professor Zlatarski set to work on it.

Zlatarski, who had first accepted a modified form of
Bury's theory,[2] now[3] followed Mikkola's first key: i.e.
somor= rat, the 1st year of the cycle, *shegor*= ox, the 2nd:
beri= wolf, the 3rd; *dvansh*= hare, the 4th; *dilom*= snake,
the 6th; *tokh*= hen, the 10th; *etkh*= dog, the 11th; *dokhs*=
pig, the 12th. The months were *alem*, 1st; *vechem*, 2nd;
tutom, 4th; *altom*, 6th; *ekhtem*, 8th; *tvirem*, 9th. These words
involve one or two alterations in the text, all very plausible, e.g. *tekuchitem* is shortened to *etkh*. Tudor Doksov's
bekhti is taken to be the 5th month. But Zlatarski has two
important emendations to make to Mikkola's and previous theories. First, he reverts to a system of lunar
years; secondly, he begins a new era in A.D. 680, when the
Bulgars established themselves south of the Danube.

It would take too long to discuss his arguments in detail.
I can only say here that they seem to me to be sound in
themselves and justified by their results. Till A.D. 680
he accepts an era of cycles beginning at the year of the
Incarnation: e.g. Avitokhol began to reign in the lunar
year A.D. 150, which is the 6th year of a cycle. From John
of Nikiou we can place Kubrat's death about 642, i.e. 662
lunar. Therefore Bezmer ended in 665 lunar; and, if we
subtract 515, for the length of the 5 reigns, we reach the
year 150 lunar. The coincidence of the first year of a
cycle with the birth of Christ seems to me arbitrary and
may be quite fortuitous; though it is curious that A.D. 679
solar (the year of the Invasion)= A.D. 700 lunar—a mystic

[1] Idem, *Die Chronologie der Türkischen Donaubulgaren*, p. 11.
[2] Zlatarski, *Imali li sa Bulgaritie sboe Lietobroenie*.
[3] Idem, *Istoriya*, i., 1, pp. 353–82, a full discussion of his views and arguments.

number that would certainly attract the attention of a Greek; and Zlatarski has shown convincingly that the List must have been written first in Greek, probably soon after Umor's death, and so almost certainly by a Greek. Zlatarski also points out that the lengths of the reigns are calculated, not accurately, but from the cyclic years in which the accessions and deaths occurred. A difficulty arises over Isperikh's accession. If Bezmer reigned 3 years with Isperikh as his successor, Isperikh's reign would begin, not in the year *beri*, but in the 5th year. Zlatarski solves it by identifying Bezmer with Baian (Isperikh is beyond question Asperuch), and by making Isperikh break off from Bezmer 2 years before Bezmer's death. This must be the approximate solution, though personally I prefer to keep Bezmer and Baian separate. Baian is a good Bulgar name, and is not very similar to Bezmer; moreover, the chronology seems to me to demand a generation between Kubrat and Asperuch.

With the year 680 a new cycle begins. Here Zlatarski works back from the date of Telets's succession, which we know from Theophanes to have been in A.D. 761–2.[1] Our interpretation of the List places it in November, A.D. 761. The first difficulty that arises is that, according to the List, the period between the Invasion and Telets's succession is $23^2 + 21 + 28 + 15 + 17 + 7 = 111$ lunar years, which is far too many. We must, therefore, abandon as inaccurate some of the stated lengths of reigns. Moreover, as the List's lengths contradict the List's dates, as we interpret them, it seems only reasonable to amend the lengths where they disagree with the dates. Measuring the years by the List's system, Zlatarski reduces Tervel's reign to 17 years, the unknown's to 6: Sevar's is raised to 16, Kormisosh's is unaltered, Vinekh's reduced to 6. This adds up to 85 lunar years, i.e. about 82 solar years—679–761. After Telets, Zlatarski inserts the 2 years of Sabin, of the existence of which at that point we are informed by the

---

[1] Theophanes, pp. 667–8.
[2] The length of Isperikh's reign after the Invasion.

Greeks; this makes Umor's year *dilom*, as it is in the List.
Without the insertion of Sabin's reign it would be *dvansh*.
Zlatarski's final results are, therefore, as follows:

Avitokhol	*began to reign*	March A.D. 146[1]
Irnik		March 437
Gostun		September 582
Kurt		February 584
Bezmer		April 642
Isperikh		February 643
His separation:		January 645
The beginning of the Bulgar era :		January 680
Tervel	*began to reign*	December 701
Unknown		May 718
Sevar		January 724
Kormisosh		October 739
Vinekh		September 756
Telets		November 761
(Sabin		October 764)
Umor		July 766

These results cannot naturally claim absolute certainty;
but the arguments with which Zlatarski supports them
seem to me to carry conviction.

Zlatarski goes on to show that Tudor Doksov and his
contemporaries also calculated their otherwise inexplicable dates by means of the Bulgarian era. Placing the
Creation in the year 5505 B.C., they began the Bulgarian
era at A.M. 6185; but for their dates after that they used
lunar years. Thus the Conversion of Bulgaria is dated in
both A.M. 6376 and 6377, but Tudor Doksov calls the year
on Etkh bekhti. Now, 6376 – 6185 = 191, which would give
the 11th year of a 12-year cycle. Moreover, as Zlatarski's
arithmetic shows, the 5th month of the lunar year 191 =
the solar year 184·62 to 184·71, which equals September

[1] The months are naturally approximate, as lunar months do not coincide
with solar.

865. Zlatarski also attempts to show that the Russian chronicler known as 'Nestor' dates Imperial events by the same system. It is inherently probable, in that 'Nestor' derived his information on the Empire from Bulgarian translations. But while Zlatarski makes clear the interesting fact the 'Nestor' was using here a system of lunar years, I do not think that it is possible to credit 'Nestor' with definitely taking over the system. Textual emendations are necessary to make several of the instances fit. I think that 'Nestor' was unaware of the intricacies of Bulgarian chronology, and simply was muddled. As evidence his dates are of little value.

There is one more point that merits elucidation. 515, the number of years that the five first Khans, Avitokhol to Bezmer, are said to have reigned, has always been taken simply to represent the traditional time spent by the Bulgars on the Steppes before Asperuch's first migration. But it is highly unlikely that they remained in one place for roughly that period. The number 515 has another significance. According to the chronological system of Africanus, commonly used at Constantinople, A.D. 680, the first year of the Bulgarian era = A.M. 6180. But 6180 years represents 515 cycles of 12 years. A Greek, aware of the Bulgars' system of 12-year cycles, but unaware of their use of a lunar year, might well inform the Bulgars that 515 cycles had passed before they crossed the Danube. The 515 cycles became corrupted into 515 years, which, again, for the sake of greater realism, were assigned to the five Bulgar Khans whose names were known; and the first two Khans received the well-rounded, but lengthy reigns of 300 and 150 years respectively, so that the number might be built up: though, as I show below, in the case of Irnik's accession there was historical justification.

This emphasizes once more the great difficulty of the List, a difficulty that its every interpreter must bear in mind. It was almost certainly written for the Bulgars by Greek slaves, and combines an Oriental system of dating with ideas based by these ignorant Greeks on superstition and an occasional coincidence. Thus no one simple theory of interpretation can suffice, and, for that reason alone, Bury's gallant mental exercise was doomed to failure.[1]

Appendix III

ERNACH AND IRNIK

IT is impossible not to be struck by the resemblance of the name Irnik, the second prince in the List, with Ernach or Ernac, the youngest and favourite son of Attila. It is, however, always a dangerous pastime to identify persons whose names chance to be similar, particularly among semi-barbarian tribes, where very often several distinct names are derived from one common root; though, on the other hand, it is extremely seldom that two distinct persons bear the same name, as happens in more civilized society.

Professor Zlatarski regards it as being wrong and pointless to seek for this identification.[2] It certainly must be conceded that we know very little of Ernach's career after Attila's death (A.D. 453). Priscus merely tells us that he, with his brother Dengisich, ruled over a remnant of Attila's empire in Little Scythia (the modern Bessarabia), whence they used to raid the Empire; and in the course of one of these raids Dengisich was slain.[3] Zlatarski points out that, (i.) according to the List, Irnik began to reign in 437, not 453, (ii.) the Balkan Bulgarians descend from an eastern branch, the Utigurs, who lived to the east of the Don, (iii.) if Ernach is Irnik, both he and Attila must have

[1] In the Godishnik of the National Museum of Sofia, 1922–5, Feher has made a profound study of the Greek evidence revelant to the dating of the List. But his results do not, I think, seriously demand an alteration in the dating suggested above.

[2] Zlatarski, *Istoriya*, i., 1, pp. 40–2. [3] Priscus, *Fragmenta*, p. 587.

belonged to the house of Dulo, whereas, actually, we never hear the name mentioned in connection with them.

Zlatarski's points are all indisputable, but they do not seem to me to provide effective arguments. (i.) and (iii.) indeed verge on the absurd. (i.) Where a prince is assigned a reign of 150 years, it is surely a little too credulous to assume that the date of his accession must be accurate. A mistake of 16 years is, under the circumstances, quite venial. (iii.) There is no reason why we should know Attila's surname. Not only do the surnames of barbarous families frequently change in the course of generations, but it seems to me that the argument would only be conclusive if we were definitely informed that Attila did *not* belong to the house of Dulo. (ii.) This is a stronger argument; I certainly agree that Kubrat's kingdom had the Utigurs as its nucleus. But here I think the Onogunduri come in. They were the remnant of Attila's empire which Ernach and his family preserved; and, under the stress of Avar rule, they either were forcibly moved eastward or migrated themselves in an attempt to escape beyond the Avar frontier. Probably it was one of their princes that headed the Bulgar revolt against the Avars, and thus acquired the command of the united Bulgar kingdom. The seat of the kingdom would naturally be in Utigur territory, as being the part of the kingdom freest from Avar attack. This theory seems to me not only to meet Zlatarski's argument, but also to explain the prominence of the name Onogunduri, which cannot be a composite name or a misnomer, but must represent a definite tribe.[1]

Under these circumstances, especially considering the remarkable similarity of the names, it is surely unnecessarily hypercritical to refuse to identify Irnik with Ernach, and not to trace the Bulgar royal line from Attila.

The question now arises whether Attila should be identified with Avitokhol. If Ernach is Irnik, this second identification is not very important. Personally, I am

[1] See above, p. 15–6.

suspicious; I regard Avitokhol, like Attila, as an elaborated form of Awit, the Turkish for ancestor, which received new meaning when Bible stories reached the Steppes, and the Turks and Khazars and Huns decided to trace their descent from Japheth.[1] (Incidentally Hungarian writers used to elaborate this descent, placing thirty-four generations between Japheth and Attila.[2]) The resultant similarity of the name with Attila's may well have fixed it firmer in the minds of the Bulgars; but actually I believe that Avitokhol was a distant ancestor, the first founder of the race. We must remember that Attila looms largely in our history because his career was chiefly directed towards conquest in the West. Ernach, whose government was definitely Eastern, may even have indulged in Eastern conquests of which we know nothing, and, anyhow, might well figure more largely than Attila in Eastern tradition.

APPENDIX IV

CHRISTIANITY AMONG THE SLAVS BEFORE THE NINTH CENTURY

BYZANTIUM has often been blamed by ecclesiastical writers for waiting till the ninth century to introduce the blessings of Christianity to the Balkan Slavs. The attack is unjustified. During the late sixth and seventh centuries the waves of Avar, Slavonic, and Bulgar invasion prevented more than fitful missionary enterprise, while during the eighth and early ninth centuries the great Iconoclastic controversy at home ruled out the possibility of a vigorous ecclesiastical policy abroad. Consequently, with one great exception, Christianity was only

[1] See above, p. 12. Attila is probably a diminutive of Awit; Okhol certainly = *oghul*, a son.

[2] e.g. de Thwrocz.

spread among the Balkan Slavs by the local influence of sees that survived the storms.

The names of these sees can be found in the semi-official *notitiae*, the lists drawn up by Epiphanius (in the seventh century), Basil (in the early ninth century), the *notitia* published by de Boor (ninth century), and that of Leo the Wise (early tenth century), and in the lists of bishops present at the various Councils. These lists have been ably tabulated by Dvornik.[1] We must remember, however, that while the *notitiae* are fairly reliable—after making due allowances for carelessness and copyists' errors—the failure of a see to be represented at a Council does not necessarily mean that the see no longer existed. An investigation of this evidence shows roughly that round the coasts of the Balkan peninsula the Christian cities lived an uninterrupted life, but, except on the Aegean coast, there was hardly any Christian hinterland. On the Black Sea coast the cities south of Mesembria appear on every list; to the north, Odessus (Varna) apparently lasted till the early ninth century, when no doubt it was finally occupied by the Bulgars; farther inland, the last see of the old Moesian provinces, Marcianopolis, lasted only into the seventh century, and then was presumably destroyed by the Bulgars. Farther south, Adrianople remained a constant centre of Christianity, and Philippopolis also, until its annexation by the Bulgars in the ninth century. Sardica, however, though certainly occupied by the Empire till the ninth century, is not mentioned; probably it was merely a garrison city without much religious life. Between Rhodope and the sea, Christianity lived on; in Macedonia, which was more exposed to invasions, only the bigger towns near to Thessalonica survived. In the Greek hinterland the Slav tribes remained pagan until they were brought under definite political control by the Empire in the ninth century. On the whole, all that we can say is that, where the Slavs were under Imperial rule, the local bishoprics

[1] Dvornik, *Les Slaves, Byzance et Rome*, pp. 60–99.

spread Christianity among them; but over the frontiers the bishoprics were extinguished, and there was no missionary enterprise save by a few isolated Christian captives at heathen Courts, such as Omortag's slave, Cinamon.

There is, however, one exception. In the *De Administrando Imperio* (pp. 148–9, 153) Constantine Porphyrogennetus tells us that the Emperor Heraclius (610–41) sent for clergy from Rome to baptize the Croatians and Serbs: which was successfully achieved. The story has been doubted[1]; but it is perfectly plausible. Heraclius was for much of his reign on excellent terms with the Papacy, and Illyricum was still then a Roman ecclesiastical province. Moreover, he was a vigorous ruler, who clearly would wish to deal with the Slavonic problem. Constantine connects the Conversion with Heraclius's political dealings with the Slavs—his recognition of their occupation of the country on condition of their recognition of his suzerainty. Constantine is almost certainly telling the truth; but he omitted to say that Heraclius's success was extremely ephemeral. In his previous chapter (written later) he shows (p. 145) the Croatians asking for priests from Rome in the ninth century: while the Serbs were certainly not a fully Christian nation till the days of Cyril and Methodius. It is most reasonable to assume that Heraclius's great missionary enterprise did, in fact, exist, but achieved nothing lasting; and certainly it cannot have had any effect at all in the Balkan peninsula to the east of Serbia.

Thus Christianity among the Balkan Slavs before the ninth century was almost certainly limited to those Slavs that were definitely under Imperial control, save round the frontiers, where the Greek (and, in the north-west, the Latin Dalmatian) cities spread their influence, and save the individual efforts of a few captive Christian slaves. Since Heraclius's day the state of the Empire, and indeed of all Christendom, had not been such as to permit of any more comprehensive evangelization of the Balkans,

---

[1] Jireček, *Geschichte der Serben*, i., p. 104.

BULGAR TITLES

A LITTLE light is thrown on to the administration of the early Bulgar Empire by our knowledge of the names of several Bulgar titles; though it is impossible to draw many conclusions from them, as it is difficult to tell which titles represent offices and which mere ornamental dignities.

The ruler in all his inscriptions is the Khan or the Sublime Khan—κάνας or κάννας, with the epithet ὑβιγή or ὑβηγη—a word which is clearly the Cuman öweghü = high, renowned.[1] The inscriptions often add the title ὁ ἐκ Θεοῦ ἄρχων, probably introduced by the Greek scribes, who considered that a necessary qualification for every prince. The title of Khan disappears after the introduction of Christianity and the Slavonic alphabet, to be replaced by Knyaz, and later by Tsar.

The main class of the nobility was the *boyars*—βοιλάδες or βοηλάδες—a name that became general among the Eastern Slavs. In the tenth century there were three classes of *boyars*, the six Great Boyars, the Outer Boyars, and the Inner Boyars[2]; in the mid-ninth century there were twelve Great Boyars.[3] The Great Boyars probably comprised the Khan's confidential Cabinet; the Inner Boyars were probably the Court officers, the Outer Boyars provincial officers.[4] Many of the individuals mentioned on the ninth-century inscriptions were *boyars*. The Kavkan Isbules and the Bagatur Tsepa were both *boyars*; but I am inclined to think that the *boyars* were civil officers.

[1] Marquart, *Die Chronologie*, p. 40.

[2] Constantine Porphyrogennetus, *De Ceremoniis*, i., p. 681. At the reception of Bulgarian ambassadors it was correct to inquire after their healths.

[3] Idem, *De Administrando Imperio*, p. 154. They were captured along with the Crown Prince Vladimir by the Serbians.

[4] I follow Zlatarski's solution—*Kvi sâ bili Vâtrieshini i Vunshni Bolyari*, passim.

The second class of the nobility, probably inferior, was the *bagaïns*. These, I conjecture, were a military caste; but their name only occurs in inscriptions, collectively (Omortag gave his *boyars* and *bagaïns* presents on one occasion), or singly where it is usually coupled with the title *bagatur*.[1] In addition to these ranks, almost every Bulgarian subject commemorated on an inscription was a θρεπτὸς ἄνθρωπος of the Khan. The θρεπτοὶ ἄνθρωποι were, no doubt, a rough order of knighthood, a nominal body guard of the Khans.[2]

The title *bagatur*—βαγατουρ or βογοτορ—is several times found on the inscriptions; while the Bulgarian general who was defeated in Croatia in 927 is called by Constantine ἀλογοβοτουρ, obviously for ἀλο-βογοτουρ.[3] This word is the Turkish *bagadur*, found in Russian as *bogatyr* = a hero. It probably represents a military rank. The prefix *alo* may mean 'chief' or 'head' (Bang equates it with the Turkish *alp*, *alyp*[4]) or merely be a proper name. The title *vagantur*, found in the list of Bulgarian legates at Constantinople in 869–70 (see below), is clearly the same as *bagatur*.

Colobrus—καλοβρός or κουλουβρός—found only in the inscriptions, was probably a title of rank, derived from the Turkish *golaghuz*, a guide.[5] The Boyar Tsepa was a *colobrus* as well as a *bagatur*.

Zhupan, once as ζουπάν and once as κοπανός, occurs in the inscriptions. On both occasions the family of the bearer is mentioned. Among the Southern Slavs generally, *zhupan* meant the head of a tribe; so Uspenski and Bury plausibly take it to mean the head of one of the Bulgar clans.[6]

---

[1] e.g. those quoted in *Aboba-Pliska*, pp. 201–2, 190–2. Enravotas, Malamir's brother, who was also called Boïnos, may have been a *bagaïn* (Theophylact, *Historia XV. Martyrum*, p. 193).

[2] See *Aboba-Pliska*, pp. 204 ff. Uspenski reaches this conclusion.

[3] *Aboba-Pliska*, pp. 190–2: Constantine Porphyrogennetus, op. cit., p. 158.

[4] Marquart, op. cit., p. 40 *n*.

[5] Ibid., p. 41.

[6] *Aboba-Pliska*, p. 199: Bury, *Eastern Roman Empire*, p. 334.

Sampses—σαμψής—does not appear on the inscription, but Saint Clement's host in Pliska was Eschatzes, σαμψής τὸ αξίωμα, two of the legates of 869–70 were *sampses*, and Symeon, Tsar Symeon's brother-in-law, the ambassador in 927, was οὐσάμψος or οὐσάμψις, which is obviously a variant.[1] Presumably the *sampses* held a post about the Court.

The title *tarkan* probably represented a high military post. It was of Turkish origin; a Turkish ambassador to the Court of the Emperor Justin II (c. A.D. 570) was called *tagma*, ' ἀξίωμα δε αυτῷ ταρχάν.'[2] Onegavon, who was drowned in the River Theiss, was a *tarkan*; so was the Zhupan Okhsun.[3] When Saint Clement arrived at Belgrade he was greeted by Boritacanus 'τῷ τότε φυλάσσοντι,' the 'ὑποστράτηγος' of the Khan Boris.[4] Boritacanus must mean the Tarkan Boris; his position was clearly equivalent to an Imperial strategus, i.e. he was the military governor of a province. I therefore hazard the conjecture that the *tarkan* may be equated with the Imperial strategus. The Bulgarian provincial governors—there were ten in Boris's reign—were called by Greek and Latin writers counts.[5] We cannot tell if this represents a translation of some Bulgar title, or if the Bulgars came to adopt the word κόμης. In 927 the Ambassador Symeon the *sampses*, the late Tsar's brother-in-law, was also called the καλουτερκάνος: while polite questions were to be put to Bulgarian ambassadors in the tenth century as to the healths of their ruler's 'sons,' 'ο κανάρτι κείνος καὶ ὁ βουλίας ταρκάνος.'[6]

---

[1] *Vita S. Clementis*, p. 1224: Anastasius Bibliothecarius, ref. given below: Theophanes Continuatus, p. 413.

[2] Menander, *Fragmenta*, p. 53.

[3] *Aboba-Pliska*, pp. 190, 191.   [4] *Vita S. Clementis*, p. 1221.

[5] 'Ταριδῆνα κόμητα,' Theophylact, op. cit., p. 201; the Bulgar who opposed the return of the Adrianopolitan captives was the κόμης of the district (Georgius Monachus Continuatus, p. 818), the father of Samuel and his brothers was a *comes* (Cedrenus, ii., p. 434), ἑνὸς τῶν παρὰ Βουλγάροις μέγα δυνηθέντων κόμητος; Bulgaria was divided ' *intra decem comitatus* ' (*Annales Bertiniani*, p. 85, ad ann. 866).

[6] Theophanes Continuatus, p. 413: Constantine Porphyrogennetus, *De Ceremoniis*, p. 681.

I think that we must obviously equate καλουτερκανος
with καναρτικεινος; both the *kalutarkan* and the *bulias-
tarkan* were officers at the head of the *tarkans*, and their
posts were probably reserved to members of the royal
family. *Bulias* may be connected with the word *boyar*;
but by itself the identification is of little value.

The most important military officer of the realm was
the *kavkan*. In Malamir's reign the Kavkan Isbules, the
Khan's παλαιὸς βοϊλᾶς (senior *boyar*?) was clearly the next
most important person to the Khan in Bulgaria. He
built the Khan an aqueduct at his own expense and accompanied the Khan to battle, apparently as his general-
in-chief.[1] In 922 we hear of Symeon being accompanied
by his *kavkan*.[2] A century later there were two *kavkans*,
Dometian and his brother; but they may not have been
simultaneous. Dometian was captured by Basil II, and
his brother soon after deserted the Bulgarian cause. Dometian was the συμπάρεδρος of the Tsar Gabriel-Radomir.[3]

The title *tabare*, or perhaps *iltabare* (the old Turkish
ältäbär),[4] only occurs among the ambassadors of 869–70.
The name Μηνικός occurs more than once. Symeon in
922 is accompanied ἄμα καυκάνῳ καὶ μηνικῷ. In 926 the
Bulgarian generals Cnenus, Hemnecus, and Etzboclia invaded Serbia. In 927 the Bulgarian embassy, besides
George Sursubul and the Kalutarkan Symeon, included a
royal relative, Stephen, and Magotinus, Cronus, and
Menicus.[5] Zlatarski makes Hemnecus a person, but
Menicus a title.[6] Personally, I think that the first passage should run ἄμα καυκάνῳ Μηνικῷ—Menicus, miscalled
Hemnecus by Constantine, being the *kavkan* of the period.
The other names that appear in the course of the history
of the First Empire we must assume, from lack of evidence
to the contrary, to be proper names, not titles.

[1] *Aboba-Pliska*, pp. 230–1, 233.   [2] Theophanes Continuatus, p. 401.
[3] Cedrenus, ii., p. 462.   [4] See Marquart, op. cit., p. 41.
[5] Theophanes Continuatus, loc. cit., and p. 413: Constantine Porphyrogennetus, *De Administrando Imperio*, p. 158.
[6] Zlatarski, *Istoriya*, i., 2, pp. 421–2, 475–6, 523–4.

In connection with these titles a word must be said about Anastasius Bibliothecarius's list of the Bulgarian legates at the Council of 869–70 at Constantinople. According to him, they were '*stasiszerco borlas nesundicus vagantur il vestrannatabare praesti zisunas campsis et Alexius sampsi Hunno*'[1]; '. . . *zerco borlas*' and '*nesundicus*' are clearly Cerbula and Sundica, the Bulgarian statesmen to whom Pope John VIII wrote a letter, and who feature in the Cividale gospel as Zergobula and Sondoke—'*borlas*' is not a misprint for '*boëlas*'[2]; '*vagantur*' is '*bagatur*,' Sundicus's title. '*Il vestrannatabare*' probably is Vestranna the *iltabare*. *Campsis* and *sampi* are both clearly *sampses*. The list therefore should run 'Stasis, Cerbula, Sundica the *bagatur*, Vestranna the *iltabare*, Praestizisunas the *sampses*, and Alexius Hunno the *sampses*.' Hunno is probably a surname. Zlatarski identifies Stasis with Peter, and Praestizisunas with the Bulgar name Presiam or Prusian. The latter identification is plausible; but the fact of Peter often appearing as Boris's chief ambassador with regard to ecclesiastical affairs does not necessarily mean that he must be Stasis.

Appendix VI

THE GREAT FENCE OF THRACE

THE great line of earthworks[3] that stretches across the northern frontier of Thrace from Develtus to Macrolivada, and is still in the main discernible, provides a problem for historians as to the date of its construction.

---

[1] Anastasius Bibliothecarius, *Praefatio in Synodum VIII.*, p. 148.

[2] See Zlatarski, loc. cit., pp. 794–800, an appendix dealing with the question.

[3] Called by the Greeks ' ἡ μεγάλη σούδα ' (Cedrenus, ii., p. 372), and now known locally as the Erkesiya (*jerkesen* = a trench in Turkish).

That it was Bulgar work we know from tradition, archaeo-
logy, and historical probability, and we know that it must
have been constructed some time between the Invasion of
679 and the Conversion of 865.

The line of the Fence runs roughly along what was
known in Bulgaro-Imperial treaties as the Meleona frontier. This frontier was first given to Bulgaria by the
treaty between Tervel and Theodosius III in 716; and it
was probably confirmed in a treaty between Kormisosh
and Constantine V.[1] Zlatarski assumes that the Fence
was constructed at the time of Tervel's treaty,[2] Shkorpil at
the time of Kormisosh's.[3] Both assumptions are plausible, but, as Bury has pointed out,[4] they leave unex-
plained a clause of the treaty between Omortag and Leo
V in 815. The treaty, which is recorded in the Suleiman-
Keni inscription, confirms the Meleona frontier-line (with
possibly one or two emendations), and then in its second
clause talks of some arrangement about various districts on
the frontier line that is to be made 'ἕως ἐκει γέγονεν ἡ ὀροθεσία,'
i.e. until the frontier delimination is completed. By
supplying the words ''Απολείφειν' and 'φρούρια' in two
doubtful places—a reading which seems to me more
convincing than Zlatarski's[5]—Bury shows that the Imperial troops were to evacuate the frontier forts while the
frontier-line was being made. This can only mean that
actual constructive operations were going to be undertaken on the frontier—i.e. a rampart was to be built. This
work would certainly need the passive co-operation of the

[1] Theophanes (p. 775) calls the treaty one between Theodosius and
Kormisosh (Cormesius). Probably there were two treaties (see above,
pp. 32–3, 35–6).
[2] Zlatarski, *Istoriya*, i., 1, pp. 179–80, 300.   [3] *Aboba-Pliska*, p. 568.
[4] Bury, *The Bulgarian Treaty of 814, passim*.
[5] The two readings are as follows, beginning in the middle of line four:
Bury : . . . μέσον τῶν β' [Απολείψειν τὰ] πολλά γε φρ[ούρια με]σον
βαλζηνᾶς κτλ.
Zlatarski : . . . μέσον τῶν β' [ποταμων επι . . . μ ?] λα γέφ[υρα και
με]σον βαλζηνᾶς κτλ.
But β' must refer to the second clause, as the first clause was undoubtedly
introduced by α'. Zlatarski inserts β' lower down, but it is foolish to reject
this β'. I am also unconvinced by Zlatarski's bridge.
U E

Imperial frontier garrisons, who, if they chose, could interfere and wreck it all.   Therefore they were for the time to be withdrawn.

The brilliant ingenuity of Bury's argument is, I think, convincing.   Nor does Zlatarski's example of the word 'ὁροθεσία' being used in a different sense—'ἡ τῶν λ΄ χρονων ὁροθεσέα' in the letter of the Oriental Synods to Theophilus (p. 368) obviously meaning the frontier-line agreed upon for thirty years—necessarily affect the obvious use of 'ὁροθεσία' here.   Indeed, I do not think the phrase in the treaty admits of any translation except Bury's, and I therefore accept his conclusions.

It is certainly difficult to see when the Bulgarians would have had time to build so vast a work except after the guaranteed security of Omortag's peace.   Moreover, if the Meleona frontier was already guarded by earthworks, it is curious that in Omortag's peace the line followed by the Fence should be so carefully stipulated as the frontier when the Fence already marked an old-established line. It is also curious (though to argue *a silentio* is notoriously dangerous) that we never hear of the Fence during Copronymus's campaigns, if it already existed by then. Actually Greek historians do not mention it till Nicephorus Phocas's reign; but, from the little evidence that we have, Imperial invaders in the late ninth and early tenth centuries seem to have kept to the coast-route.

APPENDIX VII

LEO THE ARMENIAN'S SUCCESSFUL CAMPAIGN

HISTORIANS have been unwilling to give Leo V credit even for the one successful campaign that is claimed for him—his campaign near Mesembria in 813.

This campaign is only noticed in Genesius, in Theophanes
Continuatus, and in the later chronicles derived from
them; the Continuator's account is much the most detailed. Theophanes, the Scriptor Incertus, Ignatius the
biographer of Nicephorus, and Georgius Hamartolus,
the four contemporary, or almost contemporary, historians, mention nothing about it. Their silence has convinced Hirsch and other modern writers that the story is
a myth, invented by the source that Genesius and the
Continuator used, to explain the name of the place Βουνὸς
Λέοντος—the Hill of Leo.[1]

But, as Bury has pointed out,[2] Theophanes ended his
chronicle with the capture of Adrianople, which was certainly before this campaign; Georgius Hamartolus never
took any interest in external affairs: while all of them were
so violently anti-iconoclastic, and therefore so disliked
Leo, that their silence about an event so creditable to
him is easily understood. Ignatius and the Scriptor Incertus are particularly venomous against him. On the
other hand, the detailed account in Theophanes Continuatus does not seem like a later invention.

Zlatarski accepts the existence of the campaign, but
places it at Burdizus (Baba-Eski) in Thrace, not near
Mesembria, and dates it after Krum's death. His reasons
are: (i.) only the Continuator mentions a place in connection with the campaign, and all the accounts imply
that it took place on Imperial territory; (ii.) even the
Continuator says that it took place on Imperial territory;
(iii.) Mesembria and its district were captured by Krum
in 812; (iv.) it would hardly be possible for Leo and his
army to reach Mesembria so quickly, when shortly before the troops were at Arcadiopolis.[3]

These objections depend on the assumption that Mesembria was in Bulgar hands. But there is no evidence
that Krum left any garrison in Mesembria after its

[1] Hirsch, *Byzantinische Studien*, pp. 125–6.
[2] Bury, *Eastern Roman Empire*, pp. 356–7.
[3] Zlatarski, *Istoriya*, i., 1, pp. 425–32, esp. p. 429.

capture; he seems merely to have destroyed it and deserted it—his usual practice with enemy fortresses—e.g. Adrianople. Whenever Mesembria reappears in history it is as an Imperial city.[1] Moreover, the coast-line of the Gulf of Burgas was not entirely ceded to Bulgaria till Theodora's regency.[2] Mesembria was a very important town for the Imperialists: who certainly would make an early attempt to recover it; and Leo's campaign was obviously undertaken with that object and the additional intention of then attacking Bulgaria in the flank; and the troops would be certainly moved by sea, which could be done with extreme speed if the weather was favourable. Moreover, troops working with Mesembria as their base would keep in close touch with Constantinople by sea, and so would suffer no shortage: whereas the countryside, ravaged by Krum in the previous year and probably uncultivated this season, might well produce no supplies to feed the Bulgarian army. I think, therefore, that Zlatarski's objections can easily be met, and it is unnecessary to improve upon the already quite convincing account of the Continuator. The most probable date is the autumn of 813, before Krum's death. It is, however, just possible that the campaign is the successful campaign promised to Leo by Sabbatius next year; but the story seems to show that that campaign was never undertaken.[3]

Appendix VIII

MALAMIR AND PRESIAM

A WAR has been waged by the two great authorities on ninth-century Bulgarian history, Zlatarski and Bury, over the nomenclature and the duration of the reign

[1] It certainly was Imperial when next it is mentioned, in Basil I's reign (Theophanes Continuatus, p. 308).
[2] See above, p. 90.
[3] See above, p. 72.

of the Khan Malamir. According to Bury—who followed Jireček's unelaborated theory—he reigned from Omortag's death in about 831–2 till 852 (Boris's accession), and he also had a Bulgar name, Presiam, which he discarded in the course of his reign; according to Zlatarski he reigned from 831 to 836, and was succeeded by his nephew Presiam, who reigned till 852.[1]

That Malamir existed we know, not only from inscriptions, but also from the account given by Theophylact of Ochrida, the only historian to attempt a connected account of the reigns and relationships of the Khans of Krum's family; he clearly had access to some older source now lost. He says that Omortag had three sons, Enravotas, Zvenitzes, and Malamir (Μαλλομηρός); Malamir succeeded his father, and was succeeded by his nephew, the son of Zvenitzes; a few lines below this second item he speaks of the Bulgarian Khan as 'ὀριθὴς Βωρίσης'[2] —a phrase that has usually been emended as 'ὁ ῥηθεὶς Βωρίσης.' Malamir is also mentioned as Baldimer or Vladimir in the account given of the exiles of Adrianople by the Logothete: which a few lines below suddenly mentions Michael (Boris) as Khan. But all the Logothete's information is misty; Baldimer is called the father of Symeon.[3]

This evidence provides no difficulty in assuming that Malamir was Omortag's successor and Boris's predecessor. But an inscription[4] found at Philippi speaks of '—ανος ὁ ἐκ Θεοῦ ἄρχων,' who is mentioned along with the Kavkan Isbules; and Constantine Porphyrogennetus talks, far more disquietingly, of 'Πρεσιὰμ ὁ ἄρχων Βουλγαρίας,' who fought against the Serbians about 840. Boris-Michael was, he says, Presiam's son.[5] Presiam, or more probably

---

[1] Bury, op. cit., pp. 481–4: Zlatarski, *Izviestiya*, pp. 49 ff. *Istoriya*, i., 1, pp. 447–57 (a reply to Bury's objections to his *Izviestiya* suggestions).

[2] Theophylact, *Historia XV. Martyrum*, pp. 193, 197.

[3] Leo Grammaticus, pp. 231–2 (Βαλδίμερ): Logothete (Slavonic version), pp. 101–2 (Vladimir).

[4] Villoison's inscription, see above, p. 89.

[5] Constantine Porphyrogennetus, *De Administrando Imperio*, p. 154.

Presian or Prusian (a well-known Bulgar name),[1] seems, therefore, to have been a definite Khan, the—ἄνος of the Philippi inscription.

On this evidence, Bury and Zlatarski each formed his theory—and each supported it by his interpretation of the Shumla inscription, an inscription which mentions Malamir. Zlatarski rejected the 'ὁ ῥηθείς' reading in Theophylact, saying that, as Boris's name had not yet been mentioned, it cannot be 'ῥηθείς'; Malamir was succeeded by his nephew, certainly, but that was Presiam: while Boris, as Constantine says, was Presiam's son. He took the sudden appearance of Michael's name in the story of Cordyles in A.D. 835–6 to indicate a change of Khan at that point, Michael being a misprint for Presiam. With the additional aid of the Shumla inscription, he thus built up a Khan Presiam who succeeded in 836.

Bury, however, accepted the 'ὁ ῥηθείς' reading—indeed, Zlatarski provides no adequate substitute, and his complaint as to the name not having been mentioned savours of quibbling. He showed that it is odd of Theophylact to ignore utterly a reign of some sixteen years—years probably vital for the growth of Bulgarian Christianity—and to make so much of a reign of five years, or at most ten years (Omortag might have died any time after 827); and he threw reasonable doubt on the value of any argument based on the Logothete's account. He also disagreed with Zlatarski's version of the Shumla inscription. His solution is that Malamir was Presiam, but took the official and Slavonic name of Malamir about the year 847, just after the Philippi inscription, which he agreed with Zlatarski in dating about that period. He explained Constantine's account of the Khan's relationships by saying that Boris was adopted by Presiam Malamir.

Zlatarski replied by reiterating his points, and showing up a weakness in Bury's chronology. Presiam must, in

[1] Zlatarski (loc. cit.) easily shows that Presiam is more probably Presian.

Bury's view, have changed his name between the Philippi
and the Shumla inscriptions, that is to say in 847; and all
the inscriptions bearing the name of Malamir must be
dated in the short period 847–52.[1] Here, however, he is
unfair; he only gave Malamir a reign of five years himself.
He also has difficulty in believing that any Khan took an
'official' name in the middle of his reign.

But the main battle is over the Shumla inscription.[2]
This, written (as both agree) about the year 847, tells of
a Khan's invasion of Thrace with the Kavkan Isbules.
After talking of ' Κροῦμος ὁ πάππα μου,' and of how 'my
father Omortag' made peace with the Greeks and lived
well (καλά) with them, it proceeds (line four, in the middle)

$$καὶ\ οἱ\ Γρικοὶ\ ἐρήμωσα$$
$$ὁ\ Μαλαμὶρ\ μετ(ὰ)\ τοῦ\ καυχάνου\ Ἡσβούλου\ ἐπ$$
$$.\ .\ .\ (αλα)\ .\ .\ .\ (εἰς)\ τοὺς\ Γρίκους\ τοῦ\ προβάτου\ το\ κασ$$

—and then proceeds to tell of obviously military operations, mentioning Isbules again in line nine with a deleted
passage earlier in the line. Zlatarski supplies ἔπαρχε as the
last word of line five. At the beginning of line six he says
that after 'αλα' he can read 'ε . . . ισεις,' and so supplies
'καλὰ ἔζησε εἰς.' He therefore presumes that Malamir,
too, lived in peace, and the warlike operations belong to
a different Khan, i.e. Presiam. On the fascimile of the
inscription in the *Aboba-Pliska* Album (pl. xlv.) αλα and
εις (the sign for 'ε' may also represent 'καὶ') are clearly
visible. But, if the rest of the letters that Zlatarski sees
are correct, they must certainly be completed in some
other manner. Bury's objections, I think, hold good:
(i.) Malamir's 'καλὰ ἔζησε' would precede 'οἱ Γρικοὶ ἐρή-
μωσαν' which mark the opening of a war. (ii.) καλὰ ἔζησε
does not make sense with the words that certainly follow
—Zlatarski's emendation of them is unconvincing. (iii.)

[1] Actually there are only three—the Shumla, the aqueduct, and Tsepa's
memorial.
[2] *Aboba-Pliska*, pp. 230 ff.

The mention of Isbules clearly implies military operations. All this, combined with the reference to Krum as
the Khan's grandfather and Omortag as the Khan's
father, seems to make it certain that the inscription was
made by Malamir.

For this reason and for Bury's reasons given above,
I disbelieve in Zlatarski's Khan Presiam, who reigned
from 836 to 852. There is another slight reason against it.
Isbules, when he made Malamir an aqueduct, is called
ὁ παλαιὸς αὐτοῦ βοϊλᾶς, so presumably he was of some considerable age, probably the doyen of the *boyars*. But,
according to Zlatarski, the aqueduct was built before
836; but in 847 onward Isbules went out on more than
one campaign. I prefer to think of him being allowed to
retire when he was 'παλαιός' and not having to endure
ten more years' active service.

But I am equally doubtful of an adoption by Khan
Presiam of an official Slavonic name Malamir. Rulers do
not usually change their names in the middle of their
reigns, except when, like Boris, they adopt a new religion.
This gesture towards his Slavonic subjects on the part of
the Khan makes an unconvincing story. The evidence
for there having been any Khan called Presiam seems to
me to be thin. The Philippi inscription is of small account; there are other words that end in ανος besides
Presianos; the proper name does not always immediately
precede the title ' ὁ ἐκ θεοῦ ἀρχών.' The word might
well be κάνας misspelt. Constantine's evidence is more
important. But it is at complete variance with Theophylact's, who never mentions Presiam. Constantine was
here writing Serbian history taken from Serbian sources ;
he never correlated these passages with any work on
Bulgarian history, a subject which he ignored. The
Serbs, as yet a backward race, might well mistake a splendid Bulgar general for the prince himself—and to defeat
the prince sounded far more impressive. Moreover, when
the next prince invaded, they would naturally assume
him to be the son of the former invader. The presence of

Isbules's name on both the war-inscriptions of the time implies that Malamir himself was not the general of his armies; probably, in fact, he did not even accompany them. It is unlikely, I think, that he should spend three years campaigning in Serbia. He left no son at a polygamous Court; and so his health may well have been poor. I believe that Presiam was a high military officer of the realm, a scion, probably, of the blood royal ; but he was given a princely crown and a princely son only in the ignorant imagination of the Serbs.

APPENDIX IX

THE CYRILLIC AND GLAGOLITIC ALPHABETS

THE earliest Slavonic MSS. were not all written in one alphabet; but some employed the Cyrillic alphabet, on which all the alphabets of the orthodox Slavs to-day are based, and others a more complicated script known as Glagolitic, now only surviving in a few out-of-the-way villages in Croatia. The question has often been raised as to which was the earlier and which was Saint Cyril's work.

Professor Minns has shown[1] that Saint Cyril, from a a pun that he made on a misprint in the Hebrew version of Isaiah, must have known Hebrew—Snoj's previous attempt to prove that he knew Coptic must be accounted failure.[2] If he knew Hebrew it is easy to understand from what source the Cyrillic letters were framed, for which the Greek alphabet was of no use: the sole exceptions are a few vowel sounds which bear the air of an arbitrary invention. It seems, therefore, unreasonable to

[1] Minns, *Saint Cyril Really Knew Hebrew, passim.*
[2] Snoj, *Staroslovenski Matejev Evangelij, passim.*

suppose that Cyril did not invent Cyrillic. But the whole
question has been befogged by the assumption, based
chiefly on palimpsests, that Glagolitic must have been
made before Cyrillic, and by an earnest and somewhat
uncalled-for longing to make it a development out of
Greek or Latin or Runic[1]—anything except a definitely
and arbitrarily created alphabet. The priority of Glagolitic has been also maintained because of a passage in
a MS. life of Saint Clement,[2] which said that Clement
invented an alphabet different to Saint Cyril's—Clement
therefore invented Cyrillic, it was said. But the authenticity of this passage is highly suspect.

We must consider the historical evidence. When the
Moravians asked for a teacher, the Emperor sent off
Cyril, after an infinitesimal interval during which the
saint apparently translated one of the Gospels and made
a lectionary, besides inventing the alphabet. But Cyril's
version of the Bible is written, it is now universally agreed,
in the dialect of the Macedonian Slavs, and both alphabets, Cyrillic and Glagolitic, are adapted to suit that
dialect. The only possible conclusion that can be drawn
is that Cyril, who was an enterprising philologist, had
already been experimenting with the Slavonic language in
use round his home at Thessalonica, and had evolved the
Cyrillic alphabet for it. When he arrived in Moravia,
he found that an alphabet so closely akin to Greek met
with powerful opposition; so he disguised it, reversing
most of the Greek letters, but retaining most of his invented letters, and he tidied it up into a vague uniformity
with a free use of loops.[3] From this it seems likely that the

[1] Taylor and Jagić derive it from cursive Greek, Wessely (*Glagolitisch-
Lateinische Studien*) from cursive Latin. See references in Jagić, *Grafika u
Slavyan* and *Entstehungsgeschichte*. Cursive Latin is an unconvincing source,
and Rahlfs (*Zur Frage nach der Herkunft*) has shown cursive Greek to be
historically impossible.

[2] Found by Gregorowitz at Athos in 1825. It is generally recognized now
as valueless.

[3] I follow Minns's explanation (op. cit.)—the only one that seems to
employ common sense.

Imperial Government was already planning, with Cyril's help, to evangelize the Balkan Slavs, the Bulgarians probably as well as its own subjects, when unexpected events called the great missionary farther afield, and altered the whole situation.[1]

In Bulgaria, Glagolitic MSS. are found dating from up to the thirteenth century, chiefly from the Ochrida and Rila districts. Almost certainly Clement brought the alphabet with him from Moravia; and, if there is any truth behind the interpolation in the Athos MS., it refers, not to his invention of Cyrillic, but to his introduction of an alphabet that was different from what the local inhabitants knew as Cyril's. The Bulgarians educated at the Slavonic schools of Constantinople would, however, obviously employ Cyrillic; which became the official alphabet used at Preslav[2]—Khrabr's treatise seems to refer to it, not to its rival—and which, from its greater simplicity and suitability, succeeded in time in superseding Glagolitic— an alphabet whose only merit was that it suited a particular political crisis.

Appendix X

SYMEON'S IMPERIAL MARRIAGE SCHEME

IN the couse of Symeon's second war with the Empire we hear of a marriage scheme of his to unite his family with the Imperial family. The only two references to it are very vague, but they show that it was

---

[1] Brückner (*Thesen zur Cyrillo-Methodianischen Frage*, p. 219) pushes this theory to the extent of rejecting Rostislav's mission. Bury (op. cit., pp. 396–9) takes a more temperate view.

[2] A few Glagolitic inscriptions too mutilated to read have been unearthed at Preslav and Patleïna side by side with Cyrillic inscriptions, but the latter are far more numerous.

obviously a matter of great importance. Eutychius of Alexandria, writing, a few years later, a short garbled account of Constantine VII's minority, traced Symeon's declaration of war to the refusal by the Emperor, for whom his mother Zoe governed, to permit his sister to marry the Bulgar monarch's son, as Symeon desired.[1] In the winter of 920–1, when Romanus was firmly on the throne, Nicholas wrote to Symeon reminding him that he had sought previously for a marriage-alliance with the Emperor, but the Imperial Government of the time had refused it. Now, he said, it was possible; Romanus was willing to marry either an Imperial prince to a Bulgarian princess or vice versa. Nicholas laid great emphasis on the fact that Symeon could now achieve his desire. But Symeon apparently ignored the proposal. His reply was to demand Romanus's deposition.[2]

Eutychius was almost certainly misinformed as to the persons whom it was proposed to marry. Constantine's only sister to survive childhood was his half-sister, the Augusta Anna, born well before A.D. 892, whom Leo had crowned as a stop-gap Empress after her mother's death, and whom he had proposed in 898 to marry to Louis of Provence. This marriage did not take place, but we hear no more of Anna; and this silence, considering the importance at the time of every existing member of the Imperial family, justifies us in regarding her to have died soon afterwards. It is scarcely possible that this princess was the object of Symeon's eager matrimonial suggestions. But apart, possibly, from her, there was only one unmarried member of the Imperial family living in 913–9; that was the Emperor himself.

Symeon's aim must therefore have been to marry the young Emperor to one of his daughters. This is far more convincing; as father-in-law to the Emperor, he would be in a position from which he might well reach the Imperial

[1] Eutychius of Alexandria, Greek translation, p. 1151.

[2] Nicholas Mysticus, *ep.* xvi, p. 112.

throne—just as Romanus, in fact, managed to do. And this would explain why he disdained Nicholas's proposals in 920–1. It was too late then; Constantine was already married—to Helena Lecapena, and her father was Emperor. Symeon could only demand angrily that Romanus should abdicate.

The question arises as to when Symeon put forward the proposal. The obvious occasion was his interview with Nicholas in August 914; and probably his proposal was favourably received and the marriage vaguely promised. Nicholas in his desire for peace would welcome rather than reject it. But Zoe, the Emperor's mother, would clearly hold other views. Her accession to power was therefore an excuse for Symeon to return to arms. This would explain Nicholas's silence on the subject till it was a thing of the past; considering his own promise, and the refusal of the Government that he was serving to countenance it, it would have embarrassed him to refer to it. That, I think, is the meaning of these dark references to a marriage. Symeon planned to mount the Imperial throne by first marrying his daughter to its occupant; and Nicholas half promised to enable him to do so. It was only Zoe's mother-love and the fact that the same idea had occurred to the Grand Admiral that saved the Emperor and the Empire.

APPENDIX XI

THE PEACE OF 927 AND PETER'S TITLE

WE know that by the peace of 927 the Imperial Government agreed to recognize Peter of Bulgaria as an Emperor (Βασιλεύς); Liudprand of Cremona was informed so by the Imperial chancery when he complained of the precedence given to the Bulgarian embassy[1];

[1] Liudprand, *Legatio*, p. 186.

and we are specifically told that Maria Lecapena rejoiced
in that she was marrying an Emperor.[1]   There would be
no difficulty about it, were it not for a passage in the *De
Ceremoniis*.   There, among the formulae to be employed at
the reception of foreign ambassadors, is one which refers
to the Emperor's 'spiritual grandson (πνευματικὸς ἔγγονος),
the Prince ('Αρχων) of Bulgaria,' and there is none referring to the Bulgarian monarch as Basileus.   A little lower,
among the formulae to be employed by the Emperors in
addressing letters to foreign potentates, is one from 'Constantine and Romanus, Emperors, to the Archon of the
Bulgarians'; which is followed by the remark that lately
it has been written (τὸ ἀρτίως γραφόμενον) 'Constantine
and Romanus to their spiritual son the Emperor of Bulgaria (τὸν κύριον ὁ δεῖνα βασιλέα Βουλγαρίας).'[2]   In the former
of these address-formulae the Emperor's names have almost certainly been interpolated—they must refer to Constantine Porphyrogennetus and Romanus II, who actually
only employed the second formula.   But the phrase
'spiritual grandson' in the reception-formula is not so
easily explained away.   If earthly generations are to be
taken into account, the epithet 'spiritual' is incongruous;
but there must be some meaning behind the word grandson.

Bury[3] suggested that the monarchs bound by this
relationship were Leo VI and Symeon, son of the
Emperor's godson Boris.   But Boris's godfather was
Michael III; and why should generations be taken into
account on the Bulgarian, but not the Imperial, side?
Rambaud[4] sought the solution in a physical relationship;
Peter was the grandson, through his wife, of Romanus
Lecapenus.   The Imperial title must either only have

---

[1] Theophanes Continuatus, p. 415.

[2] Constantine Porphyrogennetus, *De Ceremoniis*, pp. 681, 682, 690. There
is also a reception-formula calling the Archon of Bulgaria the Emperor's
spiritual son.

[3] Bury, *The Ceremonial Book*, p. 226.

[4] Rambaud, *L'Empire Grec*, pp. 340 ff.

been granted to him after Romanus's fall, or Romanus must have taken it away from him. Rambaud is, I think, right in insisting upon the physical relationship; and it is possible that Romanus took the title away from Peter to mark his displeasure on some occasion, or, anyhow, that he prepared a formula for use if he should wish to do so. But, from the fact that there is no reception-formula calling Peter a Basileus, I incline to think that the 'spiritual grandson' formula is a blend of two formulae, one dealing with the 'spiritual son the Archon,' the other with the 'spiritual grandson the Basileus.' The muddle only shows that the courtiers of Byzantium, usually so punctilious, regarded the assumption of an Imperial title by any monarch outside the Empire as being so ridiculous that they could treat it with disdainful negligence; and they never bothered to record it systematically, nor took much notice of it, save when they wished to irritate self-important ambassadors from the upstart West.

Appendix XII

THE CHRONOLOGY OF THE EMPEROR NICEPHORUS PHOCAS'S BULGARIAN WARS

THE chronology of Nicephorus Phocas's Bulgarian wars has often been muddled by historians' persistent attempts to co-identify the accounts given by Leo Diaconus and by Scylitzes, who, with 'Nestor,' are the only fundamental sources for them. Actually each chronicler deals mainly with separate events. According to Leo, the Bulgarian embassy demanding tribute came to Constantinople shortly after Nicephorus's triumphant return from Tarsus (which took place in October 965).

Nicephorus followed up his dismissal of it by making a demonstration over the frontier and capturing one or two forts; he would not, however, embark on a serious campaign in Bulgaria. At the same time he instituted diplomatic intrigues with the Russians, which he continued to keep up.[1] Then Leo reverts to the main interest of the reign—the eastern campaigns. Later, after the Russians invaded Bulgaria (in 967, according to 'Nestor'), he sent an embassy to Bulgaria suggesting the marriage of the Bulgar princesses to the young Emperors, and the Bulgarians begged for Imperial help against the Russians. Nicephorus, however, went off to the East, and on his return he was murdered.[2] In Scylitzes, who throughout the reign is clearly using some lost independent source, we first find a paragraph telling that Peter, after his wife's death, sent to renew the peace and gave his sons to the Emperor as hostages; it then goes on to tell of his death and of the Comitopuli—this part is certainly an interpolation.[3] Later we hear that, in June 967, Nicephorus complained to the Bulgarian Court that it allowed Hungarian invaders to pass through Bulgaria into the Empire; at the same time he marched to the frontier (to the Great Fence) and looked into the defences of the Thracian cities. Shortly afterwards the Russians invaded Bulgaria— Scylitzes here inserts an account of Calocyras's mission —in August 968 (Indiction XI.), and they came again next year.[4]

From another source, however (Liudprand, *Legatio*, p. 185), we know that there was a Bulgarian embassy in Constantinople in June 968. This must have been after the Russian invasion; therefore 'Nestor's' date, rather than Scylitzes's, must be correct. The invasion no doubt lasted into September 967, i.e. the Indiction XI.; and Scylitzes muddled the Indictions.

The key to the chronology lies in the fact—which

---

[1] Leo Diaconus, pp. 61–3.   [2] Ibid., pp. 77–81.

[3] Cedrenus, ii., p. 346.   [4] Ibid., p. 372.

neither Leo nor Scylitzes singly makes clear—that Nicephorus twice declared war; in 965 he was furious at the
Bulgarians' demands; in 967 he simply wished for a
pretext to justify him in calling in the Russians. Briefly
tabulated, the sequence of events is as follows:

965 (after October): Bulgarian embassy to Constantinople
    demanding tribute (Leo). It was just after the
    Tsaritsa's death (Scylitzes).

966 (early spring): Nicephorus invades Southern Bulgaria
    (Leo).

    (soon afterwards): Peter asks for peace and sends his
    sons as hostages (Scylitzes).

966 onwards: Calocyras intrigues with the Russians (Leo
    and Scylitzes).

967 (June): Russians being ready, Nicephorus picks a
    quarrel with the Bulgarians, and fortifies his
    frontier lest the Russians should penetrate too
    far (Scylitzes).

967 (August): Russians invade Bulgaria ('Nestor,'
    Scylitzes, and Leo). Peter falls ill (Leo).

968 (late spring): Renewed Russian invasion (Scylitzes—
    a year after the previous invasion).

    (June): Bulgarian embassy to Constantinople (Liud-
    prand). It is ineffectual.

969 (January): Death of Peter.

    (in the course of the year): Calocyras's treachery
    becomes evident. So

    (autumn): Nicephorus sends embassy to Bulgaria
    suggesting a marriage alliance. It is about the
    time of the capture of Antioch, i.e. October 969
    (Leo). Fresh Russian invasion ('Nestor' and
    Leo).

    (December): Death of Nicephorus.

Thenceforward the chronology presents no great difficulty, and we can read without hindrance of the wars that
overwhelmed the First Bulgarian Empire.
   WE

BIBLIOGRAPHY

Note—I have not attempted to cite every modern work that touches on the history of the First Bulgarian Empire, but have restricted myself to those works that I have consulted and consider to be of interest and value. Further bibliographies are given by Zlatarski (*Istoriya*, i., 1 & 2), and Dvornik (op. cit. below). I have not been able to consult works published since the end of 1929.

With regard to the Greek original sources, I have referred where possible to the editions in the Bonn Corpus, as being the most easily obtainable. The text of Theophanes, however, has been revised by De Boor (Leipzig, 1883), whose edition should be consulted on all doubtful passages.

I make use of the following abbreviations:

A.S.P.: Archiv fur Slavische Philologie, Leipzig, 1879 ff.

B.P.: Bulgarski Priegled, Sofia, 1894 ff.

B.Z.: Byzantinische Zeitschrift, Leipzig, 1892 ff.

C.S.H.B.: Corpus Scriptorum Historiae Byzantinorum, Bonn, 1828–97.

I.A.D.S.: Izviestiya na Arkheol. Druzhestvo v Sofia, Sofia, 1911 ff.

I.B.A.I.: Izviestiya na Bulgarskoto Arkheol. Institut, Sofia, 1924 ff.

I.I.D.S.: Izviestiya na Istoricheskoto Druzhestvo v Sofia, Sofia, 1907 ff.

I.R.A.I.K.: Izviestiya Russkago Arkheolog. Instituta v Konstantinopolie, Constantinople, 1895 ff.

I.R.Y.S.: Izviestiya Otdieleniya Russkago Yazyka i Slovesnosti Petrogradskoy Akad. Nauk, Petrograd, 1897 ff.

M.G.H.: Monumenta Germaniae Historica (Ss. = scriptores; a.a.: = auctores antiquissimi), Hanover, 1826 ff.

M.P.G.: Migne, J. P., Patrologia Graeco–Latina, Paris, 1857–66.

M.P.L.: Idem, Patrologia Latina, Paris, 1844–55.

M.S.H.S.M.: Monumenta Spectantia Historiam Slavorum Meridionalium, Zagreb, 1868 ff.

R.E.S.: Revue des Etudes Slaves, Paris, 1921 ff.

S.B.A.N.: Spisanie na Bulgarskata Akad. na Naukitie, Sofia, 1911 ff.

S.N.U.K.: Sbornik za Narodni Umotvoreniya i Knizhnina, Sofia, 1885 ff.

S.R.H.: Scriptores Rerum Hungaricarum, Vienna, 1746.

S.V.Z.: Sbornik v chest na Vasil N. Zlatarski, Sofia, 1925.

S.Y.D.: Spisanie na Yuridicheskoto Druzhestvo, Sofia, 1901 ff.

V.V.: Vizantiiski Vremmenik, Petrograd, 1894 ff.

Z.M.N.P.: Zhurnal Ministerstva Narodnago Prosvieshcheniya, Petrograd.

Z.R.A.O.: Zapiski Russkago Arkheol. Obshchestva, Petrograd, 1885 ff.

ORIGINAL SOURCES

A. GREEK

Agathias, *Historiae*, C.S.H.B.
Anna Comnena, *Alexias*, C.S.H.B.
Attaliates, Michael, *Historia*, C.S.H.B.

Basil II, Emperor, *Sigillia ad Archiepiscopum Ochridensem*, edited in Gelzer, B.Z. vol. ii., pp. 42–6.

Cameniates, Joannes, *De Excidio Thessalonicae*, C.S.H.B.
Cecaumenus, *Strategicon*, ed. W. Wassiewsky and V. Jernstedt. St. Petersburg, 1896.
Cedrenus, Georgius, *Compendium Historiarum*, C.S.H.B.
Chronicon Paschale, C.S.H.B.
Codinus, Georgius, *De Officiis*, C.S.H.B.

Constantine VII Porphyrogennetus, Emperor, *De Ceremoniis*, C.S.H.B.
—— *De Thematibus et De Administrando Imperio*, C.S.H.B.

Ecloga Leonis et Constantini, ed. Monfereatus. Athens, 1889.
Encomium ad sanctum patrem nostrum Photium Thessalum, ed. Vasilievski, Z.M.N.P., pt. ccxlviii., pp. 100–1.
Epistola Synodica Orientalium ad Theophilum Imperatorem, M.P.G., vol. xcv.
Euthymius Zigabenus Patriarcha, *Opera*, M.P.G., vol. cxxx.
Evagrius, *Historia Ecclesiastica*, M.P.G., vol. lxxxvi.

Genesius, *Historia*, C.S.H.B.
Georgius Acropolita, *Historia*, ed. Heisenberg. Leipzig, 1903.
Georgius (Hamartolus) Monachus, *Chronicon*, ed. de Boor. Leipzig, 1904.
Georgius Monachus Continuatus, *Chronicon*, C.S.H.B.

Ignatius Diaconus, *Vita Nicephori*, appendix to Nicephorus, *Opuscula Historica*.

Joannes Antiochenus, *Fragmenta*, ed. Muller, in Fragmenta Historicorum Graecorum, vol. iv., pp. 535–622. Paris, 1885.
Joannes Geometrus, *Carmina*, M.P.G., vol. cvi.

Leo Diaconus, *Historia*, C.S.H.B.
Leo Grammaticus, *Historia*, C.S.H.B.
Leo VI Sapiens Imperator, *Opera*, M.P.G., vol. cvii.
Leo Magister, Anthypatus Patricius, *Epistolae*, ed. Sakkelion, in Deltion, vol. i., pp. 377–410. Athens, 1883.
Liber de Re Militari, Incerti Scriptoris Byzantini Saeculi X, ed. Vari. Leipzig, 1901.

Malalas, Joannes, *Chronographia*, M.P.G., vol. xcvii.
Menander Protector, *Fragmenta*, ed. Dindorf, in *Historici Graeci Minores*, vol. ii., pp. 1–131. Leipzig, 1871.

Menologion Imperatoris Basilii, M.P.G., vol. cxvii.
Miracula Sancti Demetrii Martyris, M.P.G., vol. cxvi.

Nicephorus Patriarcha, *Opuscula Historica*, ed. de Boor.
Leipzig, 1870.
Nicetas Acominatus, *Chronica*, C.S.H.B.
Nicolaus Mysticus Patriarcha, *Epistolae*, M.P.G., vol. cxi.

Petrus Siculus, *Historia Manichaeorum*, M.P.G., vol. civ.
Photius Patriarcha, *Opera*, M.P.G., vols. ci.–iv.
Priscus, *Fragmenta*, ed. Dindorf, in *Historici Graeci Minores*,
vol. ii., pp. 275–352. Leipzig, 1870.
Procopius, *Opera*, C.S.H.B.
Psellus, Michael, *Chronographia*, ed. Sathas. London, 1899.

Romanus I Lecapenus Imperator, *Epistolae*, ed. Sakkelion,
in Deltion, vol. i., pt. 4. Athens, 1884.

Scriptor Incertus, *De Leone Armenio*, C.S.H.B.
Scylitzes, Joannes, *Historia*, copied in Cedrenus, C.S.H.B.
Suidas, *Lexicon*, ed. Gaisford. Oxford, 1834.
Symeon Magister (pseudo-Symeon), *Chronicon*, C.S.H.B.

Theodorus Studites, *Parva Catechesis*, ed. Auvray.   Paris,
1891.
Theodosius Melitenus, *Chronographia*, ed. Tafel.   Munich,
1859.
Theophanes, *Chronographia*, C.S.H.B. (revised text, ed. de
Boor. Leipzig, 1883).
Theophanes Continuatus, *Chronographia*, C.S.H.B.
Theophylactus, Archiepiscopus Bulgarus, *Historia Martyrii
XV. Martyrum*, M.P.G., vol. cxxvi.
Theophylactus Patriarcha, *Epistola ad Petrum Regem
Bulgariae*, ed. Petrovski, I.R.Y.S., vol. xviii, 6 K. 3, pp.
361–72.

Vita S. Euthymii, ed. de Boor.   Berlin, 1888.
Vita S. Lucae Junioris, M.P.G., vol. iii.

Vita S. Lucae Stylitis, ed. Vanderstuyf, Patrologia Orientalis, vol. xi.

Vita S. Mariae Novae, ed. Gedeon, in Byzanticon Heortologion. Constantinople, 1899.

Vita S. Niconis Metanoeite, ed. Lampros, in Neos Hellenomnemon, vol. iii., pp. 131–223. Athens, 1906.

Vita S. Petri Argivi, ed. Costa.-Luzzi, in Novae Patrum Bibliothecae ab Card. Maii, pt. iii., ix.

Vita Theodorae Augustae, ed. Regel, in Analecta Byzantino-Russica. St. Petersburg, 1891.

Zonaras, Joannes, *Epitome Historiarum*, C.S.H.B.
Zosimus, *Historia*, C.S.H.B.

B. LATIN

Adrianus II Papa, *Epistolae*, M.P.L., vol. cxxii.

Anastasius Bibliothecarius, *Historia de Vitis Romanorum Pontificorum*, M.P.L., vol. cxxviii.

—— *Praefatio in Synodum VIII*, M.P.L., vol. cxxix.

Annales Bertiniani, pars II. Prudentii, pars III. Hincmari, M.G.H., Ss., vol. i.

Annales Fuldenses, M.G.H., Ss., vol. i.

Annales Hildesheimenses, M.G.H., Ss., vol. iii.

Annales Laurissenses, M.G.H., Ss., vol. i.

Annales Quedlinburgenses, M.G.H., Ss., vol. iii.

Annales Weissenburgenses, M.G.H., Ss., vol. iii.

Annalista Saxo, *Annales*, M.G.H., Ss., vol. viii.

Astronomus, *Vita Hludowici*, M.G.H., Ss., vol. ii.

Cassiodorus. *Variae*, M.G.H., a.a., vol. xii.

Dandolo, *Chronicum Venetum*, in Muratori, *Scriptores Rerum Italicarum*, vol. xii.

Diocleae Presbyter, *De Regno Slavorum*, in Lucius, *De Regno Dalmatiae*.

Einhardus, *Annales*, M.G.H., Ss., vol. i.

—— *Vita Caroli Imperatoris*, M.G.H., Ss., vol. ii.

Ekkehardus, *Chronicon Universale*, M.G.H., Ss., vol. iv.

Ennodius, *Panegyricus Regi Theodorico*, M.G.H., a.a., vol. vii.

Fredegarius Scholasticus, *Chronica*, M.G.H., Scriptores Rerum Merovingicarum, vol. ii.

Gesta Dagoberti I, M.G.H., Scriptores Rerum Merovingicarum, vol. ii.

Herimannus Augiensis, *Chronica*, M.G.H., Ss., vol. iv.

Innocentius III Papa, *Epistolae*, M.P.L., vols. ccxiv.–xv.

Johannes VIII Papa, *Epistolae*, M.G.H., Ep., vol. vii.

Jordanes, *Romana et Getica*, M.G.H., a.a., vol. v.

Liudprandus Cremonensis, *Opera*, ed. Bekker. Hanover, 1915.

Lupus Protospatharius, *Chronicon*, in Muratori, op. cit., vol. v.

Manegoldus, *Ad Gebehardum Liber*, M.G.H., Ss., vol. i.

Marcellinus Comes, *Chronicon*, M.G.H., a.a., vol. xi.

Monachus Sangallensis, *De Gestis Karoli Imperatoris*, M.G.H., Ss., vol. ii.

Nicolaus I Papa, *Epistolae*, M.G.H., Ep., vol. vi.

—— *Responsa*, ibid.

Paulus Diaconus, *Historia Langobardarum*, M.P.H., Scriptores Rerum Langobardarum.

Ranzanus, Petrus, *Indices*, in S.R.H.

Reginonis Chronicon, M.G.H., Ss., vol. i.

Restius, Georgius, *Chronica Ragusina*, in M.S.H.S.M., Ss., vol. ii. Zagreb, 1893.

Sigebertus, *Chronographia*, M.P.H., Ss., vol. viii.

Stephanus V Papa, *Epistolae*, M.P.L., vol. cxxix.

Thwrocz, Joannes de, *Historia*, in S.R.H.

C. ORIENTAL

Asoghic, Stephen, *Histoire Universelle*, trans. Dulaurier et Macler. Paris, 1883.
Al-Makin, *Histoire Mahométane*, trans. Vattier. Paris, 1657.

Eutychius of Alexandria, *Annales*, trans. Pocock, in M.P.G., vol. iii.

Ibn-Foszlan, *De Bulgaris*, trans. Fraehn. St. Petersburg, 1822.

John of Ephesus, *Historia Ecclesiastica*, vol. ii., trans. Schönfelder, *Die Kirchengeschichte des Johannes von Ephesus*. Munich, 1862. Unedited extracts, trans. Nau, in Revue de l'Orient Chrétien, vol. ii. Paris, 1897.
John of Nikiou, *Chronique*, ed. and trans. Zotenberg. Paris, 1883.

Maçoudi, *Les Prairies d'Or*, trans. Barbier de Meynard. Paris, 1861.
Matthew of Edessa, *Chronique*, trans. Dulaurier, in Recueil des Historiens des Croisades, Documents Arméniens, vol. i. Paris, 1869.
Michael the Syrian, *Chronique*, trans. Chabot. Paris, 1899–1910.

Vartan, called the Great, *Vseobshchaya Istoriya*, trans. Emin. St. Petersburg, 1864.

Yachya of Antioch, *Historie*, trans. (up to A.D. 976) Krachkovski et Vasiliev, in Patrologia Orientalis, vol. xviii. Paris, 1924. Also extracts in Rozen, *Imperator Vasili Bolgaroboïtsa* (see below).

D. SLAVONIC

Bulgarian Princes' List, facsimiles of MSS. in Zlatarski, *Istoriya*, i., 1, pp. 379–82.

Chudo Sv. Georgiya, ed. Loparev. St. Petersburg, 1894.

Gregori Presbiter, preface to the Chronicle of Malalas, in Kalaïdovitch, *Ioann Eksarkh.*

John the Exarch, *Shestodniev*, in Miklosich, *Chrestomathia Palaeoslovenica.* Vienna, 1861.
Khrabr, *O Pismenikh*, in Kalaïdovitch, op. cit.
Konstantin, Bulgarian bishop, *Proglas*, in Ivanov, *Bulgarski Starini*, pp. 72–4.
Kozma, *Slovo Kozmy*, ed. Popruzhenko. St. Petersburg, 1907.

'Nestor,' *La Chronique dite de Nestor*, ed. and trans. Léger. Paris, 1884.

Simeon Logothet, *Khronika*, ed. Sreznevski. St. Petersburg, 1905.
Sinodik Tsarya Borisa, ed. Popruzhenko. Odessa, 1899.

Tudor Doksov, *Pripiska*, ed. Gorski i Nevustroev. Moscow, 1859.

Vita Constantini, in Pastrnek, *Dejiny Slovanskych Apostolu. Vita Methodii*, in Pastrnek, op. cit.

Zhitiya Sv. Nauma Okhridskago, ed. Lavrov, I.R.Y.S., vol. xii., bk. iv. (1908).
Zhivot Jovana Rilskog, ed. Novakovitch, in Glasnik Srbskog Uchenog Drushtva, bk. xxii. Belgrade, 1867.

Modern Works

Abicht, R., *Der Angriff der Bulgaren auf Konstantinopel im J. 896*, A.S.P., vol. xvii.

Aboba-Pliska: Materialy dlya Bolganskikh Drevnostei,
I.R.A.I.K., vol. x.
Anastasijevič, D.N., *Hipoteza o Zapadnoj Bugarskoj*, Glasnik.
Skopskog Nauchnog Drushtva, vol. iii. Skopie, 1928.
Antony, Archbishop, *Iz Istorii Khristianskoi Propoviedi*.
St. Petersburg, 1895.
Avril, A. d', *Saint-Cyrille et Saint-Méthode*. Paris, 1885.

Balaschev, G., *Bulgaritie prez Poslednitie Desetgodishnini na
Desetiya Viek*. Sofia, 1929.
—— *Klement Slovienski*. Sofia, 1898.
—— *Novyya Dannyya dlya Istorii Greko-bolgarskikh Boin pri
Simeonie*, I.R.A.I.K., vol. iv.
—— *Otgovor* to Mutafchev's review (see below) of *Bulgar-
itie prez Poslednitie etc*. Sofia 1929
Banescu, N., *Bulgarie et Paristrion*, in Bulletin de la Section
Historique de l'Académie Roumaine. Bucarest, 1923.
Bees, N. A., *Epidromai Boulgaron epi Tsaron Symeon Hellenikon*,
vol. i. Athens, 1928
Blagoëv, N., *Besedata na Presbiter Kozma protiv Bogomilite*,
Godishnik na Sofiiskiya Universitet, vol. xviii. Sofia,
1905 ff.
—— *Krumovi Zakoni*, S.Y.D., vol. iv.
—— *Pravni i Sotsialni Vzgledi na Bogomilite*. Sofia, 1912.
Bobchev, S. S., *Bulgaria under Tsar Simeon*, S.R., vols. vii.
and viii., Nos. 21, 22.
—— *Znachenieto za Bulgariya na Sv. Ivan Rilski*, in Godishnik
na Svobodniya Universitet, vol. i. Sofia, 1922.
—— *Nachträge zu den Notitiae Episcopatuum*, Zeitschrift fur
Kirchengeschichte, vols. xii. and xiv. Gotha, 1891–4.
Boor, C. de, *Vita Euthymii*. Berlin, 1888.
—— *Zu Johannes Skylitzes: Weiteres zur Chronik des Sky-
litzes*, B.Z., vols. xiii. and xiv.
Brehier, L., *Les Missions Chrétiennes chez les Slaves au IX
Siècle*, Monde Slave, vol. iv. Paris, 1927.
Brooks, E. W., *The Age of Basil I*, B.Z., vol. xxi.
—— *The Chronology of Theophanes*, B.Z., vol. viii.

Brückner, A., *Thesen zur Cyrillo-Methodianischen Frage*, A.S.P., vol. xxviii.

Bury, J. B., *History of the Eastern Roman Empire from Arcadius to Irene*. London, 1889.

—— *History of the Eastern Roman Empire, 802–67*. London, 1912.

—— *History of the Later Roman Empire*. London, 1923.

—— *The Bulgarian Treaty of A.D. 814*, English Historical Review, vol. xxv. London, 1910.

—— *The Ceremonial Book of Constantine Porphyrogennetus*, ibid., vol. xxii. London, 1907.

—— *The Chronological Cycle of the Bulgarians*, B.Z., vol. xix.

—— *The Treatise De Administrando Imperio*, B.Z., vol. xv.

Cambridge Mediaeval History, The, vols. i., ii., and iv. Cambridge, 1911, 1913, 1923.

Conybeare, F. C., *The Key of Truth*. Oxford, 1898.

Diehl, C., *Choses et Gens de Byzance*. Paris, 1926.

—— *Figures Byzantines*. Paris, 1906.

Drinov, M. S., *Istoricheski Priegled na Bulgarskata Tsurkva*. Sofia, 1911.

—— *Novy Tserkovno-Slavyanski Pamyatnik*, Z.M.N.P., pt. ccxxxviii.

——*Yuzhnye Slavyane i Vizantiya v X Viekie*. Moscow, 1875.

Ducange, C. du F., *Familiae Augustae Byzantinae*. Paris, 1680.

Duchesne, L., *Les Premiers Temps de l'État Pontifical*. Paris, 1911.

Dümmler, L., *Über die Aelteste Geschichte der Slawen in Dalmatien*. Vienna, 1856.

Dvornik, F., *Les Slaves, Byzance et Rome au IX. Siècle*. Paris, 1926.

Farlati, D., *Illyricum Sacrum*. Venice, 1751.

Feher, B., *Bulgarisch-Ungarische Beziehungen in dem V.–XI. Jahrhunderten*. Budapest, 1921.

—— *Vliyanie na Bulgarskata Tsurkva v Madzharsko*, S.V., vol. ii.

Ficker, G., *Die Phundagiagiten.* Leipzig, 1908.
Finlay, G., *History of Greece.* Oxford, 1877.

Gay, J., *L'Italie Méridionale et l'Empire Byzantin.* Paris, 1904.
Gelzer, H., *Der Patriarchat von Achrida.* Leipzig, 1902.
—— *Ungedruckte und Ungenügend Veröffentliche Texte der Notitiae Episcopatuum,* B.Z., vols. i. and ii.
Gibbon, E., *Decline and Fall of the Roman Empire,* ed. Bury (with appendices). London, 1909–14.
Gilferding, A., *Istoria Serbov i Bolgar.* St. Petersburg, 1868.
Golubinski, E., *Kratki Ocherk Istorii Pravoslavnykh Tserkvey.* Moscow, 1871.
Gospodinov, Y. S., *Razkopki v Patleïna.* Sofia, 1915.
Grot, K., *Konstantin Bagranorodny o Serbakh i Khorvatakh.* St. Petersburg, 1882.

Hergenröther, J., *Photius, Patriarch von Konstantinopel.* Ratisbon, 1867–9.
Hirsch, F., *Byzantinische Studien.* Leipzig, 1876.
—— *Kaiser Konstantin VII. Porphyrogennetos.* Berlin, 1873.
Howorth, H., *The Spread of the Slavs: Pt. iv., The Bulgarians.* Journal of the Anthropological Institute, vol. ii. London, 1882.
Hubert, H., *Observations sur la Chronologie de Théophane,* B.Z., vol. vi.

Ilniski, G. A., *Gramoty Bolgarskikh Tsarey.* Moscow, 1911,
—— *Kto byl Chernorizets Khrabr?* Vizantiskoe Obozrienie. vol. iii. Yuriev, 1917.
Ivanov, I., *Aksios–Velika–Vardar,* Makedonski Pregled, vol. i. Sofia, 1925.
—— *Bogomilski Knigi i Legendi.* Sofia, 1925.
—— *Bulgarski Starini iz Makedoniya.* Sofia, 1908.
—— *Proizkhod na Tsar Samuiloviya Rod,* S.V.Z.
—— *Sv. Ivan Rilski.* Sofia, 1917.

Jagič, V., *Cyrillo-Methodiana*, A.S.P., vol. xxviii.
—— *Entstehungsgeschichte der Kirchenslavischen Sprache* (2nd ed.). Berlin, 1913.
—— *Grafika u Slavyan*, Entsiclopediya Slavyanskoi Filologii. St. Petersburg, 1911.
Jireček, C., *Archäologische Fragmente aus Bulgarien*, Archäolog. Epigraph., vol. x. Vienna, Mitteilungen aus Oesten Ungarn, 1888.
—— *Das Fürstentum Bulgarien*. Prague, 1891.
—— *Die Heerstrasse von Belgrad nach Konstantinopel*. Prague, 1877.
—— *Geschichte der Bulgaren*. Prague, 1876.
—— *Geschichte der Serben*. Gotha, 1911.
Jorga, N., *Formes Byzantines et Realités Balkaniques*. Paris, 1922.
—— *Le Danube d'Empire*, in Mélanges offerts à G. Schlumberger. Paris, 1925.
—— *Les Plus Anciens Etats Slavo-Roumains*, R.E.S., vol. v.

Kalaïdovitch, K., *Ioann Eksarkh Bolgarski*. Moscow, 1824.
Khvolson, D., *Izviestiya o Khazarakh i t.d. Ibn Dasta*. St. Petersburg, 1869.
Krumbacher, K., *Geschichte der Byzantinischen Litteratur*. Munich, 1897.
Katsarov, G., *Die Gesetzgebung des Bulgarischen Fürsten Krum*, B.Z., vol. xvi.
Kuun, G., *Relationum Hungarorum cum Oriente Historia Antiquissima*. Claudiopolis, 1897.
Kuznetsov, I., *Pismata na Lva Magistra i Romana Lacapina*, S.B.U., vols. xvi. and xvii.

Lampros, S., *Historia tes Hellados*. Athens, 1898.
Laurent, J., *Sul Libro II. dei Miracula S. Demetrii Martyris*, Bessarione, vol. iv.
Lavrin, J., *The Bogomil Heresy*, S.R., vol. viii., No. 23.
Lavrov, P. A., *Nova Sluzhba Tsary Bugarskome Petru*, Juzhnoslovenski Philolog, vol. i. Belgrade, 1913.

Léger, L., *Cyrille et Méthode*. Paris, 1868.
—— *La Bulgarie*. Paris, 1885.
—— *La Littérature Bulgare au Moyen Âge*, Revue des Cours Littéraires, vol. vi. Paris, 1869.
—— *L'Hérésie des Bogomiles*, Revue des Questions Historiques, vol. viii. Paris, 1870.
Le Quien, M., *Oriens Christianus*. Paris, 1740.
Lombard, A., *Constantin V, Empereur des Romains*. Paris, 1902.
Loparev, K. M., *Dvie Samietki po Drevney Bolgarskoy Istorii*, Z.R.A.O., vol. iii.
Lucius, J., *Re Regno Dalmatiae et Croatiae*. Amsterdam, 1666.
Lüttich, R., *Ungarnzüge in Europa im 10 Jahrhundert*. Berlin, 1910.

Malyshevski, I., *Svyatye Kirill i Methodi*. Kiev, 1886.
Marquart, J., *Die Altbulgarische Ausdrücke in der Inschrift von Catalar*, I.R.A.I.K., vol. xv.
—— *Die Chronologie der Alttürkischen Inschriften*. Leipzig, 1893.
—— *Osteuropäische und Ostasiatische Streifzüge*. Leipzig, 1903.
Mazon, A., *Le Moine Chrabe et Cyrille*, S.V.Z.
Mikkola, J. J., *Die Chronologie der Türkischen Donaubulgaren*, Journal de la Société Finno-Ongrienne, vol. xxx. Helsingfors, 1914.
—— *Tyurksko-Bolgarskoe Lietoschislenie*, I.R.Y.S., vol. xviii.
Miklosich, F., *Chrestomathia Palaeoslovenica*. Vienna, 1861.
Miletich, L., *Km Samuilotiya Nadpis ot 993 God*, I.R.A.I.K., vol. iv.
Milev, N., *Kubrat ot Istoriyata i Kuber v Chudesita na Sv. Dimitriya*, in Bulgarskoto Knizhovno Druchestvo, Spisanie, bk. lxxi.
Miller, W., *The First Bulgarian Empire*, in the Cambridge Mediaeval History (see above), vol. iv.
Minns, E. H., *Saint Cyril Really Knew Hebrew*, in Mélanges publiés en l'honneur de M. Paul Boyer. Paris, 1925.

Muralt, E. de, *Essai de Chronographie Byzantine*. St. Petersburg, 1855.

Muratori, L. A., *Rerum Italicarum Scriptores*. Milan, 1723–51.

Mutafchev, P., review of Balaschev, *Bulgaritie prez Poslednitie etc.*, in Makedonski Priegled, vol. v., bk. ii. Sofia, 1929

Niederle, L., *Slovanské Starozitnosti*. Prague, 1906.

Novakovitch, S., *Legenda o Vladimiru i Kosari*. Belgrade, 1893.

Palauzov, S. N., *Viek Bolgarskago Tsarya Simeona*. St. Petersburg, 1852.

Panaret, Archimandrite, *Zhivotut na Ivana Eksarkha*. Stanimaka, 1914.

Pastrnek, F., *Dejiny Slovanskych Apostolu Cyrilla a Methoda*. Prague, 1902.

Platonov, N. V., *Patriarkh Photii*. Moscow, 1891.

Popov, N. A., *Imperator Liev Mudry*. Moscow, 1892.

Prokič, B., *Jovan Skilitsa*. Belgrade.

—— *Die Zusätze in der Handschrift des Johannes Skylitzes*. Munich, 1906.

Rački, F., *Bogomili i Patereni*. Zagreb, 1869–70.

—— *Documenta Historiae Croaticae Periodum Antiquam Illustrantia*, M.S.H.S.M., vol. vii. Zagreb, 1877.

Rambaud, A., *L'Empire Grec au Xme Siècle*. Paris, 1870.

Rapoport, S., *On the Early Slavs, The Narrative of Ibrahim Ibn Yakub*, S.R., vol. viii., No. 23.

Rozen, V. P., *Imperator Vasili Bolgaroboïtsa*. St. Petersburg, 1883.

Rösler, R., *Rumänische Studien*. Leipzig, 1871.

Runciman, S., *The Emperor Romanus Lecapenus*. Cambridge, 1929.

Safarik, F., *Slovanské Starožitnosti*. Prague, 1837.

BIBLIOGRAPHY 321

Schlumberger, G., *L'Epopée Byzantine à la Fin du Xme Siècle*. Paris, 1896–1905.
—— *Sigillographie de l'Empire Byzantin*. Paris, 1884.
—— *Un Empereur Byzantin au Xme Siècle*. Paris, 1890.
Shkorpil, K., *Bieliezhki za Starata Bulgarska Stolitsa Preslav*, I.A.D.S., vol. iv.
—— *Pametnitsi iz Bulgarsko, I Trakia*. Sofia, 1888.
—— *Purvata Bulgarska Stolitsa do Aboba*. Varna, 1901.
—— *Starobulgarski Pametnitsi*, in Dobrudzha. Sofia, 1918.
Shopov, A., *Edin Dokument za Bulgarskata Istoriya*, S.N.U.K., bk. ii.
Šišič, F., *Geschichte der Kroaten*. Zagreb, 1917.
—— *Prirucnik Izvora Hevatske Historije*. Zagreb, 1916.
Snoj, *Staroslovenski Matejev Evangelij*. Ljubljana, 1922.
Snopek, F., *Die Slavenapostel*. Kremsier, 1918.
Sobolevski, A. I., *Cherkovno Slavyanskitie Stikhotvoreniya*, V., IX.–X. Viek, S.N.U.K., bks. xvi.–xvii.
—— *Episkop Konstantin*, S.N.U.K., bk. xviii.
Sokolov, M., *Iz Drevney Istorii Bolgar*. St. Petersburg, 1879.

Tafel, T., *De Thessalonica Ejusque Agro*. Berlin, 1839.
Tougard, S., *De l'Histoire Profane dans l'Actes Grecs des Bollandistes*. Paris, 1874.
Trifonov, I., *Besieda na Kozma Presbitera*, S.B.A.N., bk. xxx.
Tunitski, N. L., *Sv. Clement Episkop Slovenski*. Sirgiev Posad, 1913.

Uspenski, F. I., *Nadpis Tsarya Simeonie*, I.R.A.I.K., vol. iv.
—— *Pogranichnyi Stolb mezhdu Vizantiei i Bolgariei pri Simeonie*, I.R.A.I.K., vol. iii.
—— *Rusi Vizantiya v X Viekie*. Odessa, 1888.
—— *Staro-bolgarskaya Nadpis Omortaga*, I.R.A.I.K., vol. iii.

Vasiliev, A. A., *Arabski Sinaksar o Bolgarskom Pokhodis Imperatora Nikifora*, in Novoi Sbornik v chest V. I. Lamanskago. St. Petersburg, 1905.
—— *History of the Byzantine Empire*. Madison, 1928.
Xe

Vasiliev, A. A., *Istoriya Vizantii.* Petrograd, 1917.
—— *Proiskhozhdenie Imperatora Vasiliya Makedonyanina,* V.V., vol. xii.
—— *Slavyane v Gretsii,* V.V., vol. v.
—— *Vizantiya i Araby.* St. Petersburg, 1900, 1902.
Vasilievsky, V. G., *K. Istorii 976–986 Godov,* Z.M.N.P., pt. clxxxiv.
—— *Khronika Logoteta na Slavyanskom i Grecheskom,* V.V., vol. ii.
—— *O Mnemon Slavyanstvie Gunnov,* Z.M.N.P., pp. 222, 226.
—— *Odin iz Grecheskikh Sbornikov Moskov. Sinod. Biblioteki,* Z.M.N.P., pt. ccxxviii.
—— *Soviety i Razkazy Vizantiiskago Boyarina XI. Vieka,* Z.M.N.P., pt. ccxii.
Vogt, A., *Basile I, Empereur de Byzance.* Paris, 1908.
Vondrak, V., *Zur Frage nach der Herkunft des Glagolitischen Alphabets,* A.S.P., vols. xviii. and xix.

Wessely, C., *Glagolitisch-Lateinische Sprache.* Leipzig, 1913.
Westberg, F., *Ibráhím's Ibn Ja'kûb's Reisebericht über die Slawenlande.* St. Petersburg, 1898.

Zachariae von Lingenthal, K. E., *Beiträge zur Geschichte der Bulgarischen Kirche.* St. Petersburg, 1864.
Zlatarski, V. N., *Bulgarski Arkhiepiskopi-Patriarsi priez Pervoto Tsarstvo,* I.I.D.C., bk. vi.
—— *Dva Izviestny Bulgarski Nadpisa,* S.N.U.K., bk. xv.
—— *Die se Namiral Grad Dievol,* I.I.D.C., bk. v.
—— *Die Bulgarische Zeitrechnung,* Journal de la Société Finno-Ongrienne, vol. xl. Helsingfors, 1924.
—— *Istoriya na Bulgarskata Durzhava.* Sofia, 1918, 1929.
—— *Izviestiyata za Bulgaritie v Khronikata na Simeona Metaprasta,* S.N.U.K., bk. xxiv.
—— *Izviestieto na Mikhaila Siriüski za Prieselenieto na Bulgaritie,* I.I.D.C., bk. iv.
—— *Izviestieto na Ibrahim-ibn-Yakuba,* S.B.A.N., vol. xxii.
—— *Koi e bil Tudor Chernorizets Doksov,* B.P., bk. iii.
—— *Koi za bili Vátrieshni i Vunshni Bolyari,* in Univ. Sbornik v chest Bobchev. Sofia, 1921.

Zlatarski, V. N., *Kum Istoriyata na Otkritiya v Misstnostata Patleina Munastir*, I.B.A.I., bk. i.

—— *Novi Izviestiya za Nai Drevniya Period na Bulg. Istoriya*, S.N.U.K., bk. ii.

—— *Pervy Pokhod Simeona na Konstantinopol*, in Recueil d'Études dediées à M. Kondakov. Prague, 1926.

—— *Pismata na Nikolaya Mistika do Simeona*, S.N.U.K., bks. x.–xii.

—— *Pismata na Romana Lacapina do Simeona*, S.N.U.K., bk. xiii.

—— *Poslanie na Photiya do Borisa v Slavienski Prievod*, B.S., bk. v.

—— *The Making of Bulgaria*, S.R., vol. iv., Nos.

X_E*

INDEX

Note : Except in the case of princes and prelates, where a definite surname, not merely a title, is known, the person is given under the surname.

326 INDEX

Ashot, Prince of Taron, 228–9,
232, 239–40
Asperuch (Isperikh), Khan, reign,
25–30; dates, 273–8; 3, 4, 16,
17, 19, 20, 21, 24, 43, 51, 58,
202, 261
Atelkuz, 249
Athanasius, Saint, 139
Athens, 251–2
Attica, 229
Attila, is Avitokhol? 279–81; 4,
5, 12, 35, 51
Austria, 149
Avars, conquer Bulgars, 10; Bul-
gars revolt from, 14–15; in
Pannonia, 19, 50–2; 3, 23, 24,
27, 28, 67, 68, 80, 97, 280,
281
Avitokhol, Khan, is Attila? 279–
81; dates, 273–8; 11
Azmak, River, 73
Azov, Sea of, 3, 6, 7, 12, 20

Bagdad, 169
Baian (Batbaian), Khan, 3, 16, 17,
276
——, boyar, 39, 40
Bakadzhik, 32, 33, 36, 74
Balathistes, forest, 241
Balaton, Lake, 97, 115
Baldric, Marquis of Friuli, 83
Baltic Sea, 22, 99, 150, 186
Baltzene, 72–3
Bardas, Cæsar, 99, 101
Bari, 270
Basil I, the Macedonian, Emperor, relations with Rome,
112–14, 117, 119–20; and Slavonic Liturgy, 124–6; 118, 123,
135, 261
—— II, Bulgaroctonus, Emperor,
character, 223; First Bulgar
campaign, 224–5; campaign in
Macedonia, 227–8; yearly campaigns in Bulgaria, 234–8,
240–4; final campaigns, 245–9;
Bulgaria submits to, 249–52;
his settlement of Bulgaria,
255–6; 198, 219, 222, 226, 257,
267, 268, 269
——, writer, List of, 282
—— the Bogomil, 194
—— the Paracoemomenus, 212,
223
Bavaria, 19
Belgrade, 81, 95, 118, 126, 144

Belisarius, Imperial general, 9
Belitsa, 136
Benedict VII, Pope, 226
Benevento, 21
Benjamin, Bulgar prince, 177, 189
Berat, 252
Berrhoea in Thrace (Beroë) 47, 59
—— in Macedonia, 226–7, 228,
229, 235, 247
Berzetians, Slav tribe, 41
Bessarabia, 12, 26, 27, 80, 81, 279
Bezmer, Khan, dates, 273–8; 16,
27
Bithynia, 32, 38, 128
Bitolia (Monastir), 243, 249
Bizya, 166
Blachernae, quarter of Constanti-
nople, 67, 156, 179
Black Sea, 7, 21, 27, 38, 40, 52, 60,
66, 143, 171, 186, 202, 225, 235
Boa, Queen of the Sabirs, 7
Bobus, Paul, Magister, 234
Boeotia, 229
Bogas, John, Patrician, 159–60
Bogdan, Bulgar official, 249
Bogomil, Pope, heresiarch, 190–6,
259, 260
Bogomils, heretics, tenets, 190–6;
writings, 271–2; 220, 231, 239,
256, 260
Bohemia, 97, 149
Boris I (Michael), Khan or Prince,
reign, 90–130; conversion, 102–
6; joins Roman Church, 108–13;
deserts Rome, 113–14; abdi-
cates, 130; returns, 134–6;
second retirement, 136; during
Magyar invasion, 146; death,
152; 143, 144, 150, 157–8,
258–9, 261, 266, 270, 286,
293–4, 302
—— II, Tsar, reign, 205; captured
in Preslav, 209–10; abdication,
215; death, 220–1; 200, 204,
217, 219
——, Tarkan, 126, 286
Bosnia, 196
Bosograd, 247
Bosphorus, 64, 161, 166
Boteniates, Theophylact, Imperial
general, 241, 242
Bourbon family, 258
Bovianum, 21
Boyana, 246
Branichevtsi, Slav tribe, 82
Branimir, Prince of Croatia, 119
Bregalnitsa, 129, 135–6

Hemnecus, 175, 287
Heraclea, 61, 65, 165
Heraclius, Emperor, 13, 14
Heristal, 81, 82
Herod, King, 193
Hexabulius, Imperial official, 64
Hiung-nu, 4
Hohenstaufen, family of, 258
Hungary, Hungarians, 50, 233, 270, 281. *See* Magyars
——, Princess of, wife of Gabriel-Radomir, 233–4, 257
Hunno, Alexius, the *sampses*, 288
Huns, 4–16, 22, 135, 261, 281

Iberians, 8
Ibn-Foszlan, writer, 18
Ibrahim-ibn-Yakub, writer, 186, 198
Ignatius, Patriarch of Constantinople, deposed, 99; reinstated, 112–14; biography, 268, 291; 117, 118
——, biographer, 268
Igor, Grand Prince of Russia, 186, 209
Illyricum, 101, 112, 117, 173, 283
India, 197
Ioannupolis, name for Preslav, 210
Irene, Saint, Empress, peaceful policy, 47–50; 43, 52, 59
——, Ducaena, Empress, 258
—— of Larissa, Tsaritsa, 222, 233–4, 244
——, Lecapena, Tsaritsa. *See* Maria.
Irenupolis, name for Berrhoea, 47
Irnik, Khan, is Ernach, 279–81; dates, 273–7; 11
Iron Gate, pass in Stranya Planina, 90
—— of the Danube, 238
Isaac I, Comnenus, Emperor, 257
Isbules, Kavkan, 84–5, 88, 94, 284, 287, 293, 295–7
Isernia, 21
Isker, River, 27
Isperikh. *See* Asperuch.
Italy, 112, 130, 150, 159, 198
Ivatza, Bulgar general, 246, 250–1

Jacob, Bulgar Prince, 133
Japheth, 11, 281
Jeremiah. *See* Bogomil
Jerusalem, 99

Joachim, Saint, 192
John the Evangelist, Saint, 192
—— of Rila, Saint, 189, 204
—— I, Tzimisces, Emperor, Bulgar wars, 206–16; death, 218–19; 221, 267
—— VIII, Pope, 116–21, 125
—— X, Pope, 174, 288
——, Patriarch of Bulgaria. *See* David.
——, Bulgar prince, 177, 188
——, Bishop of Nikiou, writer, 13, 275
—— of Antioch, writer, 7
——, Bulgar ambassador, 168
—— the Chaldee, 249
—— the Exarch, writer, 139, 141–2, 197
—— Geometrus, poet, 222–3, 225
—— the Presbyter, Papal legate, 118–19
—— -Vladislav, Tsar, reign, 244–9; death, 248–9; 231, 257
Jordanes, writer, 270
Joseph, Paracoemomenus, 215
Julian the Apostate, Emperor, 129
Justin II, Emperor, 286
Justinian I, Emperor, 6, 8–9, 22
—— II, Rhinotmetus, Emperor, 30, 31, 34, 261

Kadi-keui, inscription, 58
Kama, River, 18, 81
Kardam, Khan, reign, 48–50; 51, 52, 61, 258
Karnobad, 36
Khazars, 17, 18, 30, 281
Khrabr, writer, 139, 197, 271, 299
Kiev, 202, 205, 214
Kocel, Moravian prince, 115
Kormisosh, Khan, reign, 35–7; 33, 39, 59, 273, 277, 289
Kosara, Bulgar princess, Princess of Dioclea, 233, 245, 251
Kouria, Petcheneg chieftain, 214
Kozma, writer, 191, 196–7, 271
Kraina, 245
Krakra, Bulgar general, 238, 240, 246, 247, 248–9
Krum, Khan, reign, 51–70; wars, 52–68, 291–2; legislation, 68–70; death, 68; 71, 72, 74, 76, 79, 80, 89, 90, 94, 130, 170, 214, 258, 261, 266, 295; family of, 215, 216, 231, 238
Kuber, Bulgar chieftain, 20
Kubiares family, 83

Symeon, Tsar (*continued*)—
177; result of reign, 177–8, 183;
130, 134, 183, 184, 188, 189,
197, 199, 200, 215, 259, 261,
267, 268, 286, 287, 293, 302
——, brother-in-law of Tsar
Symeon, 178, 286, 287
——, the Asecretis, 151–2
Syrians, 35, 224

TABARI, CHRONICLER, 148
Tagma, Turkish Ambassador, 286
Taman peninsula, 6
Taridin, Count, 129, 286
Taron, theme of, 257; princely
family of, 228, 249
Tarsus, 199, 303
Tcheslav, *boyar*, 126
Telerig, Khan, 41–3
Telets, Khan, 37–9, 273, 276, 277
Tempe, Vale of, 229
Terbunia, 233
Tervel, Khan, reign, 30–4; peace
treaty with Theodosius III,
32–3, 59, 63, 70, 73, 289; dates,
273–7; 43, 58, 144, 261
Tetraxite Goths, 6, 8
Theiss, River, Bulgar frontier,
50–2, 81, 97, 149; 69, 83, 286
Theodora, Saint, Empress-Regent,
80, 90–1, 102, 292
——, Empress, wife of Romanus
I, 166
Theodore, Stratilates, Saint, 212
——, Bulgar prince, 257
——, Abbot of Studium, 61, 80
——, Bulgar ambassador, 147
——, Tarkan, 152
—— the Bogomil, 194
Theodoric, Ostrogothic King, 5, 6
Theodorocanus, Imperial general,
235
Theodorupolis, name for Preslav,
214–5
Theodosiopolis (Erzerum), 35,
257
Theodosius III, Emperor, 32, 33,
59, 289
——, Bishop of Nona, 120
——, Protovestiarius, 147
—— of Melitene, historian, 257
Theophanes, Saint, historian, 153;
works, 7, 15, 25, 26, 36–7, 42,
54, 265–6; 276, 291; Continu-
ator of, 266–7, 291
——, Protovestarius and Para-
coemomenus, 179–80

Theophano, Empress, 198, 204,
206
——, Western Empress, 180, 226
Theophilus, Emperor, 85–6, 290
Theophylact, Lecapenus, Patriarch of Constantinople, 190,
191, 195, 268
——, Archbishop of Bulgaria,
writer, 256, 268, 293–4
——, Papal legate, 180, 226
Thermitsa, 246
Thermopylae, 9, 229, 251
Thessalonica, sieges by Slavs, 20,
23, 24; trade-route to, 95; Bulgar trade diverted to, 144, 148;
sack by Leo of Tripoli, 151–2,
167, 269; attacked by Samuel,
228, 229; visited by Basil II,
227, 243, 246; 30, 33, 34, 87,
101, 129, 140, 159, 188, 234,
236, 238, 240, 241, 282, 298
Thessaly, 41, 221–2, 224, 236,
238, 251, 252
Thirty Years' Peace made, 72;
ended, 88; 74, 75, 78, 84–5, 87
Thomas, rebel, 75
Thrace, invaded by Telets, 38,
by Kardam, 48, by Krum, 61,
63, by Symeon, 145, 146, 147,
156–7, 161, 164, 166, 167, 169;
Asiatic colonies in, 107, 169,
192, 217; Great Fence of, *see*
Fence; 22, 32, 34, 37, 40, 47,
58, 88, 159, 171, 172, 206, 207,
231
Thracian Chersonese, 9
Tiberiupolis in Bithynia, 129
—— in Macedonia, 128–9
Tiberius, Emperor, 31
Timok, River, 237; Timocian
Slavs, 81–2
Timothy, Saint, 129
Tirnovo, 77, 260
Tirpimir, Prince of Croatia, 92
Tokt, Khan, 40
Tomislav, King of Croatia, 175–6
Tomor, Mount, 128, 250
Trajan, Emperor, 80
——, Bulgar prince, 257
—— Gate of, defile, 224, 235
Transmarisca (Turtakan), 76
Transylvania, Bulgar Empire in,
50, 51, 80, 95; lost to Magyars,
149–50
Tsepa, *boyar*, 84, 284, 295
Tsigat, Bulgar ambassador, 41
Tsok, *boyar*, 71